CASE*METHOD^{SM}

Function and Process Modelling

About the Authors

Cliff Longman was born in Harrow, England, in 1959. He attended Lanchester Polytechnic, where he studied Computer Science.

He spent the early part of his career designing database and realtime systems in the manufacturing, travel and communications industries. After a time working in Europe, he joined Oracle as a consultant, where he helped to develop the training and education services of the Company. Cliff has led analysis teams on some of the largest strategic studies undertaken by Oracle. He later joined the CASE Product Development Group, where he helps to develop CASE*Method and acts as the chief architect for the computer tools to support it.

Cliff is married with two children and lives in Surrey, England.

Richard Barker was born in Sheffield, England, in 1946. He went to Edinburgh University where he studied Chemistry, but realized that his interests lay outside the realms of pure science.

He has gained insight into many aspects of information systems through work in manufacturing industry and the Health Service, and the early introduction of database and data dictionary software whilst working with a major hardware company. Subsequently, Richard led a consultancy team specializing in strategic analysis and systems development using structured methods. He is currently a main board director of Oracle Corporation UK Limited, and a Senior Vice President of Oracle Europe, responsible for the Oracle system development method, CASE*Method, and the development of Computer-Aided Systems Engineering (CASE) and Application Package software using the ORACLE RDBMS. He established the UK Training Division to provide education for clients and Oracle staff alike in the use of Oracle products, methods and strategic thinking, and has lectured widely on network and relational database technology, distributed databases, CASE and user involvement in systems development.

Barbara Barker was born in Coleraine, Northern Ireland, in 1946. She studied Biochemistry at Edinburgh University. She has worked in a laboratory, been a teacher, a technical editor and an environmental activist, with a continuing involvement in wildlife conservation work. Richard and Barbara are married with three children, and live in Berkshire, England. They have worked together for several years on this series of books.

Cliff and Richard have worked together for nearly ten years on methods, training, strategy studies and the development of CASE tools. They are both members of the Oracle architecture committee, which determines the direction of all Oracle's products.

CASE＊METHOD℠

Function and Process Modelling

RICHARD BARKER
CLIFF LONGMAN

Addison-Wesley Publishing Company

Harlow, England • Reading, Massachusetts • Menlo Park, California
New York • Don Mills, Ontario • Amsterdam • Bonn • Sydney • Singapore
Tokyo • Madrid • San Juan • Milan • Mexico City • Seoul • Taipei

ORACLE®

The Relational Database Management System

Cover designed by Hybert Design & Type, Maidenhead.
Printed in the U.S.A. by R.R. Donnelly & Sons Company.

First printed in 1992. Reprinted in 1994 and 1995.

Written by Richard Barker, Cliff Longman and Barbara Barker.
Edited and illustrated by Barbara Barker.

ISBN 0-201-56525-0

British Library Cataloguing in Publication Data
A catalogue record for this book is available from the British Library

Library of Congress Cataloging in Publication Data is available

Other books available in the CASE*Method series:

Entity Relationship Modelling
Tasks and Deliverables

When ordering this book through Oracle Corporation please quote the Part Number 6867-10-0892. Contact:

Oracle Corporation UK Ltd	World Headquarters
The Oracle Centre	Oracle Corporation
The Ring, Bracknell	500 Oracle Parkway
Berkshire, RG12 1BW	Redwood Shores, CA 94065
UK	USA

FOREWORD

Never before have the challenges facing organizations been so great as they are today. Every collective human venture, commercial, social and governmental, is affected by a dramatic coincidence of change. From the accelerated effects of the social revolution started in the west during the 1960s, especially in the fields of education and politics; through globalization of businesses and the interdependence of national and geographical economies; to the enormous political unheavals of recent years and the desire of many ethnic populations for autonomy; and increased environmental awareness set against a backdrop of apparently inexorable environmental degradation, no endeavour remains untouched. All of this has been hastened by technological and media innovation.

To survive in this continuously changing environment, organizations must develop and evolve good business support systems, and to do this they must be able to articulate accurately the very nature of the business they are in or want to be in and the changes to which they are susceptible.

To meet these challenges there is a need for structured techniques which can be applied effectively together as a coherent set, aimed in the first place at describing the business itself and subsequently using that definition to drive the use of technology in an applicable way.

CASE*Method Function and Process Modelling describes a collection of such techniques for modelling what a business does or needs to do. The practical experience gained from their use in the field has been recorded by Richard and Cliff by means of a variety of examples: simple examples are used to introduce the techniques and their associated concepts, and more complex examples illustrate them at their capacity. In particular, these techniques can be used to focus rapidly and effectively on the critical aspects of what a business needs to do and to help guide the practitioner towards the development of relevant business systems.

In a world characterized by turmoil, complexity and continuous change, techniques for accurately understanding a business are a crucial asset in the business development armoury.

Mike Harrison,
Managing Director, Oracle Corporation UK Limited.

PREFACE

This, the third book in the series, was in many ways the hardest to write, the main reason being that Cliff and I only write books in our spare time and we don't have much of that these days. Our main occupation of designing methods and software is more than a part-time job. In fact, it is more than a full-time job! Another reason is that the material covered is so wide. In retrospect, we could possibly have split it between two volumes but we wanted to cover the ground in one relatively comprehensive book. With the added distractions of frequent business trips abroad, house moves and serious illness in both families, maintaining continuity of example and style has been difficult. We hope that the end result is coherent and that the joins are not too obvious.

Over the years, we have found that information systems departments have been predominantly driven by either data analysis or systems analysis. In our experience both are needed: people must be kept focused on what the **business** really does need to achieve. We have endeavoured to balance the concepts of data, function and business direction as each, on its own, is incomplete and of uncertain relevance. We have also encountered the classic 'battle of the methods' between dataflow zealots and event-modelling zealots. Each technique is relevant, useful and appropriate in some circumstances. We have written Chapter 15, "When to Use What", on this specific issue, to help you determine when to use each technique.

Life is not static and we will need to refine these techniques continually, replacing some, adding others. The advent of object modelling has been beneficial to the implementation of graphical and other software solutions, but understanding its role when modelling businesses and systems has been slower to develop. We have not covered this topic in this volume, but hope to return to it in the future.

Major technological changes will come with the exploitation of massively parallel processors, powerful miniaturized workstations, cellular-telephone-based networks, highly generic flexible CASE tools, generators for portable applications, flexible integrated application packages, and the convergence of structured data, free-format text, analogue data and multi-media technology. New approaches and techniques will be needed, creating opportunities to model businesses and systems in innovative ways. These technologies are associated with perhaps the fastest peaceful economic, political and social changes the world has seen. The only certainty in this environment is the certainty of change. A key goal for us is, therefore, to develop accurate, useful ways of thinking about the world and elegant modelling techniques to enable decision makers to have informed clarity of thought before committing to change.

Many of these new techniques will impinge on how people work together, relate to their environment, and establish cultural models to help in their business or private lives. This is a realm fraught with difficulty, inevitable given the conflicting goals, attitudes and approaches of diverse groups and individuals. These issues must be addressed as organizations become more cosmopolitan and many traditional boundaries weaken. My personal goal is to seek a balance between the conservation and ecological needs of the planet and the formidable forces of global business and politics.

Acknowledgements

I would especially like to thank Cliff for contributing the lion's share of the original text in this book and his wife Jeanette who helped with this initial writing. I would like to thank Barbara, who took these first drafts and edited them, added to them, and produced the pictures and the desktop-publishing files. I would like to thank our colleagues and customers for their encouragement and our families for their tolerance. We would also like to thank Synergix, the company whose activities we modelled for the realtime aircraft refuelling example in Chapter 13.

We hope you will find the book useful and would welcome constructive criticism and suggestions for this and any other topic associated with building the best systems we can for the businesses we support.

Richard Barker
September 1992

CONTENTS

1

INTRODUCTION

Function Modelling is a set of techniques for describing what your business does. As most businesses and organizations **do** something, these activities turn out to be very useful in helping to determine job descriptions and organization structures, and defining functional requirements for new or revised systems that accurately meet your business needs. In its simplest form, function modelling involves identifying what a business does (**functions**), what triggers those activities (**events**), and which things of significance (**entities**) or properties of those things (**attributes**) are acted upon by the functions. But this is only of value within the context of what the business is trying to achieve (**business objectives** and **aims**).

Other techniques, such as Entity Relationship Modelling, are covered by other books in this series. *CASE*Method Tasks and Deliverables*[1] describes all of the tasks that need to be carried out when going through the life-cycle of engineering a system. It suggests when various techniques should be used, along with covering project control and the important issues of building in **quality**.

Objectives of Function Modelling

The main objectives of producing a function model of an organization are:

- To provide an accurate model of the functional needs of the organization, which will then act as a framework for development of new or enhanced systems.

- To provide a model that is independent of any mechanism or processing method, allowing objective decisions to be made about alternative implementation techniques and coexistence with existing systems.

| **Generic Models** | Modelling has always been accepted by engineers, scientists, artists and accountants as an invaluable technique for presenting ideas, aiding understanding and giving insight, and even predicting new ways of doing things. Indeed, scientific theories are models not hard facts, designed on the basis of the evidence available at the time they are put forward. Many models are refined in the light of further evidence and some are finally discarded when their limitations are discovered. |

Arguably our own perception of the world is an elaborate model we create in our brains from the information we have gathered. We then hold it in such a way that it can be used to help us explain and cope with novel situations. Our imaginations and creative thinking make full use of our intellectual model of the world.

Good modelling techniques are supported by rigorous standards and conventions to remove ambiguity and aid communication. Function and process modelling involves a number of such techniques, applicable to the functional needs of any organization.

| **Complexity** | Function modelling requires the use of a variety of techniques, sometimes used in combination, to cover the different ways in which an organization may work. Each technique is applicable in different circumstances and there is a degree of overlap, just as there is in the different techniques used in geography to model the world with different types of maps, contour models, cross-sections, and so on. |

All organizations will have simple functions, such as 'hire an applicant for a job', which are relatively easy to model as descriptive text. Others will require sophisticated modelling techniques to model such things as realtime requirements. (The term business function is synonymous with function in the context of function modelling.)

| **Function Hierarchy** | The simplest and most useful technique for modelling functions is to produce a hierarchy of them, where each function is described by a simple unambiguous sentence, starting with a verb. A hierarchy is similar in layout to a family tree or organization structure. Each parent function in the hierarchy is then described in more detail by its child functions. If we take the example mentioned above ('hire an applicant for a job'), we could describe it in more detail in the form of a hierarchy as shown in Figure 1-1. |

Even this simple form of modelling can enable us to ask questions such as: *"Is this complete? What have we missed?"*. This questioning helps us to establish the complete business requirement quickly. (The function hierarchy is covered in detail in Chapter 5.)

Figure 1-1
A Function Hierarchy

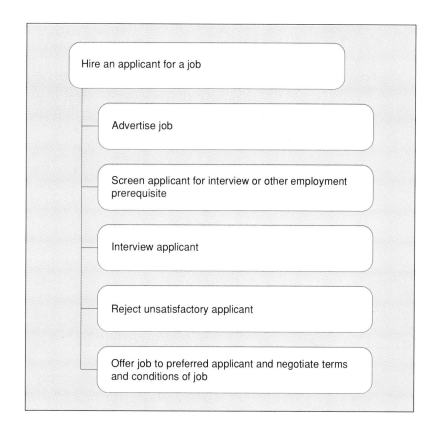

Hire an applicant for a job

Advertise job

Screen applicant for interview or other employment prerequisite

Interview applicant

Reject unsatisfactory applicant

Offer job to preferred applicant and negotiate terms and conditions of job

Events

Most organizations also have interdependent functions, which will require the additional concept of **events** (the triggers for functions). These events include external, realtime and system events.

External events are very common and are often associated with some form of communication arriving at our organization from a third party; for example, the receipt of an application for a job. This event may trigger a series of business functions, such as 'check application for accuracy', 'check availability of required job or position' and 'check qualifications or experience of applicant'.

A realtime event, as the name implies, is when a specific date and time have been reached. For example, in most organizations a whole series of business functions is triggered when real time reaches the start of a new financial year. Another example would be that when real time reaches the last Thursday in a month the function 'pay all employees on the monthly payroll' may be triggered.

System events may occur when something in the business reaches a particular state. For example, if the stock of a product at a site reaches the state where it is less than or equal to the reorder level we may trigger a function to reorder that product. System events may also be defined as occurring when one or more particular business functions have been completed, in which case other functions are triggered. (Events are covered in more detail in Chapters 3 and 7.)

Function Dependency

Function Dependency Modelling is the technique used to model the interdependencies between functions and the events that cause each function to be carried out. It is particularly useful when we need to model **cause and effect** and know what happens when some external influence affects the organization. A function dependency diagram tells us what an organization does when reacting to an event in an attempt to achieve some outcome. For example, on receipt of an application for a job, the desired outcome might be to set up an interview or reject the application within five days of receiving it. (Function Dependency is covered in detail in Chapter 7.)

Dataflow Modelling

Interdependence between functions can also be shown by the use of another technique, called **Dataflow Modelling**. Often functions cannot be carried out until information is made available from some other source: the information may come from other functions, or it may come from somewhere external to the business. Imagine you are responsible for ordering goods for a group of shops. Before you place an order you may need to know how much stock you have sold, how much you have left and how quickly you have sold various items, before you decide when and how much to order.

Dataflow modelling shows this interdependence between functions by defining real or virtual flows of data (information) between functions. This technique is particularly important when modelling some existing, complicated, flow-oriented process in a business, such as dealing with an insurance claim. It is just as useful when defining a new flow-oriented process. (Dataflow Modelling is covered in detail in Chapter 11.)

Realtime Modelling

The other major technique is **Realtime Modelling**, which is used to handle operations that are continuously changing as a result of external influences.

Let us take Newton's Laws of Motion as applied to landing a space shuttle as an analogy. These laws work pretty well in everyday circumstances: we can take details about initial velocity, mass, acceleration, and so on, and predict the way in which things will move, how far, with what final velocity and in what time. When used in laboratory conditions the scientists will normally try to eliminate other influences to enable the laws to be used accurately – they often talk about experiments where friction does not play a part. However, a lot more needs to be considered if you are responsible for safely landing a space shuttle on to the Earth during a force ten gale! A **realtime** system would continuously monitor all the relevant external events, such as change of wind direction, and relevant internal ones, such as change of mass as fuel is used up, and react dynamically and instantaneously to correct the process and hopefully achieve the desired result.

Realtime modelling is, therefore, a technique that enables us to describe the complex interactions of various events and the status of things in a system accurately, and show what functions or processes are carried out under different conditions (typically by a diagram). In really dynamic situations a process may be part of the way through completion of some discrete task when factors change, causing the process to be aborted or modified in some way. This type of modelling is particularly useful when modelling control systems. (Realtime Modelling is covered in detail in Chapters 12 and 13.)

Function Logic

What a function must do under different circumstances often has to be described in precise detail. This detailed logic is defined using a technique that states the step-by-step process. The steps may need to be in a particular sequence, iteration may be needed, and often there is a choice of alternative steps. This would be a procedural means of defining detailed function logic. Alternatively, the logic may be defined by stating the required outcomes and the conditions under which different outcomes would be achieved. This non-procedural way of detailing function logic is also very useful, and often relates better to systems that use fourth-generation languages and Structured Query Language (SQL).

**Business,
System or Program**

Each of the function modelling techniques described above can be used at different levels of abstraction. When an existing system needs to be replaced, these techniques are often used to model the existing system to gain an understanding of what is currently done, to model a new system, and then to model the various detailed system components, such as computer programs or clerical procedures. On a larger scale, however, it is more appropriate to model what the organization or business actually does or needs to do. Given **that** understanding, new or refined systems can then be modelled to reflect this business need.

The business level is thus what the organization does or needs to do. The resulting models will be strongly influenced by what the executives in the organization believe should be done, balanced by the pragmatism of expert practictioners.

The system level is how these business requirements may be logically supported by some mixture of processes that can subsequently be computerized or implemented in some fashion. Systems are major differentiators between companies and organizations, and are strongly influenced in their design by innovators, visionaries, consultants and other practical exponents in the industry concerned.

The program or procedure level is how a system may be physically implemented by a combination of clerical, computer or other mechanisms. The choice of implementation techniques will be based on cost, availability, applicability to the problem, technology strategies, ease of use, and a variety of other factors.

The following table provides an overview of when these techniques are generally applicable. The symbols below show the representation used for functions at each level. When you meet these techniques in the book only one symbol will be used, but the technique may also be used at the other levels as indicated. The applicability is restated in the introduction of the detailed definition of each technique.

Figure 1-2
When to Use the Various Modelling Techniques

Modelling Technique	Business Level	System Level	Program/ Procedure Level	
Function Hierarchy	p	p	p	Acts as scope for all functions
Function Dependency	o	p	o	Interdependent functions
Dataflow	o	p	o	Flow orientation
Realtime	–	p	p	Event driven
Function Logic	p	p	o	Detail for any of the above requiring explicit logic definition

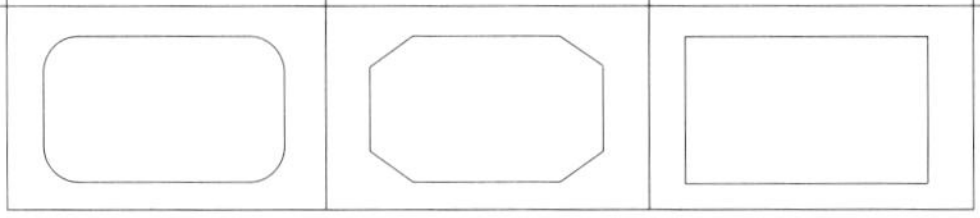

Key
p – primary technique
o – optional technique

The Key Issues

To be effective, the techniques mentioned above need to be used in a focused manner. A number of key issues need to be addressed before you can successfully model what a business does or needs to do and subsequently develop any systems.

Figure 1-3
The Key Issues

Key Issues

- Functions, What Your Organization Does
- Management Commitment
- Conventions
- Unambiguous Definition
- Independence from Mechanisms
- Pre-empting Change
- Common Functions
- Attitude and Quality
- Applicability
- A Means, Not an End

Functions – What Your Organization Does

Every organization exists to fulfil some purpose. This may be measured by the aims and objectives it is trying to achieve, usually in a product or service sense. A manufacturer of electrical goods may want to produce and sell a certain number of washing machines and refrigerators each year; a youth counselling service may set a target to have seventy percent of its clients able to cope with their problems after eight visits to a counsellor. The ultimate aim of one organization is financial and that of the other humanitarian. Both can be referred to as businesses, and the techniques of business modelling are of benefit to all types of organization.

It is vital to thoroughly understand **what** a business has to do to achieve its objectives. Function modelling is the process of defining this, in a manner that is independent of the organization structure, people or mechanisms that may be deployed to fulfil these functions. Given such a pure model, it is possible to evaluate how well existing clerical and computer systems are meeting the business needs.

New or replacement systems can then be designed, taking into consideration constraints such as organization structure, and the resources and technologies available. Subsequently, system design may be modified to take advantage of new technology or to cater for a new organization, using the original function model as the framework. Unless the essence of the business changes in some way, the function model stands the test of time. Functions must be modelled, at the business level, within the context of what the organization is trying to achieve, and in a manner that allows alternative system implementations to be considered or deployed.

Management Commitment

The benefits from any business modelling technique will be limited unless the executives and opinion leaders contribute towards their accuracy and 'buy into' the implications. Objective, apolitical models often suggest rationalizations that may be beneficial to the organization. Management must be fully involved in the business modelling process and any consequent decisions, and committed to such change if it is to be adopted successfully.

Conventions

These powerful modelling techniques must follow rigorous conventions, as illustrated throughout this book. But experience has shown that rigour alone is not enough. To lead to tangible benefits to the business, the conventions used must also be clear, unambiguous and easily understood by users and executives as well as data processing people. There must be no compromise in ensuring that the functions are described in pure English (i.e. where English is the primary spoken language), using the terminology of the organization and avoiding jargon. When in Germany, obviously German must be used; and for that matter when in Texas, or Scotland, or Australia, the form of the language should be relevant to the participants (i.e. the appropriate local variant). Attention to this level of communication detail pays real benefits in the speed and quality of building appropriate systems.

Unambiguous Definition

Function definitions must represent the essence of **what** the business does, as opposed to **how** it does it. The appropriate technique must be employed to model different types of function – simple, realtime, flow-oriented and so on. A simple test can be used to check the degree of understanding and ambiguity of any function definition – if we give the definition to several different users **will they all have the same understanding**, perhaps illustrated by different but equally valid examples? And will our data processing people also have the same understanding? If not, later on they will get comments from their users such as, *"That is not what I asked for!"* .

Independence from Mechanisms

At the business level, functions should be defined in a manner that is independent of how they will eventually be carried out (the mechanisms). Thus the business model can remain valid, and the eventual system can evolve to reap the benefits of advances in the enabling technologies or be more easily adapted to other changes in circumstances. For example, there must be different ways in which a company can place an order: verbally across the table, by telephone, by letter, by facsimile, and so on. As technology extends, new ways are being found. Nowadays, with some companies, you can place an order via a device attached to your television set or via electronic mail from systems in a customer organization connected directly to a major supplier. This does not change **what** the business does (placing the order), only **how** it is carried out.

Pre-empting Change

As businesses evolve and move into new markets or add new levels of service, they tend to expand into areas that are closely aligned to what they already do and know well – a low-risk expansion policy. A good analyst or designer can often produce powerful generic models that will cater for such evolution with little or no change. This is mainly a matter of identifying similar patterns of data or reusable functionality and processes. Systems that are built to support generic functionality are more flexible and responsive to change, and at a much lower maintenance cost. Change can also be pre-empted by using opinion leaders, and creative thinkers and modellers to expand any model to a wider picture of what might be possible. Executives can then select the areas that are most likely to be useful and let the systems designers build in flexibility in some key areas.

Common Functions

In any business, identifying duplication of effort and common functionality can be of benefit. It can help the system designer to produce simpler, clearer and more useful models. It can also enable us to take advantage of reusable processing logic, giving more modular designs, which are inherently flexible to change. Similar benefits can be made in business terms; in particular, by eliminating redundant activity, streamlining processes, learning from others and refocusing effort.

Finding common functions can assist rationalization of the business, simplification of function models, and the production of more flexible systems that cost less time and money to develop.

Attitude and Quality

Function modelling gets very close to what people actually do in their day-to-day work, so the approach must be apolitical; it must be seen as totally independent from personal, organizational or other interests. The danger is that a weak analyst will be persuaded to model exactly what is done today: managers who see any new way of doing things as a threat will insist on their own style of accuracy. The analyst's attitude must be objective, persuasive and educational, and of course the models must be obviously correct, useful and appropriate.

To get a high level of quality and accuracy various guidelines should be followed. The source of information is key: analysts must have access to the most knowledgeable, visionary, responsible and pragmatic users. They must be allowed to observe what is done and get to know the business to synthesize models of how it could be done – a type of business prototyping. You need to understand what happens now to avoid missing vital aspects of the current business often forgotten in the haste of thinking about how things could be. Later on, during system design, practical issues must be considered, and cost effectiveness, usability, acceptability, maintainability and other factors need careful balancing.

Quality and completeness are invariably improved by cross-checking against other related models, against checklists and against models from other similar organizations. Selected quality checkers can add tremendous value – these could be systems people from other projects, specialists or people who are good at role-playing different viewpoints. The acid test and the ultimate quality input come from the users, who need to be encouraged to find omissions, errors, inconsistencies and improvements in the wording. Given this level of emphasis on quality at this stage, the likelihood of producing a high-quality, acceptable system will go up by an order of magnitude. But beware: there is a danger of analysis paralysis from unnecessary insistence on absolute perfection and involving every person that may be affected. A small representative group with the necessary balance of skills and experience is the most effective way to deliver quickly and adequately. Results should be forthcoming on a six-to-twelve week cycle to keep momentum going, users involved and team morale high.

Applicability

The applicability of function models can make a real difference to the time taken to develop systems, the ability to reuse concepts and the appropriateness of solutions. If asked to replace an inventory system, for example, an analyst can usefully model quite widely around the subject area, without of course missing any of the salient aspects of the subject. In this process we invariably find commonality that will allow economies of scale and reuse of concepts. The downside is that no one is prepared to go ahead with anything until the whole scope has been covered. Systems are like businesses: people must make decisions – balanced judgements to enable progress to be made. And the scope is often a balance between cost, benefit, reusability, scale, timeliness, priorities and other factors.

To get appropriate and applicable system models you need to involve people who are good at making balanced business decisions.

A Means, Not an End

Some people enjoy function modelling so much that they lose sight of what they are trying to do! Function and process modelling is just one of a set of useful techniques that enable us to understand requirements, devise good systems designs and create cost-effective, appropriate systems. There is no point in producing perfect function models whilst a company goes into liquidation for lack of a new mission-critical system. The end is the operational availability of the right systems, on time, within budget. Function modelling is only a means.

Benefits of Function Modelling

The most obvious benefit from a good function model is a clear understanding of what is required before we start designing and building a system. In the last thirty years a large proportion of systems have been rejected by their users because, quite simply, the systems departments did not have a clue what was really needed. Understanding what is required leads to huge savings in cost and time as it is relatively easy to build something and get it right (more or less) first time when you have a clear objective and definitive design. The system will also have credibility with its users.

Identifying reusable components and generic solutions can also save time and money. Such components can also lead to solutions that can cater for change in the business **without** changing the system.

Secondary benefits can come from unexpected quarters though some may be difficult to quantify. For example, users from different parts of an organization may, for the first time, actually understand what each does individually and how they can work together. Many organizations have used function models to help them assess what different departments do, how appropriate job and role definitions are, the effectiveness of organizational structures and how much redundancy of effort there is within the organization. This can be a catalyst to changes that lead to significant improvements in overall productivity and effectiveness, with the useful backdrop that the systems that subsequently appear will fit the organizational changes being made.

Quantum Improvement

Many organizations are critically re-examining what they do and how they do it. They are looking for quantum improvements in profitability, cost utilization, market penetration, service level, or some other business parameter. Radical changes in the business process are often needed. Sometimes, this means taking the same events that affect the business and their required outcome, and totally re-engineering the process by which this is attained. On other occasions, improving some small, but critical, part of the process will provide a radical improvement. This activity is sometimes referred to as business process re-engineering.

The function and process modelling techniques shown in this book can and should be used as a catalyst to change. They can be focused on the four or five really key processes that the business must get right to meet its goals. The techniques can be used, in particular, to model and therefore prototype possible new ways of running the business. This work **must** be done with the executives responsible for corporate direction, and when done well can have enormous benefits to an organization. Such changes must nearly always be accompanied by careful change management in organizational, cultural and other areas.

The best way of finding the benefits of function modelling is to talk to companies and organizations that have gone through the process and seen the results. They will also have discovered the costs as well as the benefits, and a bonus from such references may be a list of things to avoid and other lessons they have learnt.

Reminder

Function modelling should never be conducted in isolation. It must always be accompanied by a clear understanding of the objectives, aims and priorities of the business, which give a context and applicability to the models. It should also be mirrored by a comprehensive information model (entity relationship model) where each item of information has corresponding functions that act upon it. Conversely, each function must refer to and possibly affect some item of information.

How to Use This Book

This book is designed to give the novice insight and understanding into the modelling process and to provide the expert with advanced techniques and useful guidelines.

Chapters covering the basic techniques are marked with a ▭ in the margin. If you are new to the techniques, try to follow the examples and have a go yourself as soon as possible, but do not worry about the advanced examples or detailed quality checks until you feel more confident with the primary aspects of the techniques. More advanced sections and appendices are marked with a ▬ in the margin.

The appendices provide additional information and guidelines about the techniques, and function models for the main examples used throughout the book. A glossary covers all the important terms, and the extensive index and contents list provide alternative entry points to the information in the book.

2

A SIMPLE EXAMPLE

Before diving into the full rigour of function modelling, let us look at an example and how we might model it. We will then have a look at why a function model is useful, by considering two possible systems that might result from our example. This approach is particularly applicable to the business level ⬜, but it can also be applied to the system level ⬜. The full set of definitions, rules and guidelines for function modelling follows in Chapters 3, 4 and 5.

Throughout the book we will be using a variety of everyday examples to illustrate the different concepts and techniques. With the first example, which is based on the airline industry, you will find that your personal knowledge of air travel, problems at airports, and what you would deduce goes on behind the scenes will be of value when working through it. We start by looking at the process of making a reservation.

The Example

When travelling by air it is normal to reserve a seat on a flight before turning up at the airport. Consider a hypothetical airline called 'Atlantis Island Flights' and a business traveller trying to get from Atlantia, the capital city of the island group Atlantis, to Honolulu in Hawaii for a business convention.

Our businessman enlists the services of a travel agent, who telephones the airline reservations desk on his behalf to make the reservation.

**Figure 2-1
Requesting a
Reservation**

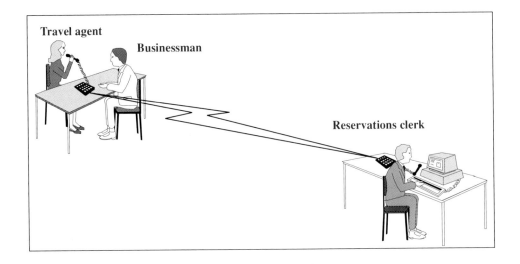

*The reservations clerk asks for the details of the traveller's itinerary – he
wants to get from Atlantia to Honolulu in time for the start of the
convention at 10.30 a.m. on Monday 12th July. The clerk then makes an
enquiry on the company's flight information computer and finds that there
is a flight arriving at 8.30 p.m. on Sunday 11th July.*

**Figure 2-2
Flight Enquiry Screen**

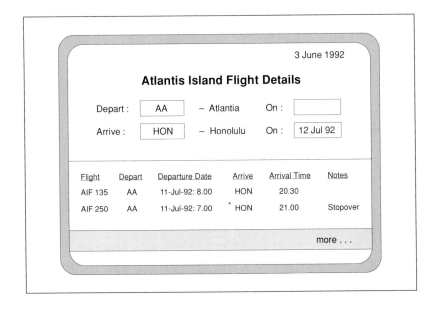

*The agent says that this flight would be fine, so the reservations clerk
checks for availability of seats.*

Figure 2-3
Availability Request

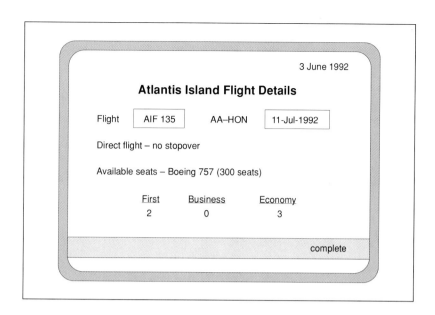

The Function Model

The function that the clerk is trying to carry out is that of reserving a seat on a particular flight, and, as you have already seen, this is performed in a number of steps. The steps we have identified so far can be modelled as shown in Figure 2-4; each box represents a business function.

Figure 2-4
The Basic Function Model

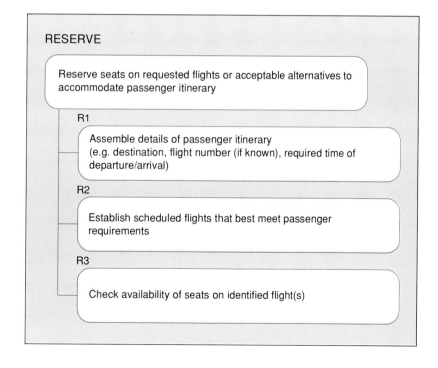

Each function is a structured sentence describing something that needs to be done in the business, and is of the form:

verb object . . .

for example, reserve seats . . .

We avoid stating **how** the function is to be carried out; that is decided during the design of a system to support chosen business functions. You will notice that the words computer and telephone are **not** used, as both are just alternative ways of carrying out the function. Nor is the agent mentioned, as the functions could be carried out directly, or via some other organization unit; these are implementation issues.

This basic model has four functions in it. The top-level function describes the part of the business we are modelling (reservation of a seat on a flight that accommodates the passenger's itinerary). The three functions immediately below it show components of the function in more detail. This process of subdivision into smaller steps is known as **decomposition** of a function into its sub-functions; that is, the top-level function is achieved by these three more detailed functions.

We can also consider the detailed functions as a simple list of sentences that describe **what** is done. A higher-level function is then just a natural grouping that seems to make sense, enabling us to ask questions such as:

"Have we missed any detail here?"
"What exceptions might there be which need to be catered for?"
"Is there anything else that might be necessary in order to carry out the function?"

Or we might observe the following:

"Oh yes, and I always prefer to fly on XYZ airline so I can get a frequent flyer credit."

We could record this as a function to take account of the preferences of prospective passengers.

So functions are just simple, clear statements of what is done, and are easy for anyone to understand.

The Example
(continued)

The first-choice flight is fully booked for business class, but there is an earlier flight that includes a connection at Los Angeles and gets into Honolulu at 9.00 p.m. Our businessman would prefer the original flight if possible, so he is put on a waiting list (or 'waitlisted') for Flight AIF 135 and a firm reservation is made for a seat on Flight AIF 250 (change at Los Angeles). The reservations clerk links the two requests so that the reservation on Flight AIF 250 can be given up to somebody else if the waitlist place becomes available.

The remaining details are taken, including our traveller's request for a seat in the non-smoking section and a vegetarian meal, and the booking is complete for now. The tickets will be sent out two weeks before departure.

Figure 2-5
The Extended
Function Model

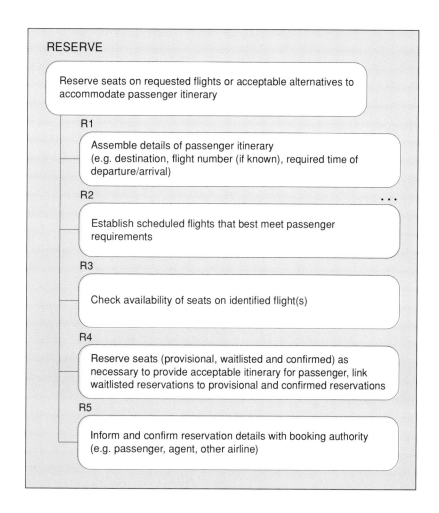

The Function Model (continued)

The telephone call with a request for a reservation is an **event**; it causes the Atlantis Island Flights reservations clerk to respond with a procedure for reserving a seat on a flight. The event, in this case, is an external happening that causes the business to react in some way. The reaction to an event is the execution of one or more business functions. In our example, the phone call triggers a series of functions, establishing enough information for the clerk to check on the flight availability. One of these

(R2 in Figure 2-5) is in fact quite complex and needs to be decomposed (subdivided) into more detail, indicated by the points of ellipsis (. . .) at the top-right of the box labelled R2.

Let us take a look at the detail of this function, R2. Notice that it can be subdivided into functions in a similar way to the decomposition of RESERVE. Each box is still a function, but they are becoming more and more detailed as we go down this hierarchy. The event has been added as a hollow arrow pointing to the function it triggers (causes the business to carry out), in this case the highest level function on the diagram, R2.

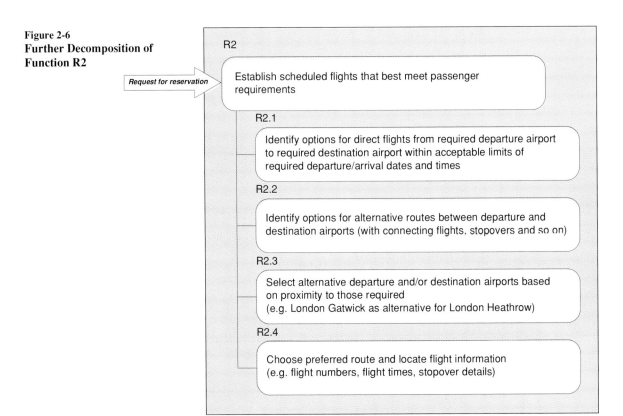

**Figure 2-6
Further Decomposition of
Function R2**

A Short Summary

Before moving on, let us recap on what we have found so far. An **event** (the agent telephoning to request a reservation) caused the airline reservations clerk to carry out a series of **business functions**. This was modelled by describing what was being done overall (RESERVE Function), which was then decomposed into its component parts (R1 to R5). One of these functions (R2) was subsequently decomposed further as more details became known. A full function model for this part of the business would look something like Figure 2-7.

Figure 2-7
Full Function Model
(showing three levels)

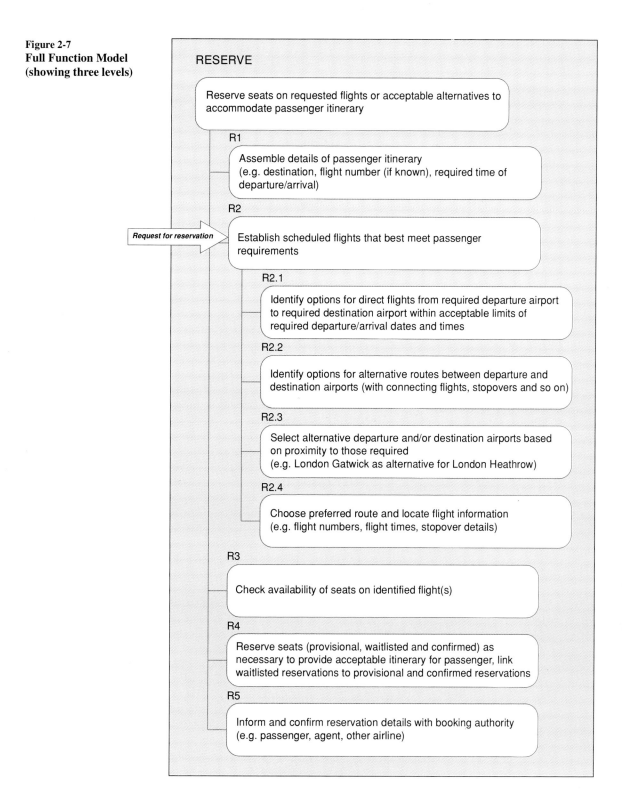

RESERVE

Reserve seats on requested flights or acceptable alternatives to accommodate passenger itinerary

R1

Assemble details of passenger itinerary (e.g. destination, flight number (if known), required time of departure/arrival)

R2

Request for reservation →

Establish scheduled flights that best meet passenger requirements

R2.1

Identify options for direct flights from required departure airport to required destination airport within acceptable limits of required departure/arrival dates and times

R2.2

Identify options for alternative routes between departure and destination airports (with connecting flights, stopovers and so on)

R2.3

Select alternative departure and/or destination airports based on proximity to those required (e.g. London Gatwick as alternative for London Heathrow)

R2.4

Choose preferred route and locate flight information (e.g. flight numbers, flight times, stopover details)

R3

Check availability of seats on identified flight(s)

R4

Reserve seats (provisional, waitlisted and confirmed) as necessary to provide acceptable itinerary for passenger, link waitlisted reservations to provisional and confirmed reservations

R5

Inform and confirm reservation details with booking authority (e.g. passenger, agent, other airline)

A Simple Example   19

Once again you will notice that when describing the event we do not mention that the request was made by telephone. The telephone is one means of requesting a reservation but there are lots of alternatives. We could fax the request; it could be done completely by computer; or even verbally from a reservation clerk across the room. How an event or function is carried out is called a mechanism. Mechanisms have also been removed from the business functions, so no references to the computer system or any other way of doing a function remain. This enables the function model to stay valid as a statement of requirement, even when the mechanism changes; as new technology appears, for instance. It also caters for the fact that there may be several alternative ways of carrying out the function, each of which is perfectly acceptable to the organization.

Let us now extend the model a little further.

Back to the Example

This financial year Atlantis Island Flights has an objective to increase its annual revenue from business ticket sales by five percent. The company has decided to improve business class travel in a number of ways: it will provide a personalized seat allocation for regular business travellers, a special executive lounge in the main airport at Atlantia, and follow these two services up with some direct marketing and advertising.

Returning to our business traveller; he has just arrived at the check-in desk and is about to have a seat allocated to him. Because he has a confirmed ticket, the airline knows there will be sufficient seats on the plane, but the time has come to allocate a specific, numbered seat to our passenger. The airline representative checks for the availability of seats in business class and sees that there are plenty of unallocated seats, and that the traveller has previously stated a preference for an aisle seat in the non-smoking section. This is confirmed with the traveller by asking whether he would like his 'usual seat'. One of the available aisle seats in the middle of the business class section is selected and allocated to him. In addition, the airline representative notices he requested a vegetarian meal and confirms that this is still required.

Let us examine the overall function 'allocate seat to passenger'. We can now indicate specifically why this is important to the business, by including reference to a business objective; for example, 'allocate seat to passenger to achieve stated preferences wherever possible (e.g. known preferences for a regular traveller)'.

We can then break this down further as shown in Figure 2-8 opposite.

Figure 2-8
The Function
'Allocate Seat to Passenger'

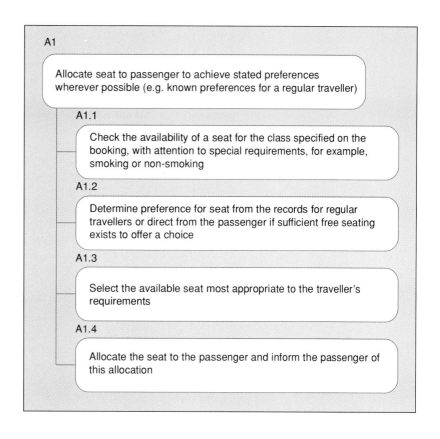

Referring to regular travellers' personal preferences for seat allocation is one of the ways in which the airline hopes to make business travel more pleasant, and thus achieve its objective of an increase in its share of the business travel market. A business objective is some measurable target that a business has set itself to achieve within a defined timescale*; in this example:

> *to increase its annual revenue from business ticket sales by five percent by the end of the financial year.*

Focusing on a specific objective helps in understanding **why** a business function is significant, and provides a tangible basis from which to develop relevant business support systems.

---

*   To see whether the objective has been attained, we could make a note at this point to add some functions into the model to set business objectives and measure actual achievement against business objectives. Generic functions of this type occur frequently; Appendix E may help you identify extra ones.

Figure 2-9 summarizes the whole function model. This time it has been presented in an alternative layout to make it easier to read and take up less space. Other styles of layout are discussed in Chapter 5.

Figure 2-9
The Function Model to date

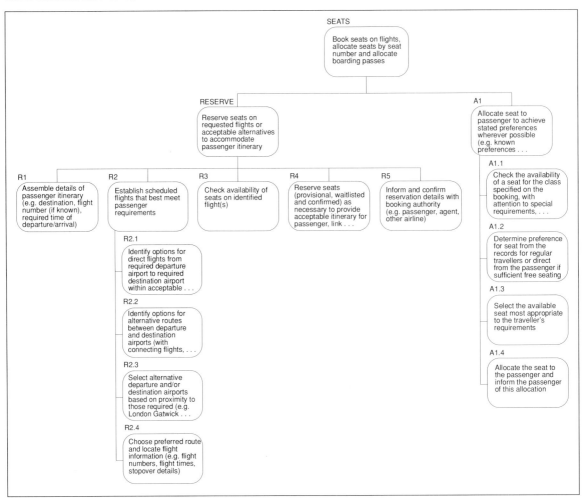

System Implementation

Having established what the **business** does, or needs to do, we can examine alternative ways in which a **system** (not necessarily a computer system) could support the function 'allocate seat to passenger'.

A Computer System

Figure 2-10 shows a computer screen used to implement the 'allocate seat to passenger' function. The seating arrangement of the aircraft on which we want to reserve a seat is shown graphically, with seats that have

Figure 2-10
Seating Allocation Screen

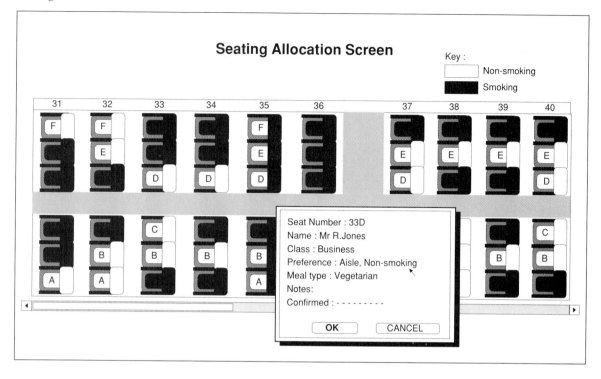

already been reserved in a darker shade. The operator of this screen uses a mouse as a pointing device to indicate which of the non-reserved seats to allocate. The passenger's details are shown as a pop-up box, which includes any special requirements. Having indicated which seat to reserve, the operator will point to the OK button with the mouse and click here to make the reservation. As the computer makes the reservation, it will print the number of the seat that has been reserved on the boarding card for the passenger.

A Manual System

Now let us consider an alternative implementation for this function. A diagram of the seat layout is positioned at the boarding gate for the flight, and as passengers arrive the airline representative points out which of the seats on the diagram are still available. Passengers make a choice and the airline representative peels a piece of adhesive coloured paper with the seat number on it from the diagram and sticks it onto the boarding card. This single operation simultaneously allocates the seat to the passenger and shows, by the blank space, that the seat is no longer available.

Figure 2-11
The Sticky Paper Version

A Note on Performance

What is important here is the performance and integrity of the system, as a whole, in achieving the business function, not how fast a screen responds to any particular request (although, of course, that has a distinct bearing on how usable a screen is). How long does it actually take to reserve a seat for a passenger? And can we ensure that a seat is not allocated twice?

In all systems, functions will tend to be implemented by a mixture of processes – clerical, computerized and many that are just done in the mind (cerebral activity). Together, these achieve something of use to the business. Any specific performance requirements can be recorded against the business function; for instance, it might be important that the function 'allocate seat to passenger' be achievable within thirty seconds and that each seat be allocated to one passenger only for a given flight.

**So What
Have We Found?**

Function models are used to represent what a business does, or needs to do, to meet its objectives and respond to events:

- A business function is something that the business does, or needs to do, and is represented on a diagram by a box with rounded corners.

- An objective is something quantifiable (you can measure it) and is something that the business has set out to achieve. The importance of business functions is made more visible when they are tied to specific objectives.

- Functions are arranged in a hierarchy, with increasing detail at the lower levels; this is for convenience and as a navigation facility, giving a context to a function when it is being read (i.e. it needs to be done to achieve its parent function). This arrangement also helps us to check for completeness.

- We describe functions in a way that is independent of any possible implementation mechanism; that is, we record **what** the function is, not **how** it is to be carried out.

- Events are happenings, often external to the business, which trigger business functions and are shown as hollow arrows.

Function models are constructed in a manner that is independent of any implementation technique and organizational implications. The computer and manual examples illustrate just two alternative ways that a functional requirement can be implemented. The description of a function can thus be used to describe the business requirement unambiguously, and when implemented by some computer process, for example, can be used to check that the chosen mechanism adequately meets the user needs.

So function models are really useful ways of clearly describing what a business does so that users, analysts and system engineers can agree on the requirement. They are also independent of mechanisms or organization, and thus can be used for many years, even if the organization changes or new mechanisms are found.

This chapter has dealt with a simple example, and it is interesting to note some of the more sophisticated things that we may need to consider to satisfy the modern business requirement. We may need to worry about safety and security aspects such as whether the passenger actually boards the aircraft, whether the luggage is put on the correct plane and how to cater for passengers who did not show up. In all cases, however, the analyst must model **what** is done, not **how** it is done.

3

BASIC CONVENTIONS AND DEFINITIONS

This chapter describes the basic conventions and definitions for business objectives, business functions, elementary business functions and events, all at the business level ⬜. More advanced conventions and definitions are addressed in Chapters 7, 9, 11, 12 and 13. A very brief overview of the entity relationship modelling technique is given in the section on 'Information Modelling' on pages 34-37.

Business Objective

We often talk rather loosely about business aims and objectives, goals and mission statements. In this method, a goal and objective are considered to be one and the same thing, and a mission statement is a global objective of an organization, perhaps covering a three or four year period. For now, let us only consider aims and objectives; both are statements of intent. Aims refer to targets that may be measured subjectively. In a business situation this could be an intention to 'go up market'. On a personal level you might aim to improve your personal 'standing in society'. But what do you intend to do to achieve these aims?

Business Objective Definition

A business objective is a **quantifiable** goal or target that a business is trying to achieve. To focus on the most important aspects of the business, it must be **measurable objectively** – it must be possible to ascertain whether or not the objective has been achieved.* Such objectivity also allows a business to measure its progress towards an objective at a point in time or for a given period of time.

* It is useful to check whether an objective is SMART; that is: Specific, Measurable, Achievable, Relevant and Trackable.

To realize the aims we stated above, we need to set some objectives. The business might decide to diversify its product set (an aim) by achieving a portfolio of thirty products by the end of the year (an objective). We can then measure progress, success or failure in achieving this objective, by simply counting the products. In personal terms you might set yourself an objective of reducing your bank overdraft by a half (let's not be too ambitious) before your next birthday: again success is easily quantified. How you will achieve either objective is another matter!

Our make-believe airline Atlantis Island Flights has an objective:

> *to increase annual revenue from business ticket sales by 5% by the end of the next financial year.*

'Annual revenue', 'business ticket sales' and 'the next financial year' all need to be defined, so that progress towards the objective can be measured. This is done in terms of the information or objects available to the organization, which we would model using an entity relationship model (see pages 34-37). Useful entities or objects of interest here might be a target and a financial period. More information would be held about each of these and how they relate to other objects. A specific target might be to achieve a certain minimum amount of revenue within a specific financial period, such as the second quarter of the financial year. Functions can then manipulate these objects, for example, to 'set target for the business for the required financial period'.

**Figure 3-1
A Business Model**

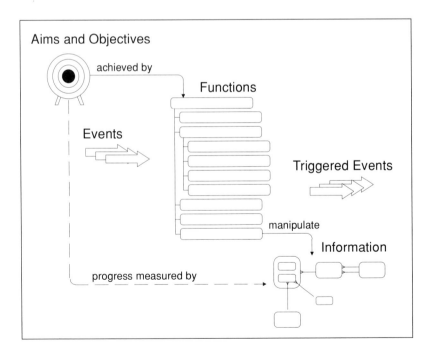

Relevance to Function Modelling

Knowledge of objectives is a key aspect of function modelling. If a business function does not help to achieve the stated objectives of the business, we would question whether, in fact, it is necessary at all. Of course, good analysts will question whether they have understood **all** the objectives before disposing of a business function, thereby capitalizing on a useful cross-check between the different aspects of the business model.

Business Function

Business Function Definition

A business function is something an enterprise does, or needs to do in the future, to help achieve its objectives. Business functions might be:

- from a car rental company – *agree the terms and conditions of a rental agreement with customer (e.g. hire charge, insurance cover)*
- from a credit company – *identify customers with overdue payments*
- from a charity – *allocate and distribute available monies to chosen causes*
- from a pharmaceutical company – *test new product through toxicological studies, pre-clinical trials, clinical trials or other means to ensure safety for use by customer*
- from a health service – *carry out planned, routine and emergency operations on patients*
- from a government department – *set levels of taxation in line with government policy.*

They all start with a verb and actively describe **what** is done, or needs to be done, using only terms in daily use in the business. As a useful shorthand, throughout this book the term 'function' is also used to mean 'business function'.

Figure 3-2 A Business Function

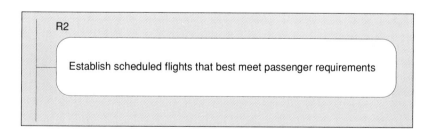

R2

Establish scheduled flights that best meet passenger requirements

Function Representation

A business function is shown as a softbox (a rectangle with rounded corners) with its full name written inside the box, and a short name or label outside the top left-hand corner of the box. Points of ellipsis (. . .) are placed outside the top right-hand corner when a function has been decomposed into more detail, but that detail is not currently shown on this diagram (usually for brevity or for presentation purposes).

Function Names

From the example used in Chapter 2 you will already have realized that function names are not simple names in the conventional sense of a word by which a thing is known, but more a sentence describing something that needs to be done.

The name of the business function should be a full and descriptive text, using terms familiar in the business whilst, at the same time, being terse, accurate and only referring to concepts defined in other parts of the business model (see section on information modelling later in this chapter). This balance of accurate description and brevity has been found to provide an engineering discipline to the modelling process, and the resulting clarity helps to get the models right more quickly.

Abbreviations, acronyms, jargon (except maybe one or two terms, widely used and unambiguous in the particular business) and other language not in common use should be avoided. Above all, the name must be clear and understandable: you are going to have to present this material to have it checked!

A good practice to adopt is to use a consistent format for writing all the function names. This makes the hierarchy easier to read. Each name should be a structured sentence, starting with a verb. Adopt the same form of the verb through the hierarchy – the imperative is recommended. It should continue with the object of the verb, followed by any further detail required to qualify these. The essential parts are the 'do' and the 'what'. For example, using the function shown in Figure 3-2, these would be:

Establish (scheduled) flights

with the rest of this function further qualifying the object *flights*.

It is sometimes useful to include an example to clarify part of the function. For instance:

. . . confirm reservation details with booking authority
(e.g. passenger, agent, other airline).

Function Labels

The function label is simply a short name or tag that is used for convenience, so that the function can be referred to without resorting to its full and lengthy name. The label is usually less than a dozen characters, and is either a short mnemonic (say, RESERVE) or a number indicating the business function's position in the hierarchy (e.g. R1.2.4. would be the fourth function under the second function under the first function under RESERVE).

Function Hierarchy

Business functions are arranged in a hierarchy, starting at the top with a single business function describing the entire business or the scope under study. This overall 'parent' function is split into other business functions, each of which represents, in more detail, a part of its parent. Any business function in the hierarchy should be described **completely** by the detail below it: that is, nothing **other** than its detail should be necessary to carry it out and all functions below it do help to carry it out. For those of you familiar with menu systems on a computer, think of it as a menu where each of the options appears once only. Later on in the book we find a new concept called a common function, which is analogous to having the same menu option appear in different parts of the menu hierarchy.

Decomposed Functions

The decomposition symbol (. . .), placed outside the top right-hand corner of the softbox, indicates that further details of this function can be found below this level in the function hierarchy. Typically, in a paper-based documentation system, a piece of paper will be found which has this function at the top of the page with decomposition on the page below it. In computer-aided documentation tools, multiple levels of decomposition can often be viewed at the same time on a workstation screen.

Sub-functions

A sub-function is a useful term for any function that has a parent. Two or more sub-functions provide the detail for the parent function.

Figure 3-3
Part of a Large Function Hierarchy

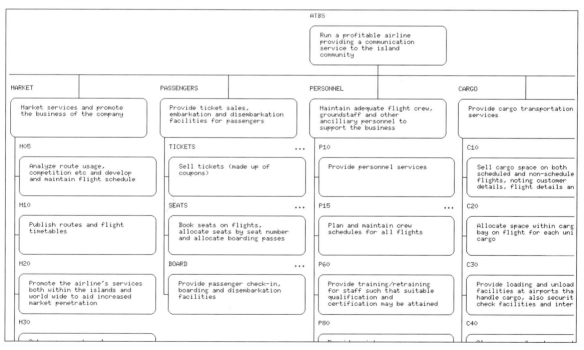

Function Modelling Rules	In the early stages of constructing a hierarchy and defining business functions, we have found it helpful to use more than one verb in the function name. This extends the scope of the function and helps to ensure that nothing is missed; as in 'define and maintain standard crew profiles'. This would affect the functions in the decomposition, since functions both to define **and** maintain standard profiles would be required.

As a general guideline, refer to things in the function name in the singular (this becomes easier as functions become more detailed) – use 'check in passenger and baggage for a specified flight' in preference to 'check in passengers and baggage for specified flights'. It helps to reduce the ambiguity of the function name and will make checking against the other parts of the business model easier. However, if you look back at the functions used in Chapter 2 you will notice that in many cases plurals are unavoidable (rather than the authors not sticking to the rules).

As far as possible, ensure that each function, described by its full name, appears in the function hierarchy only once.

Conditional Functions	Sometimes business functions are only carried out under certain conditions. When constructing function models, those conditions are included in the full name of the function. At a more detailed stage, they can be taken out and recorded formally. But to avoid losing important conditions, it is best to record them as they become known; for example, 'identify alternative flights **if requested flight is full**'.

An Acid Test	The purpose of a function modelling exercise is to understand **what** the business does, or needs to do, to achieve its objectives. Imagine taking the chief executive officer (CEO) of the enterprise through each of the functions that you are documenting and ask yourself:

> *"Have I understood what is going on and captured the essence of the business in the words that I am writing?"*

> *"Will the CEO recognize the business, as described by the function hierarchy?"*

Removing Mechanisms	**How** the business carries out the functions to achieve its objectives is a mechanism. There are various classes of mechanism, for example:

- cerebral (done in your head)
- computer (done electronically)
- mechanical (done by machine)
- manual (done by people).

There is almost always more than one alternative mechanism for implementing a given function, so it is important to keep function names free of mechanisms whilst creating a function model. Take the function 'issue ticket to passenger': this could be done by post, courier, even by hand, or by delivery to the departure airport for collection by the passenger. And nowadays, the ticket could even be in the form of a magnetic recording resembling a credit card, instead of the usual piece of paper or card. The purpose of function modelling is to record **what** is required in business terms, not to pre-empt **how** that requirement is to be satisfied.

People are usually more comfortable talking in terms of mechanisms or examples rather than functions, so part of the analyst's job will be to remove mechanisms from the information gathered for the function model and replace them with the corresponding functions.

To remove a mechanism, ask yourself the questions:

> *"Have I defined **how** something is being done rather than **what** is being done?"*

> *"Could the same outcome be achieved in a different way?"*

The phrase 'put baggage on conveyor belt' superficially resembles a function, but further analysis reveals that it is a mechanism (a how to do). Ask why are we putting the baggage on the conveyor belt (the what to do)? The business function here is to transport the baggage to the aircraft. There will of course be numerous mechanisms for doing this, one of which will be the conveyor belt. Another mechanism, for the passenger who arrives at the last minute, is to carry the baggage into the cabin.

We are in search of the underlying business requirement. If this can be found and documented, alternative mechanisms for supporting it can be considered as design options. Removing mechanisms from the model leaves our options open: the model will be more robust, since changes in mechanisms will rarely cause changes in the function model itself. And when we come to designing systems (i.e. designing mechanisms), multiple alternatives can be considered and the decision on which to use can be made on the basis of constraints such as:

- people
- performance requirements
- skills
- organization
- suitable technology
- and of course cost.

Putting Mechanisms Back!

Bear in mind that, having removed a mechanism in this way, you may have removed the comfortable feeling that someone had when they spoke about it. It is a common trap to abstract to such a point that the meaning of the business function is lost or becomes ambiguous and difficult to read. To retain clarity, one or two mechanisms can be reintroduced as examples to illustrate **how** the function is currently performed or could potentially be implemented:

> *Transport baggage to aircraft; for example, by conveyor belt, porter, trolley.*

A Benefit

It is quite interesting to note that this simple modelling discipline of removing mechanisms from the function name can often prompt the system engineer to say, *"Well, what new ways **could** I implement this function?"* On many projects this has led to innovation in the design of resulting systems.

Information Modelling

When discussing function names, we said that they should refer only to concepts defined in other parts of the business model. The other major modelling technique used in most system development methods is that of information modelling (also known as entity modelling or entity relationship modelling). The purpose of an entity relationship model is to describe the information needs of an enterprise accurately; and it is this information that business functions manipulate.

We model this information using three main concepts: **entities, attributes** and **relationships**. Just as business functions should be recorded free from mechanisms, the information model is recorded free from data-storage and access methods. This means that decisions on possible implementation techniques for the business systems being developed can be taken objectively. Full details of how to apply this technique can be found in *CASE*Method Entity Relationship Modelling.*[2] What follows here is an overview of the technique.

Take the function:

> *Assign aircraft to fly a scheduled route between two airports.*

Entity

An entity is a thing of significance about which information needs to be known or held. So this function refers to three entities: aircraft, scheduled route and airport.

These entities (represented by the upper-case names in boxes) are shown in Figure 3-4, a small part of the information model for Atlantis Island Flights. This pictorial presentation of the information model is called an Entity Relationship Diagram.

Functions can sometimes be decomposed to sub-functions, and, similarly, entities can sometimes be subdivided into sub-entities (sub-types). Two are shown here for the entity FLIGHT, but on a simplified diagram you could hide this extra information and just use FLIGHT.

Attribute

An attribute is a description of a thing of significance: that is, any detail that serves to classify, quantify, qualify, identify or express the state of an entity.

For the entity AIRCRAFT the attributes (represented by the lower-case names in the boxes) include registration number and name. For the entity FLIGHT two attributes are shown on this diagram: date of departure and time of departure. Attributes may be mandatory (they must have a value), shown by a '*' on the diagram, or optional, shown by a small 'o'.

Figure 3-4
Example Entity Relationship Diagram

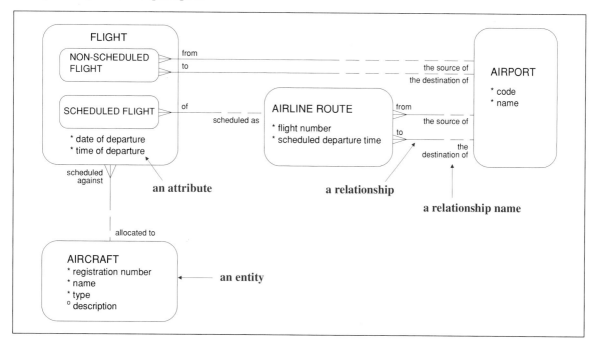

Business Relationship

A relationship is any significant way in which two entities may be associated, represented on a diagram by a line between the entities. Each end of a relationship has certain properties and a name, which must be shown on the diagram, allowing relationships to be 'read'. For example, from the diagram shown in Figure 3-4, we can read:

Each AIRCRAFT may be allocated to one or more FLIGHTs

and from the other end of the relationship:

Each FLIGHT must be scheduled against one and only one AIRCRAFT.

The words 'may be' indicate an optional relationship, represented by a broken line; the words 'must be' indicate a mandatory relationship, represented by a solid line. A degree of many, read as 'one or more', is shown by a 'crowsfoot' $\succ\!\!-$ on the diagram. A degree of one — is read as 'one and only one'. Reading round more of the diagram we get:

Each AIRPORT may be the destination of one or more AIRLINE ROUTEs, each of which may be scheduled as one or more SCHEDULED FLIGHTS (further described by their date of departure)

and from the other end of the relationship:

Each SCHEDULED FLIGHT, which is a type of FLIGHT that must be scheduled against an AIRCRAFT, must be of one and only one AIRLINE ROUTE, which must be from one and only one AIRPORT and must be to one and only one AIRPORT.

Cross-checking

During a business modelling exercise, you will need to check that the function model is consistent with the information model. It is useful to ask the questions:

"Are there any functions that refer to concepts not mentioned in the information model?"

to indicate missing detail from the entity model, and

"Are there functions to create, update and delete instances of each entity, attribute and relationship in the information model?"

to indicate missing detail from the function model. A matrix such as the one in Figure 3-5 opposite is frequently used for this purpose. Look out for blank rows and columns: they indicate that the model is incomplete.

Event

Event Definition

An event is a thing that happens or takes place or is an outcome or result.

It is the arrival of a significant point in time, a change in status of something, or the occurrence of something external, which causes the business to react in some way. We split events into four categories.

External Event

An external event occurs as a result of something happening outside the control of the business or outside the scope of the business systems which is, nevertheless, significant to the business in some way. If bad weather or a strike by air traffic controllers causes the cancellation or diversion of flights, these are external events outside the control of the business.

Figure 3-5
Business Function to Entity Matrix

Business Function to Entity Matrix. Business functions (diagonal labels): P154 | Allocate an individual to a st; P156 | Allocate a crew to a flight; P158 | Adhere to statutory/country; P159 | Make provision for staff acc; P15A | Identify crew shortages and; P60 | Provide training/retraining for; P80 | Provide maintenance crews,; PASSE | Provide tickets sales, emb; PERSO | Maintain adequate flight cr; R02 | Acquire sufficient routes to a; R03 | Run down services on route; R04 | Define staffing and other res; R10 | Define aircraft to route; R1 | Assemble details of pass; R2 | Establish scheduled fligh.

Entity	P154	P156	P158	P159	P15A	P60	P80	PASSE	PERSO	R02	R03	R04	R10	R1	R2
AEROPLANE															
AGENCY															
AIRCRAFT														✓	✓
AIRCRAFT SERVICE															
AIRCRAFT TYPE													✓		
AIRLINE														✓	
AIRLINE ROUTE	✓											✓	✓	✓	✓
AIRPORT															✓

Perhaps the most common external event in system terms is **whim**. This is when someone within the organization simply decides to do something, such as conduct an audit, check security, replace a member of staff, do a spot check. We identify these events by words such as 'on demand', but do not tend to show them on the diagrams.

Change Event

A change event occurs when the status of something changes, as a consequence of which some business function may be triggered. The simplest example is when a new instance of something is created, such as a reservation for a flight. More complex examples would include when a flight becomes fully booked, in which case we might close the flight. Status changes are often the creation or destruction of an instance of an entity, when the value of some attribute changes or when a relationship is changed: another useful cross-check to the entity relationship model.

Time or Realtime Event

A realtime event occurs when time reaches a significant point, such as:

- the departure time of a flight
- a regular aircraft service falls due
- every Monday at midday
- the end of the financial year.

System Event

This occurs when something significant happens within the control of the business: either the completion of a business function, or a condition in the information known to the business being met; such as, flying hours for an aircraft reaching the maximum allowed under international legislation.

Event Representation

Events are shown on function diagrams as hollow arrows, big enough to contain the name of the event, shown in bold italics. The arrow points at the function triggered by the event. If more than one function is triggered, the event appears at each function. Alternative representations may be used with CASE tools, as advanced computer-drawn graphics should be available; for example, a clock icon could be used for a realtime event. Care should be taken with naming events to distinguish them from the associated functions. For example, 'issue boarding pass to passenger' is a function, but 'boarding pass issued to passenger' is an event.

Figure 3-6
An Event

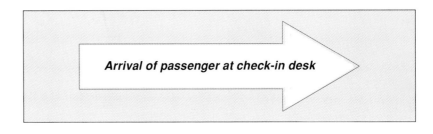

Arrival of passenger at check-in desk

Triggers

Events are important in function modelling because they trigger (or inhibit) functions. When an event occurs, it will possibly cause a number of business functions to be carried out. The arrival of the passenger at a check-in desk may cause three functions to occur:

Weigh, record, label and accept personal baggage.
Allocate free seat to passenger for flight.
Issue boarding pass to passenger.

We say that the event 'arrival of passenger at check-in desk' triggers these functions. In the example opposite in Figure 3-7, the event 'reservation of seat' is a system event, generated by the function R4. This is known as a triggered event and may in turn trigger other functions.

Syntax

Events and the functions they trigger can be recorded using the syntax:

*On the **event-name** event, the **business-function-name** function is triggered.*

For instance:

On the 'arrival of passenger at check-in desk' event, the 'weigh, record, label and accept personal baggage' function is triggered.

**Figure 3-7
Triggering
a Function**

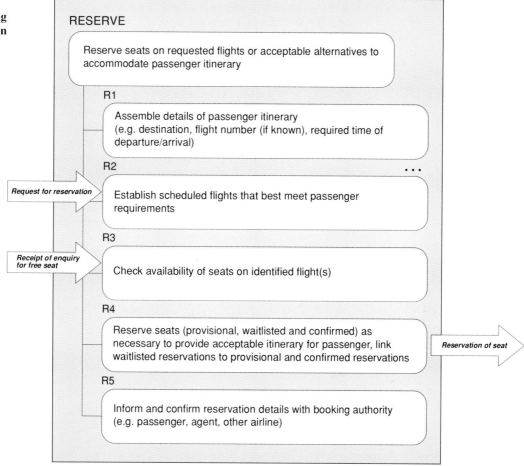

RESERVE

Reserve seats on requested flights or acceptable alternatives to accommodate passenger itinerary

R1

Assemble details of passenger itinerary
(e.g. destination, flight number (if known), required time of departure/arrival)

R2

Request for reservation

Establish scheduled flights that best meet passenger requirements

R3

Receipt of enquiry for free seat

Check availability of seats on identified flight(s)

R4

Reserve seats (provisional, waitlisted and confirmed) as necessary to provide acceptable itinerary for passenger, link waitlisted reservations to provisional and confirmed reservations

Reservation of seat

R5

Inform and confirm reservation details with booking authority (e.g. passenger, agent, other airline)

Inverted Syntax

*The **business-function-name** function will only ever be triggered after the **event-name** event, is that true?*

For instance:

The 'weigh, record, label and accept personal baggage' function will only ever be triggered after the 'arrival of passenger at check-in desk' event, is that true?

An Alternative Syntax

To be really rigorous you might like to try an apparently simpler syntax:

*On/at **event-name**, **function-name**.*

Our example would now read:

On arrival of passenger at check-in desk, weigh, record, label and accept personal baggage.

However, the equally valid event name – passenger arrives at check-in desk – will not work. It can be difficult to meet the constraints of this more rigorous syntax, but the effort is really worthwhile for critical areas.

Elementary Business Function

As function models become more and more detailed, it helps to identify **elementary business functions** as a quality and completeness check on the model.

Elementary Business Function Definition

An elementary business function is a function which when triggered must either be completed successfully or, if for some reason it cannot be completed successfully, must 'undo' any effects that it had up to the point of failure. An alternative definition is that an elementary business function must take the business from one consistent state to another, or not change the state of the business at all.

The business function 'check in passenger and baggage' could be composed of a number of subordinate functions (as illustrated above under triggers):

Weigh, record, label and accept personal baggage.
Allocate free seat to passenger for flight.
Issue boarding pass to passenger.

If the function to weigh, record, label and accept the baggage was carried out successfully but the subsequent allocation of a seat to the passenger failed for some reason (e.g. there were no non-smoking seats left and the passenger elected to travel on an alternative flight), it would clearly cause some business disruption if the baggage remained labelled with the flight number from the initial flight. We might, therefore, decide that 'check in passenger and baggage' represents an elementary business function. In this example, if its effects were not undone it would leave the business in an **inconsistent state**. The consequence to a passenger of this inconsistent state might well be the loss of his or her baggage. The consequence to the airline might be that all the baggage would have to be unloaded to ensure that baggage without a corresponding passenger was removed – often necessary with modern security rules.

Elementary business functions tend not to be decomposed further in the hierarchy but, as just illustrated, this is not always the case. If elementary business functions can be identified throughout a hierarchy, the understanding of the business being modelled will be improved. A word of warning, though: do not do this too early in the modelling exercise, especially when the hierarchy is still subject to large modifications, or the effort of keeping track of these functions will be high.

Summary of Concepts

We have already defined a number of concepts:

- Objective – a goal or target that the business is trying to achieve and which we can measure quantitatively

- Business function – something the business does or needs to do to achieve its objectives

- Sub-function – a business function that has a parent function

- Mechanism – a way in which a business function can be carried out

- Entity, attribute and relationship – the structure of the information manipulated by the business functions

- Event – something happening which triggers one or more business functions

- Elementary business functions – business functions which cannot be left part-way through. They must be completed, or their effects completely undone, to leave the business in a consistent state.

These concepts interrelate in a single unified business model comprising the three components shown below: a function model and an information model, both devised within the context of the business direction model.

**Figure 3-8
The Business
Model**

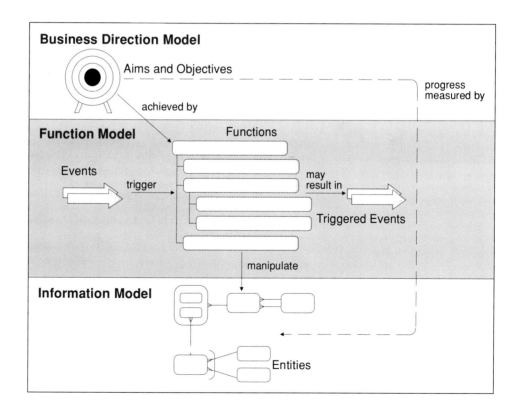

Function Decomposition

Reading though this chapter so far, you should now be comfortable with the concept of a business function and could probably think of a number of business functions from your own company or organization without too much trouble (if you are going to try this, write each one on a separate piece of paper, as it will make reorganization easier). In fact, one of the problems you will soon have to face is how to manage enormous numbers of functions!

Do not panic – help is at hand in the form of the **Function Hierarchy**. This is used to locate, consolidate and control the large numbers of business functions that are found during a function modelling exercise. How to perform function decomposition and create a function hierarchy is fully explored in Chapter 5, but this is an overview to get you started.

Start at the Top

A function hierarchy starts with a single business function that expresses the entire scope of the business being modelled. This is called the **Root Function** and appears at the top of the hierarchy. Beneath it are about seven or eight business functions, each of which describes an area of business within the scope of the root function. Each of these business areas is then broken down further, in much the same way, to produce another seven or eight more detailed functions. If this process is carried through to its limits, then the minute detail of the business will appear at the bottom level (sometimes called atomic or leaf functions) – it does not take a mathematical genius to work out that there could be an awful lot of these bottom-level business functions. The lower-level functions can be thought of as children of the function above them in the hierarchy, and that higher-level function can be called a parent function. (We do not, however, take this to its limits backwards and refer to grandparents and great-grandparents!)

What Makes a Hierarchy so Useful?

Constructing a hierarchy as a kind of framework to hold business functions is useful for a number of reasons. It serves as an easy access mechanism when you need to find your way around large numbers of functions and it facilitates completeness checking (*"Have I identified all the business functions?"*). It is also a means of checking the quality and consistency of each business function.

Two simple checks can be applied to each level in the hierarchy:

- Is it relevant?
- Is it complete?

Constructing a Hierarchy

You might like to have a go at writing a single function to describe the business that your company is in right now. It is not as easy as it sounds. But the great thing about having a hierarchy is the ease with which changes to functions and the structure of the hierarchy can be made, whilst still retaining control of the whole process. So, have a go at producing a top-level function for your company and then think of seven or eight functions that this can be split into (but don't use the organization structure as a template for this). Have a look at some company literature – marketing or sales information, employee handbooks and so on – as a source of business functions. Try to do two or three levels, but do not worry if you run out of ideas before you get seven or eight functions at each level. This is known as top-down decomposition, which produces a basic framework.

Additional functions can be added later, evolving and expanding the hierarchy with each one. In doing so, you may find that a decomposition that started with seven detailed functions quickly grows to twenty or thirty functions, all under the original parent function. This imbalance can be rectified by assembling these business functions into seven or eight groups. The criteria for grouping is subjective, so it is worth trying out various ideas to see how they work out. A single function describing the scope of a group can then be written for each group. So now, under the original parent, the hierarchy has seven or eight new functions, each of which is a group of a handful of the original twenty or thirty functions.

Throughout this process, reorganizing whole legs of the hierarchy and rewording functions is quite normal. New functions can be slotted in and the hierarchy will evolve as you do so. If you have been trying this whilst reading the chapter, you will probably appreciate why it helps to have each function on a different piece of paper or to use a CASE tool designed for this task.

General Guidelines

Experience has shown that when it is necessary to decompose a function into more detail it is best to have between three and eight sub-functions.

It is often convenient to arrange the functions so that they follow the life-cycle of something, as in our example of following the life-cycle of a booking.

Summary

We have introduced and defined the basic concepts of function modelling and explored the technique of constructing a business function hierarchy. A theme throughout has been one of modelling a **business** requirement that will still be valid for the foreseeable future. We have done this with the expectation of having it verified at a senior executive level. The aim is to produce a robust and rigorous model, free from details of the mechanisms for performing the functions. If these were included in the model they could prejudice the eventual choice of mechanisms, and would reduce the longevity of the model as it could be overtaken rapidly by technical change, even though the actual business content might still be valid.

Chapter

4

IDENTIFYING BUSINESS FUNCTIONS

In this chapter we address the business level ⬭ and how to identify business functions: our initial aim is to take the minimum time possible to identify all relevant business functions. Constructing a function hierarchy is examined in Chapter 5, and checklists for testing the quality and completeness of functions are given in Appendix A.

Identifying Business Functions

Business functions can be identified from a number of sources; the first, and most important of these, is the interview.

Interviewing

An interview is a conversation, driven by a number of questions, which seeks to uncover an understanding of a business. Future plans, expectations and the **good ideas** of the people who run a business are rarely available from any source other than an interview. This may be the only chance there is to uncover them, which makes interviewing one of the most important analytical skills to master.

Typically, an interview with a senior business manager or executive is conducted by two analysts, one acting as the interviewer and the other as note-taker. The interviewer aims to keep the interviewee talking about business topics by asking open questions (i.e. those to which there is not a simple yes or no answer). The note-taker records the answers, sifting and analyzing responses, and checking for ambiguities, exceptions, completeness and general understanding; looking all the time for objectives, functions, events, entities, attributes and relationships.

Taking notes in an interview situation is a demanding and skilled job that warrants more than can be given to the subject here and, as with other skills, practice is the best way to become proficient. The notes are the only tangible deliverable from an interview. (You may have gathered that note-taker is the more important of the two analyst roles: it is often the role taken by the **more** experienced analyst.) If you find yourself in a situation where your first interview is imminent, so time to practise is short, try taking notes from a newscast on television or radio – it will give you some idea of the speed with which you will have to write to keep up! Above all, be prepared; an interview is a marvellous opportunity to collect information, so do some background research into the business area of interest and the person being interviewed before the interview starts. Organize the way in which notes are to be taken. Write on one side of the page, for example, so that consolidation is made easier on the facing page, and practise as much as possible before starting (especially for the first time).

Figure 4-1
Example of Interview Notes after Consolidation

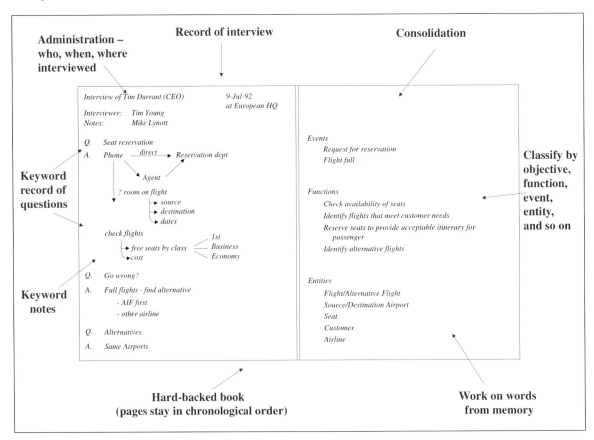

A transcript of an interview from which the example hierarchies in Chapters 2 and 3 were derived might look something like this. Note the open questions encouraging the **interviewee** to talk at length about the business, while the interviewer will spend most of the time listening.

Question *Could you tell us a little about the process of reserving a seat?*

Answer *Well, typically, somebody will telephone our Reservations Department, either personally or through an agent, and ask if we have any room on a flight from, say, Atlantia to Honolulu. We would then check, via the reservations computer, to see what flights go between those two airports on the dates required, and we can tell from a reservations enquiry how many seats are free in first class, business class, economy and so on. We typically tell the passenger this and he would make a choice based on how much it costs, the most convenient flight times, or any other criteria that are relevant to him. Once the passenger has made up his mind, we would reserve a place for him and this would be confirmed by sending out a ticket at a later date, usually within two weeks of the departure date.*

Question *O.K., what can go wrong with that process?*

Answer *Well, I am not sure what you mean by wrong, but quite often the flights are full and we have to look around for an alternative, which can sometimes get quite complicated. We would try to keep the business by checking Atlantis Island Flights first, but we may have to resort to using another airline if we have no seats at all that satisfied the passenger's requirements.*

Question *You mentioned alternatives; what makes one flight an alternative for another?*

Answer *Well, obviously, the same flight between the same two airports but at a different time or date might be acceptable, if the passenger is prepared to travel a day earlier or later; this is the most obvious alternative. However, you might consider other alternatives such as flying to a different airport or from a different departure airport or by a different route.*

Analyzing the Notes

Unless your note-taker is highly proficient at shorthand, the notes from an interview will not look quite like this! Usually they are written in haste, difficult to read and only contain key words, which are all the note-taker has time to record during the interview (more like Figure 4-1). As a result, to get the best from interview notes, try to consolidate them as soon as possible after an interview has finished, extracting relevant functions and other concepts (objectives, events, entitites and relationships, for instance) – a good note-taker will even do a certain amount of this during 'quiet points' in the interview. (A trained note-taker is, after all, an analyst and not simply a proficient reporter.)

The aim of analyzing the notes, from the perspective of this book, is to identify as many business functions as possible, and to gain a good general understanding of the business as a whole. Working from the interview transcript above, notice there are few immediately obvious functions – there is quite a lot of work to do here. You might like to try extracting some functions yourself before reading the next section.

Extracting Business Functions from Interview Notes

An initial scan of the interview notes, picking out the verbs, is a good starting point. Disregard anything outside the scope that has been set; for example, you should not include a function for the **passenger** to decide which flight best suited him or her, since the passenger's decision-making process is not within the scope of the Atlantis Island Flights business. As you do not want to prejudge any eventual solutions, you need to remove all references to computer systems, examples and other mechanisms. Now apply some common sense to synthesize a sentence that describes what is going on, based on your current understanding of the business.

Referring to the transcript, the answer to the first question:

"... *somebody will telephone our Reservations Department ...*"

reveals an event – someone contacting the airline to make a reservation. The interviewee then goes on to describe what Atlantis Island Flights does in response to this event. The first function is found in the statement:

"*We would then check, via the reservations computer, to see what flights go between those two airports ...*"

Removing references to the current computer system, the named airports and working on the words a little, we might try:

Check flights between requested airports.

But this is not precise enough. We may have a flight between the requested airports on the date required, but we also need to check if there are still seats available on it! So, from our current understanding of the business, we would change this to something like:

Check availability of seats on flights between requested airports.

Carrying on in this way, we might identify the following additional functions in the first answer:

Inform passenger of flights, availability and other flight details.

Reserve seat on identified flight for named passenger.

Confirm reservation (e.g. by sending tickets two weeks prior to flight departure).

The answer to the second question gives us a further function:

Locate alternative flights that satisfy passenger's criteria, by considering alternative departure airport, arrival airport, airline, and so on.

Synthesis

It is impracticable to gain **everything** explicitly from interviews (or any other single source for that matter): that would take far too long. Instead, **most** of our information about functions is obtained from the interview, but common sense is used to synthesize functions that we suspect must exist, even though we have not been told about them. Use your powers of logical deduction – and if it is **obvious** that a function must exist, then define it anyway. The more experienced and comfortable you become at identifying functions, the easier the process of synthesizing business functions becomes. At this stage you need not worry about synthesizing functions: many different cross-checks will be applied to the function model as it is developed, so anything that is incorrect or irrelevant is removed and anything that is missed is picked up at a later date.

Other Sources

There are some other sources of information that can be used to find functions. These tend to be less productive and less reliable than the interview process; however, they are still a valuable source of cross-checking material. In particular, existing documentation, observing people at work, generic hierarchies and 'having a go' at a business activity are the most useful.

Documentation

Nowadays, any enterprise has a lot written about it. Its marketing literature, sales literature, employee handbooks, internal procedures, existing systems documents, and so on, can all be used as a source of business functions. Be careful, however, because these functions usually describe current systems; they rarely, if ever, contain any information on future requirements, and are quite frequently wrong, out of date and misleading.

Text, which can be treated in the same way as interview notes, and photographs, diagrams and schematics can all be used as a source of information about functions. For example, a marketing brochure for a rental business, showing a photograph of a high-street shop, might reveal a range of products available to rent, special offers, promotions, options to buy, and so on. A graduate careers promotion leaflet might say:

"On joining the Company as a graduate recruit, you will attend a full induction programme involving a period in each of three departments to familiarize you thoroughly with how the Company operates . . ."

Observation

Observation can be a useful source of information. It involves watching people at work in their normal day-to-day jobs; but again, it is the current system that is being studied. Observation is a skill in its own right. It requires an ability to assess **what** is being done whilst observing **how** it is being done.

Figure 4-2
Observation

This is especially useful for a business where there is an amount of geographical distribution or local variation on a central business theme. For instance, in the television and video rental business all outlets would try to respond to customer demands, so in a retirement community the business might concentrate on reliability and technical service, whereas in a community with a high percentage of young professionals it might concentrate on offering a wide choice of the latest equipment. And in the health business, orthopaedic surgeons in the first community might find they perform a higher level of hip arthroplasty, while in the second community they might have to set rather more broken legs (as a result of skiing accidents).

Unfortunately, people under observation tend to behave differently from normal, making it more difficult to apply this technique successfully. We all have a tendency to become self-conscious and to want to present ourselves in a favourable light. You may drink rather less coffee and spend rather less time chatting to colleagues when being observed, in the belief that these will be seen as time wasting. Yet apparently casual conversation in a corridor may form a vital part of communicating and sparking off new ideas. A theoretical chemist was once asked to justify the amount of time he spent each summer apparently lounging in the sun in his garden. He was, in fact, thinking.

You can encounter a similar problem in interviewing. Again, we all have a tendency to want to present ourselves in a favourable light. Are **you** totally honest if you have to fill in a survey form on your eating habits or how much exercise you take? Or do you report that you eat rather more salads and rather less junk food than you really do? A skilled interviewer observes your body language, as well as the words you use to answer questions, and sets you at ease so that you can relax and give really honest answers, rather than protective ones that tell only part of the truth (possibly out of a sense of loyalty to your business). Remember, your job, later on, is to build or improve systems that fit into the real world.

Observation, interview notes and questions, and the functions you synthesized in your role as analyst can all be used to cross-check and confirm each other. Where results from these techniques conflict, questions can be prepared for subsequent interviews to resolve this conflict.

Aside

On one project with a senior executive in a power station, the interviewee had himself come carefully prepared and for two hours insisted on giving us a highly detailed technical insight into how a nuclear power station works. He forcibly resisted all attempts to find out what people did or what needed to be done; but we did learn a lot about the theory of controlled nuclear reactions!

It was obvious after an hour that attempts to pull the interview around had failed, but we had to keep going for two hours as this had been pre-set in everyone's mind as the **minimum** time for an in-depth interview. The questioning therefore changed direction – the objective was now to exhaust the interviewee of everything he wanted to tell us, whilst of course learning as much as we could in the process. At the end of the interview we thanked him and said, *"You know we have never been around a nuclear plant. Is there anyone with your level of experience who could show us around?"* He volunteered immediately, relaxed, handed out 'hard hats', warned us about safety procedures, and took us on a three-hour guided tour.

Being good analysts we took a keen interest and, of course, restarted the interview. The questions nearly all took the form: *"What happens here? What is that for? What does he/she do?"* We simply used everything and everybody that we observed as a reason for an open question. He really enjoyed it. We took down over forty pages of notes, compared with the one and a half pages we took in his office. And of course we not only identified hundreds of functions, events and so on, but got a set of really practical examples to use later on.

Figure 4-3
Taking Notes the Hard Way

Visual impressions and smells are often retained better than voice and can subsequently be recalled easily to help verify an idea. The only hard part was for the poor note-taker trying to take copious notes whilst climbing ladders, leaning over high parapets, running through the rain and passing through huge noisy work areas. An unforgettable interview/observation session.

Commonly Occurring and Forgotten Functions

Appendix E contains some example functions that apply to a wide range of businesses. These can be used as a completeness check, to see whether anything has been forgotten. A word of warning: these functions will not automatically apply to all businesses so, unfortunately, you cannot use them straight out of the book without exercising great care. Test their relevance out thoroughly before you incorporate them into a hierarchy – your career might depend on it.

Having a Go

If you really want to understand a business, have a go! It is becoming quite common for Information Technology Departments to put their new recruits through a period of training and experience in other parts of the business before taking up their full-time positions. Wise old sayings such as *"there is no substitute for experience"* and *"nothing like being at the sharp end"* are true.

Practical experience gained by doing a job for a period of time is an ideal way of getting to understand a business. Unfortunately, the cost involved is potentially high – firstly, there is the obvious amount of time that it takes to become familiar with a new role and, secondly, there is a risk that inexperience may result in mistakes. Despite this, an exercise to get involved in the day-to-day running of the business is a good way to gain understanding, an opportunity to observe others at work, and to collect relevant background information and documentation. It is also, perhaps, an ideal way of introducing a new and less experienced member of a team into an analysis project.

Your attitude towards this venture is critical to its success. Pretend that you are going to work in this area and take a genuine interest in the business you are analyzing. What do you expect to find? What problems do you see? How might it be done better? This approach, coupled with rigorous analysis and good CASE tools, will help you get it right faster.

Summary of Other Sources

Documentation, observation, generic hierarchies and practical experience can all provide a good source for additional functions. Compared with the interviewing process, however, they are expensive – they take a long time for little additional value – and neglect one very important aspect of function modelling: that of future business requirements. We recommend using these sources as a **bottom-up** check of a set of functions already discovered by interview and synthesis. Having said that though, never pass up an opportunity to collect information, whether it be a chance meeting with a manager in the car park (an ad hoc, casual interview) or a glance at a draft for a new marketing brochure – all information is a valuable cross-check.

A Word of Warning

In some organizations internal politics are rife, so you need to be wary of the skilled manager (or perhaps we should use the term manipulator) deliberately feeding you invalid data, which you might inadvertently use, furthering the political intent of this person. Avoid getting involved in this type of activity, carefully cross-check key assertions and continually work on questioning techniques and other approaches that cut through the politics to find out what the business actually does or needs to do, as opposed to how the politics work.

Summary

We have looked at a variety of ways of gaining information about the organization under analysis and identified a number of sources from which functions can be found. Interviewing is recommended as the primary source, with cross-checks from existing documentation, observation, practical experience and generic hierarchies.

At this point in an analysis you may have hundreds of pages of notes, highlighted documents, mental images, and so on. You will already have done some consolidation to arrange the information into categories such as events, functions and entities. You will also have rewritten what you have been told (or understood) into unambiguous functions, which are independent of the organization structures, roles or mechanisms. Now you must turn these into a function model.

A Short Modelling Exercise

Before reading the next chapter you might like to try modelling a familiar situation such as getting ready for work each day. Produce a function hierarchy starting with a suitable root function, perhaps:

The Trigger and the Root Function

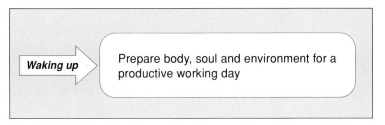

Waking up → Prepare body, soul and environment for a productive working day

Remember to remove mechanisms as you go.

5

THE FUNCTION
HIERARCHY

The simplest and, arguably, most useful modelling technique for functions is the construction of a function hierarchy. This technique is very fast to perform and yet can enable a good analyst to clearly define a very wide scope which is easy to check, agree and use as a framework for subsequent work. Remember, the purpose of function modelling is to **understand** what the business does now, or needs to do in the future, to achieve its objectives, and to document that understanding in a way that can be passed on to others.

In this chapter we examine the process of constructing a function hierarchy, then explore a variety of techniques for testing it for accuracy and completeness, and finally look briefly at how to present the function model. The technique of producing a hierarchy is of general applicability; whilst only illustrated at the business level ⬚, it is also applicable at the system ⬚ and program/procedure level ⬚.

**Constructing a
Function Hierarchy**

Having conducted an interview and studied other sources of information you may be confronted by a large number of business functions. But where should you start the construction of the function hierarchy?

It is both productive and a good quality check to approach the exercise from two different directions. Initially, you will start producing the function hierarchy from a top-down perspective and then cross-check it from a bottom-up perspective.

Figure 5-1
Top-down Plus
Bottom-up

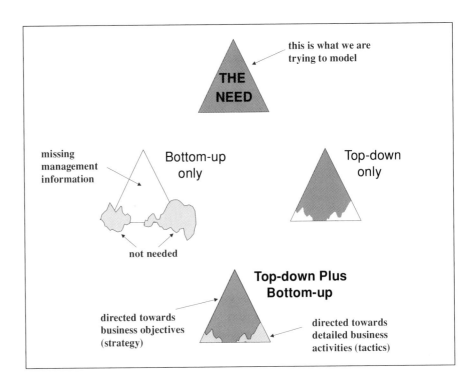

Top-down Modelling

Top-down modelling involves starting with a blank sheet of paper and coming up with a single sentence (expressed as a business function) which represents the essence of the business as a whole – the business strategy or mission. Then, a number of components for this are produced, each one a business function in its own right. These must fit with the way people in the business perceive their enterprise (seven or eight functions at the next level down is a simple guideline for the number of components). This process is repeated with each of the component functions. At each stage ask yourself a number of questions:

"Is anything else needed which is not already in its decomposition in order to carry out the parent function?"	If so, add a function to represent it.
"Is there something in this decomposition which is not necessary to achieve the parent function?"	If so, move it to somewhere it **is** necessary.
"Does each function help to contribute to one or more business objectives?"	If not, check for missing objectives and question whether the function is significant.

"Do the words used fit with the terms that are used in the business?"	If not, scrap and rewrite the function.
"Have I understood what is really meant by this function?"	If not, do some more analysis on it, or perhaps use it as a question in the next interview.
"Would I feel happy talking a chief executive through this business function?"	If not, rewrite the function.

Go ahead now and try this on your own company's business – it only takes about fifteen minutes to come up with a basic structure. Then you can check it out with the questions above.

The Anatomy of a Function Hierarchy

All hierarchies correspond to the following structure:

Figure 5-2
The Function Hierarchy

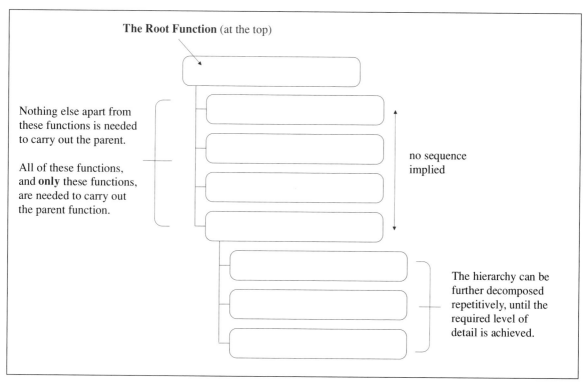

The Root Function (at the top)

Nothing else apart from these functions is needed to carry out the parent.

All of these functions, and **only** these functions, are needed to carry out the parent function.

no sequence implied

The hierarchy can be further decomposed repetitively, until the required level of detail is achieved.

In this way, a basic framework in the form of a hierarchy can be built from the top down. Now it needs to be thoroughly checked, and to do that you need to work from the bottom up.

Objective Modelling

If we assume that a business only carries out functions in order to achieve its objectives, a good way to get that initial framework for a hierarchy is to start with the objectives identified so far. For each objective, ask, *"What functions need to be done to achieve that?"*, and use those functions as a starting point for the seven or eight sub-functions of the highest-level function. The term 'essence of a business' is often used to describe a summary of the main things that need to be done (asking for a description of the essence of the business is a good open question for an interview of a senior executive). The top-level function in a hierarchy should capture this essence, and the level immediately below should make it obvious what the most essential functions are and why they are essential (i.e. they should include references to the objectives in them). The aim is to show the top level of the hierarchy to a senior executive and get the comment, *"Yes, that is a good, concise way of describing what we do, and it reflects what we are really trying to achieve."* Conversely, if the executive says, *"That's rather wishy-washy; it could describe any company!"*, you will know that you need to think more clearly about what **this** business does and how it is trying to achieve it.

For example, it would certainly not be right to have a hierarchy for an airline which does not have a function to fly passengers to their destination, a hierarchy for a training organization which does not have a function to deliver a training course, and a hierarchy for a health service which does not have a function to treat a patient. (And don't laugh, this happens a lot. Strategists can get so carried away with writing generic functions that they forget what business they are working in.)

Cross-checking by Using One Technique against Another

Conversely, you can look at all the functions you have identified and ask yourself whether there are any obvious objectives or aims that you have not been told about. Record any missing aims or objectives, check them with the users, and ask them to refine them. This is an example of using one modelling technique to cross-check another one. More importantly, it can help to fill gaps and promote new ideas. And these were just simple models, a list of objectives and a list of functions – even greater value comes when more structured modelling techniques are used.

Bottom-up Checking

Initially, this should be used as a cross-checking mechanism. Compile a list of business functions from all sources of material, such as interview notes, business literature, marketing material and employee handbooks; anything, in fact, which **does not** follow the top-down decomposition.

Take each of the functions in the list and see if there is a convenient place in the top-down hierarchy for it. Quite often there is no obvious position in the hierarchy for a function, but a space can be made, by:

- rewording an existing function – extending the scope it covers, so that a new function fits into its decomposition

- fitting the function in on its own as a new 'leg' at the top level

- disposing of the function completely (it was not relevant anyway)

- rewording an existing function to include the essence of the function being added

- completely regrouping and reorganizing the hierarchy to accommodate the new function more comfortably.

The aim of function decomposition is to gain a thorough understanding of what the business does, or needs to do, to achieve its objectives. By reworking the hierarchy again and again you will become more familiar with what was really meant by each function, so do not be afraid to scrap a hierarchy at any point in time and rework it from scratch again.

**Figure 5-3
Creating a
Hierarchy**

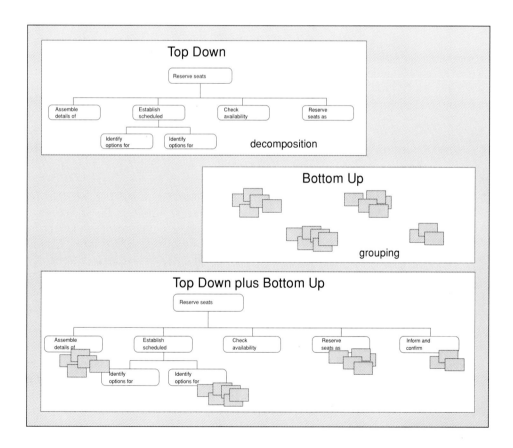

When to Stop!

A function hierarchy needs to be:

- accurate and self-contained at each level

- complete (i.e. it covers the intended scope)

- succinct in its use of words and its interaction with the information model

- balanced enough to make it easy to read.

When to stop is somewhat subjective and frequently has more to do with how much time there is left on a project! If you stop at too high a level the reader is left feeling there is a huge amount of detail unexplored. Aim to get to a level where each function is helpfully descriptive of something that needs to be done in the business. A simple test to use is to ask if a function can be done by more than one person at a time. If the answer is yes, try decomposing further. This is not a hard and fast rule but can be a useful general guideline.

If functions still run to a number of sentences, have lots of 'ands' in them and contain more than one verb, another level of detail is probably in order. Good candidates might be:

Check Atlantis Island Flights scheduled flights and availability of seats on them which satisfy passenger itinerary and book seats in requested class.

Record arrival of passenger for departure, weigh and examine baggage according to local and company security requirements, and allocate passenger a seat.

If a function has become terse and obvious to an extreme, you could have safely stopped one level higher:

Revise flight arrival time.

Change standard fare of airline route.

Modify cargo capacity of aircraft.

Beware, however, because the terse wording may be hiding something far more significant to the business. 'Revise flight arrival time' might trigger a function to ensure there are crew changes to cover the number of flying hours, in which case it is important to retain the detail. (See Chapter 7 for more detail about modelling functional dependencies and triggers.) To gain the full benefit of a function model, the model must be interesting, relevant, easily read and comprehensive.

A Few Tips

To prevent reworking the model becoming time consuming and demoralizing, you can try some of the following:

- Write the functions on individual sheets of paper (small sticky notelets are ideal); this makes periodic reorganization and regrouping much easier.

- Defer labelling functions until you are happy that the hierarchy will not change radically.

- Get used to challenging your own work. Never pretend that it is as good as it possibly can be, but continually try to improve every function every time you come into contact with it.

Testing a Hierarchy

Try testing a hierarchy from a number of alternative viewpoints. These tests can be carried out fairly quickly (perhaps half an hour each), and each may uncover a small number of flaws or give rise to minor improvements to the hierarchy. Try asking some 'reality' questions:

"If I were one of our customers and I read this, would I recognize the business and would it cover all interactions with me?"

"If I were an accountant, would I find that it covered revenue, cost, budgets, profit and loss, balance sheets, capital expenditure, . . .?"

"If I were a safety officer, could I spot the safety issues?"

"Is my own job described in the hierarchy somewhere?"

Using Generic Hierarchies

A business is a complex and changeable organization of people, machines, buildings and other resources trying to achieve some objectives. A look at a number of businesses in detail will show how very different they can be; even those operating in the same industry will have different cultures, styles of operation, objectives, organization structure, and so on. Despite these differences, however, a great deal of commonality exists across all businesses. For example, virtually all businesses have functions to set goals and objectives to achieve in each operational period. In a commercial concern this objective setting is likely to be of a financial nature, such as:

Set revenue, cost and profit objectives for the next financial period.

In a state-run health service the objectives may be more like:

Set objectives for average length of time a patient must wait for a class of operation, such as a kidney transplant.

Most businesses will have functions to:

- set goals and objectives for the business to achieve
- acquire funding (e.g. by borrowing or retaining profit)
- set up and maintain an infrastructure (e.g. organization, recruitment, acquisition of buildings)
- research and develop products and/or services
- market and sell products and/or services
- manufacture products
- deliver and support products and/or services
- review progress against plans.

It is, therefore, possible to create a useful generic hierarchy showing functions that are frequently found in most businesses. To use it as a cross-check for a function hierarchy you have built, you would take each of the functions in the generic hierarchy, tailor it to the business you are modelling (using the understanding you have gained to date), then check to see whether you have the resulting function covered somewhere in your hierarchy. The procedure is illustrated in Figure 5-4.

Figure 5-4
Using a Generic Hierarchy to Test a Function Model

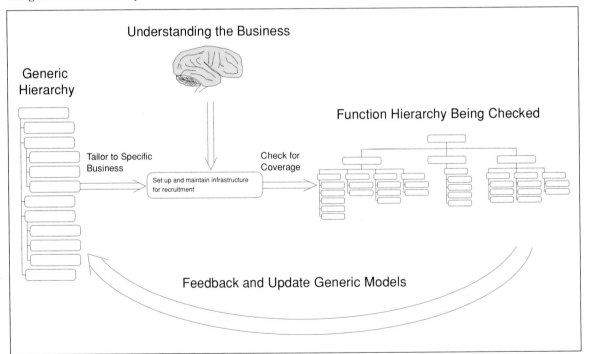

Appendix E includes some commonly occurring and often forgotten functions that can be used as a cross-check on your models. As you become more proficient and experienced at function modelling you will build up your own set of general functions (in your mind, if not on paper). You can put them to good use as a cross-check, and with each new modelling exercise they can be improved and expanded.

Entity Life-cycles

An entity life-cycle is a method for checking a function hierarchy by examining the way in which we expect information to be manipulated. Consider an entity from the Atlantis Island Flights information model – a CREW, for example. From our knowledge of the business we would ask ourselves what stages a crew goes through in its lifetime. We might end up with something like:

Figure 5-5
An Entity
Life-cycle

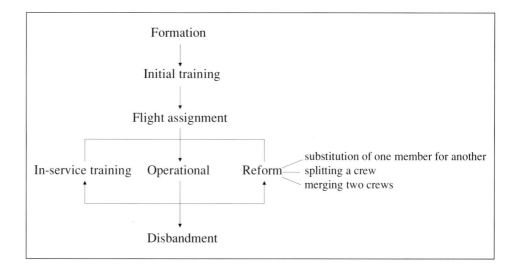

There should be functions to take a crew into each of the stages above, for example:

Form crew from available staff.

Train crew for standard and emergency procedures for aircraft type normally to be flown by crew.

Assign crew to flight.

Substitute crew members (either temporarily, e.g. to cover illness, or permanently).

Disband crew, reallocating staff to other crews or positions as necessary.

Analogies

A hierarchy can be tested by analogy. We could compare our airline function model with the business of, say, manufacturing a car. The manufacturing process will include such things as designing the car, purchasing raw materials, setting up the machines on the production line, allocating people to work them, producing the components of the car, final assembly, stock control and shipping to customers. Some of these will have analogues in the airline business. (We do not need to add functions for the design and production of new aircraft: these belong to a different industry.) Perhaps preparing an aircraft for flight could be an analogue of setting up a machine; assigning a crew to a flight could be an analogue of assigning people to work the machines and so on. This is most useful when something is discovered that had not been thought of before and which clearly is significant (or could be). Perhaps thinking about retooling a machine on a production line makes you think of refitting an aircraft, which may have been omitted from the hierarchy by accident.

For the analogy to be most effective:

- you must know the subject well
- you must spot some relevance or connection to the business being modelled very quickly
- it should **not** be too closely aligned to the business.

Almost anything at all can act as an analogy; often the things that seem the most unlikely candidates turn out to be the most useful! Here is a list of things that might start you thinking about analogies:

- the company you worked for previously
- your favourite hobby
- having an extension built on your house
- the last major trip you organized (holiday, attending a conference, going on a training course, taking a school class on an outing)
- the company you rate as giving you the best service
- reorganizing the contents of your kitchen cupboards
- what you have to do to start up a new project.

On the face of it, many of these things are obscure, irrelevant or, at least, somewhat personal! That is the power of using the analogy as a technique though – it tries to force your brain to make slightly odd associations (something the brain is inherently very good at) and then rationalize and learn from them.

The secret of this technique is to 'think through' the analogy quickly. See if three or four parallels between your model and the analogy come easily to mind: if not, try an altogether different analogy. If you do find that a number of things seem to have a reasonable parallel, then think through the analogy in more detail. For instance, what would happen if you changed something in this analogy: how would it affect the equivalent thing in the business? Having established a relevant analogy, you can use it as a rapid cross-check to a function hierarchy by looking for a parallel in the business for each element of the analogy. Most will probably exist in your hierarchy already; some will not have parallels that you can think of; but a few will make you think of things that you had missed, forgotten or simply not thought of before and the analogy becomes a source of new functions.

Proactive Function Modelling

Think of how someone senior in a business feels about seeing a description of that business abstracted into a hierarchy – well-presented and carefully cross-checked, but with all mechanisms, examples, organization, responsibilities and roles removed from it. This is a new way to view a business and, as such, is interesting, motivating and thought-provoking – people rarely think about their business in this way. As a result, it is possible that presentation of a function model will promote ideas and ways to **change** the business. A mark of a good function hierarchy is that it causes people to think about their business differently and is well enough structured to enable proposed changes to be incorporated easily. Encourage proactive function modelling; it may not lead to any changes actually being made to how a business works, but it is an excellent aid to understanding what is really going on.

An Event List

From the same set of interview notes, and other sources used to build a function hierarchy, you can identify a list of events. These events should trigger the business functions in your hierarchy. Put the hierarchy to one side and consider each event in turn, asking the questions:

"What functions should be carried out when this event occurs?" and
"What does the business want to happen when this event occurs?"

Write a list of functions triggered by each event and then use the list as a cross-check to see where each one would fit in the hierarchy.

Role Playing

Imagine you are a passenger with Atlantis Island Flights. Take an imaginary trip and note down everything that happens to you on a sheet of paper. The more detailed you make this, the better. Now reread the notes you have made and ask yourself what each part of the notes says about the Atlantis Island Flights business. In fact, treat this imaginary script in the same way that you would treat interview notes: searching, analyzing and consolidating from memory.

When we wrote this book, for example, as a way of generating some of the material for Chapter 2, we produced a number of imaginary scripts based on our knowledge of how airlines typically operate. Here is one example:

> *"I booked a ticket for my family and me with Atlantis Island Flights for our holiday this year. We had a great trip – we booked early, almost nine months ahead, and paid for the flight (via our agent) in three instalments. We got the tickets in the post about three weeks before we were due to fly, which is just as well – they had booked us into the wrong airport in London! Anyway, that was changed without delay and replacement tickets arrived in plenty of time. On the day we were due to travel we heard a local radio announcement of flight delays because of a hurricane, so we phoned ahead to check on the situation and were told, to our relief, that flights from London were not affected at all. We drove to the airport and took the courtesy bus from the car park to the departure building. The first thing to do was to check in and get rid of all our baggage – you wouldn't believe it was just for a fortnight! We were twenty kilograms over the baggage limit, but the check-in clerk said the flight was not full and did not charge us extra – I just hoped that they would be as understanding on the way back. Having checked in, we looked around the duty-free shops and had our boarding passes duly stamped for the perfume we bought for Aunt Maude. Talk about security! They wouldn't let us carry the duty-frees around with us, but insisted on delivering them to the departure gate as we boarded – I suppose it makes you feel that much better about travelling with an airline that is so cautious. We made it to the gate as soon as the announcement board started to show 'Boarding' and hardly had to queue at all. The stewards checked the boarding passes, gave us the duty-frees and directed us to our seats.*

> *As we taxied to the runway, the stewards and stewardesses told us (again) about the emergency procedures (I suppose it must be new for somebody!), and pretty soon we were airborne. After an hour or so we were served lunch and the children spent half their holiday money on an Atlantis Island teddy bear each."*

You can see how this could be used as a source of functions. In role playing you are making everyone in the organization available for interview in your own mind.

Now try from a different viewpoint, assuming the role of:

- maintenance engineer
- pilot
- steward(ess)
- reservations clerk
- security guard
- supplier of spare parts for aircraft, and so on.

Each role-play need only take five or ten minutes, including time for the cross-check; it is surprising how much extra this can find. This list consists of types of job. You might argue that a passenger is hardly a job type, but if things go wrong it can feel like hard work!

You might also like to work through some different scenarios for the business and imagine how they would affect the role you are playing. For instance, if you were a marketing executive, what would the following scenarios mean to you?:

- the introduction of a new product
- the phasing out of an old product
- different seasons in the year (i.e. time)
- taking over and integrating a competitor.

Obviously, the roles or scenarios will vary, depending on the business being modelled.

Extending a Function to Other Areas

Business functions are structured sentences of the form 'verb object . . .' and asking what else the verb in a function might act upon can help you to identify missing functions. For example, the function 'transport baggage to the aircraft' might lead you to investigate what else might need to be transported (and to where).

Similarly, you could ask what else we might need to do to an object. In the case of the baggage, it may need to be transferred between flights if the journey involves more than one flight, and the baggage will have to go through security screening. You may have specified the provision of food and drinks for a flight, but neglected to specify transporting them to the aircraft.

For the function 'locate alternative flights . . .' there may be other things you need to do to an alternative flight once you have located it, such as:

- check seat availability on it
- inform the passenger of its details
- highlight differences between the alternative and the original flight.

You could also extend more of this function, and ask what else the business might need to locate alternatives for:

- the pilot or another member of staff
- the aircraft (following breakdown)
- an airport (perhaps even consider a permanent route change)
- a supplier (e.g. of spare parts)
- a seat (for a passenger), and so on.

Figure 5-6
Testing a Hierarchy

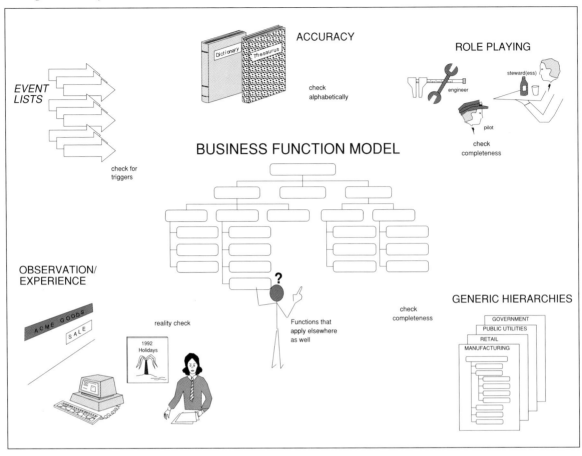

A Story

On one project with a company that rented televisions, after four interviews we had identified about four thousand potential functions. The question was simple: *"How could we organize these into a hierarchy – quickly and accurately?"* The process was as follows:

1. We wrote them all on separate sticky notelets, improving the definitions during the rewriting and adding any new ones that came to mind.

2. One of us stood in front of a very large clean glass window* and arbitrarily selected one notelet. This was placed in the centre.

3. The same person, working alone, processed all the notelets, placing them above the central one if they were earlier in the life-cycle and

---

*   Why glass? We once tried this exercise on a papered wall. When we came back after lunch all the stickies had fallen to the floor!

below it if later. Grouping was encouraged (though obviously this was subjective). Further detail was grouped to the right and new groups organized on the left.

4. Frequent reorganization of groups occurred, including overlapping common areas.

5. At any time new functions or groups could be added.

6. When all the notelets had been used, the analyst switched to synthesis mode and grouped the groups by defining new higher-level functions. This process continued until a new top was reached.

7. This bottom-up synthesis of the hierarchy was compared with the results of the top-down process. The hierarchies were merged to give a more comprehensive model. (At this point any of the checking techniques already described can also be deployed.)

The exercise took about sixteen hours, which is incredibly fast for processing such a vast amount of information. It had to be done by one person as it relies on retention of concepts in the analyst's head. The notelets were then carefully labelled, removed and the functions recorded in a CASE tool for subsequent manipulation, checking and use.

Quality of the Model

It is key to the success of any modelling exercise that the model is as accurate and representative of the subject of the model as possible. Good function models are not easy to produce, but here are some pointers that will help improve the quality of any model and that can be applied as a cross-check when a hierarchy gets close to completion. As you gain experience, you will be able to apply these quality measures as you are building a hierarchy.

Aside

Sometimes the production and checking of a function hierarchy can have immediate and unexpected effects. In an engineering organization that was responsible for quality assurance, the following function appeared in the middle of the hierarchy:

Accept plant or part.

This seemingly innocuous function caused a heated debate. When conducting interviews and observing the inspection engineers at work it was obvious that their job was to inspect pipes, motors, turbines or any other plant or parts on behalf of a third-party company that was buying them. The engineers worked diligently and samples were tested rigorously. On a satisfactory result the engineer would complete an acceptance form, cross-referenced to the buyer's contract, signed by the engineer, and copies would be given to the supplier and the buyer: the engineers actually accepted the plant or part.

This process had been going on for at least twenty years. The problem was that the engineers did not have the **right** to do it! They were a third-party quality assurance organization who were paid to check things; however, they had **not** been given the right to act on behalf of the buyer. When this came to light it was obvious something needed to be done so new functions were suggested.

Accept plant or part on behalf of buyer if, and only if, delegated rights have been agreed.

Notify buyer that plant or part has satisfactorily passed appropriate test.

Recommend buyer to accept plant or part.

You will notice that in the end the major change was that the verb accept was replaced by the verb recommend – a distinct change of meaning. Resolving this issue caused significant contractual changes in the way the business was conducted, major changes to what the engineers did and, coupled with other changes in the organization, eventually led to a higher level of quality assurance.

Words

It is really important to use the right words so a good dictionary and thesaurus are a sound investment on any project. People who enjoy word games (crosswords, anagrams, etc.) often make good function modellers. Natural languages tend to be expressive, so think of alternative phrases and, eventually, you will find one that clearly and unambiguously captures what you mean. The rules of good writing should apply to function modelling as to any other form of writing, and given the nature of function names there should be little room for grammatical errors! But a careless choice of words can break a hierarchy, so in choosing your words it is worth heeding the advice of Fowler to be *"direct, simple, brief, vigorous, and lucid"* .[3]

Remove acronyms, abbreviations and anything else that will reduce clarity or cause ambiguity, and then check for meaning to ensure that the functions accurately define what you believe should be done in the business. Then, when you check the functions with the users, they can work with you to 'get it right'. Later benefits appear in improved procedures and more appropriate systems.

The following extract from a model of a freight haulage company has a number of weaknesses:

Provide facilities to load cargo for onward transportation.
Provide facilities to clear cargo through customs.
Provide facilities to invoice customer and collect dues.

Someone joining part-way through this project pointed out that 'provide facilities to . . .' was superfluous. Arguably, it was actually wrong, since the essential business activities were to load and clear cargo, and to invoice customers and collect dues. (The original modeller had fallen into the trap of constructing lots of functions with an identical structure.) Simply removing the redundant phrase from each function made the wording direct and precise, and the style more vigorous.

Sequence of Functions

At this stage of developing a function model, no sequence is intended within the decomposition of a function (this will be dealt with later in Chapter 7). In the previous chapter we examined the function 'check in passenger and baggage' and identified the sub-functions:

> *Weigh, record, label and accept personal baggage.*
> *Allocate free seat to passenger for flight.*
> *Issue boarding pass to passenger.*

You might have paused to consider the order in which these functions would need to be done. It does not matter at this stage in which sequence you list sub-functions under a parent. However, there are dependencies between these functions (anyone who has flown will know that the boarding pass has the seat number on it, so we have to allocate the seat before we can issue the boarding pass), and we will deal fully with dependencies in Chapter 7. Initially, create your decomposition free of any implied sequence.

A Story

In one large insurance company, a particularly forceful executive on the main board would not accept the model until a whole leg of the function hierarchy, previously three levels down, was elevated to the top level. *"That's better,"* he said. *"**Now that really reflects the emphasis that we are trying to place on timeliness.**"*

This change occurred at a feedback session to the board, when the primary business functions, information needs and other findings were being presented to the executives for correction and acceptance. The presenters fought against the change at first, as it was already in 'the most logical position' (in their view). In the end they submitted to the pressure and the model was changed.

Did it matter? Well, yes, it did for a variety of reasons. This influential executive 'bought in' to the procedure. Current business priorities were emphasized. Other executives also wanted to make their impact on the model – so their attention increased and the model became correspondingly more accurate.

Did it matter that the hierarchy was now drawn differently? Well, not really. The objectives of a hierarchy are to identify **all** the functions, to check for completeness and consistency, to be able to handle a vast number of concepts in a convenient and acceptable manner, and ultimately to find all elementary functions that need system support. It does not actually matter what the groupings are, so long as the objectives are met. You could give the same list of functions to two equally good analysts and they would inevitably produce different groupings – that is perfectly okay so long as the above objectives are met. After all, aircraft designers use their skill to produce different designs, each of which (hopefully) adequately meets the needs but each also reflects different emphasis, bias and ideas. (To use a singularly unpleasant vernacular saying, there's more than one way to skin a cat!)

Job Definitions

A similar thing applies to grouping functions into the jobs people do. For instance, there is no necessity to have all the job functions of a steward or stewardess described in one place in the hierarchy. We set out to understand and document what the **business** does, or needs to do, to achieve its objectives, regardless of how it is currently organized, who currently does what job, and what mechanisms are currently used to implement the functions.

Organization Structure

A potentially more difficult task is to keep the function model free of any current organization structure. It is not necessary to put all of the functions carried out by the 'current' sales and marketing division under a function called 'Sales and Marketing'. It is, in fact, far better to avoid this because the structure of organizations frequently changes. A good hierarchy is accurate, regardless of the structure of the organization.

A word of warning, however: once you have removed all of the structure that reflects the current organization, executives responsible for an area of functionality will find it much more difficult to locate 'the bits that they do'. This is intentional! We have found from experience that grouping hierarchies by organization causes many problems:

- Excessive duplication of functions.
- The cross-check of *"Is the parent completely satisfied by its sub-functions?"* cannot be used (especially in cases where one or more of the sub-functions is the responsibility of another department).
- It can become a vehicle for 'empire building' if people think that having responsibility for a bigger part of the hierarchy entitles them to more resources to manage it.
- As soon as an organization changes its structure, the hierarchy will become out of date.

There is great value in helping executives understand what the other parts of the organization do, instead of their limiting themselves to the parts they are personally responsible for.

Approach

The way a function modelling exercise is approached will affect its success. If you intend to seek verification from very senior business people that a hierarchy is a reasonable understanding of the business requirements, anything in it must be of a sufficiently high quality to be presented at that senior level. Imagine the chief executive is looking over your shoulder while you are carrying out the exercise and aim to get it right first time, every time – ambitious, yes, but to produce quality work you need to aim high.

Learn to be humble: this is not the contradiction to the last aim that it may seem at first glance. The less protective you are about your model, the more likely you, and other people, are to spot flaws early and adopt improvements; get used to challenging, redrawing and reorganizing the hierarchy. The effort will be worth it in the end.

Team Work

It is usual to work in teams on this kind of analysis exercise. To be effective, the majority of time should be spent function modelling rather than on non-productive activities, such as arguing with one another! It is easy to fall into the trap of defending a model because it happens to represent the way **you** first thought about it, and a challenge to the model can quickly become a lengthy and costly debate. Each member of an analysis team may well have a different viewpoint; this can be put to good use by getting someone with an alternative viewpoint to rearrange 'your' hierarchy or create and improve the existing hierarchy from time to time. Aim to get the best from everybody in the team rather than sticking to one individual viewpoint. It is beneficial for the team members to agree the approach to be adopted in cases of joint modelling, so that everyone is clear that periodic reorganization of a hierarchy is useful.

Presentation

We have spent a lot of time in this chapter looking at a wealth of techniques that can help us make sure that we have identified all relevant functions and that the hierarchy is consistent and logically complete. We now need to ensure that we have got it right – from the users' viewpoint. They need to correct it, approve it and 'buy into' any implications of this interesting model of their business.

It is, therefore, important to explain the function hierarchy to people who know the business well, so that it can be checked for relevance and applicability. It will be used to decide which areas of the business are to receive systems support. A function hierarchy will often contain hundreds, or even thousands, of functions, which poses an interesting presentation problem. The hierarchy, however, also has a number of advantages when you come to present it, since it provides a natural context at each level in which to focus a limited functional requirement. In practice, presenting the hierarchy from the top (one leg at a time) and offering the opportunity to comment, discuss and modify the words and the structure is an effective way of checking your understanding of the business. The top-level function establishes that the correct and agreed scope is being addressed and that the essence of the business has been captured at a very high level, while the decomposition allows you to check that the functional detail of the business has been understood.

In order to present the decomposition of the top-level function effectively, the ground rules for the hierarchy need to be understood by everyone at the presentation. This only takes a few minutes to explain, and the key points are:

- Each function is something the **business** does now, or needs to do in the future.

- The 'who', 'when', 'where' and 'how' have been removed. This is best explained as:

      no mechanisms (e.g. fax, telephone)
      no organization structures (e.g. department, team)
      no job titles (e.g. salesman, researcher, mechanic).

- The decomposition of a function is **all** that is needed to carry it out.

- Each function that is in a decomposition is **necessary** to carry out the parent function.

Once the ground rules are understood after discussing a few real examples to illustrate them, individual business managers can be left to review and comment in their own time on the areas of the function model with which they are most familiar.

Changes at lower levels in the hierarchy generally have somewhat less impact than those at the higher levels. The function model can be used to great effect in conjunction with its accompanying information model. It is best to split the information model into sub-models (ideally with overlap so that they can be easily linked together) which support different parts of the function hierarchy. In this way, function and information model can be presented and discussed in small, coherent, easily digestible sections.

Overview Model

Quite often, presenting the function model as a hierarchy only is rather dry and boring, so a high-level dependency diagram may be used to summarize the functions in a decomposition. This kind of diagram is discussed in Chapter 7 but might look something like Figure 5-7.

Figure 5-7
Presenting an Overview

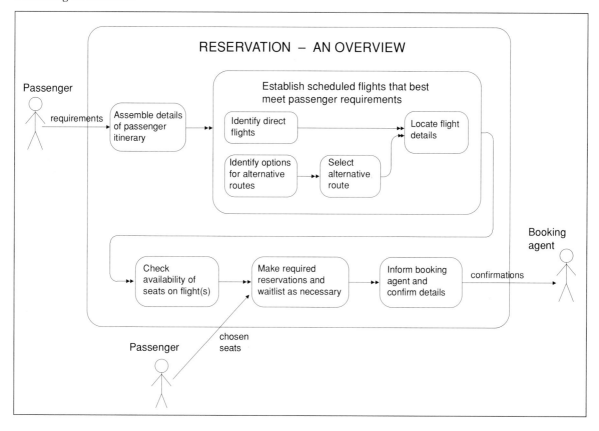

Each line shows a business function (to the left) which needs to be done before another (on the right) can be carried out. The overview diagram need not be rigorous to be very useful. It can, for example, be used as a kind of menu, which gives a context within which to discuss an area of the business. Notice this reintroduces the notion of sequence of the functions; this is discussed fully in Chapter 7.

Layout

In most western societies, hierarchies are read from the top down and from left to right to illustrate going from the general to the detailed or more specific. All the examples of layout shown below assume this pattern, but if users are from a society where some alternative pattern is more appropriate a different layout approach needs to be considered for speed of acceptance and understanding of the model. The objective of a good layout is to convey correct structure, understanding and clarity, to aid checking for accuracy and completeness and to facilitate active discussion of issues.

Automatically produced hierarchies, such as those from a CASE tool, will give layouts like those shown in Figures 5-8 to 5-10 below. These will be excellent for most purposes.

Figure 5-8
Vertical Layout

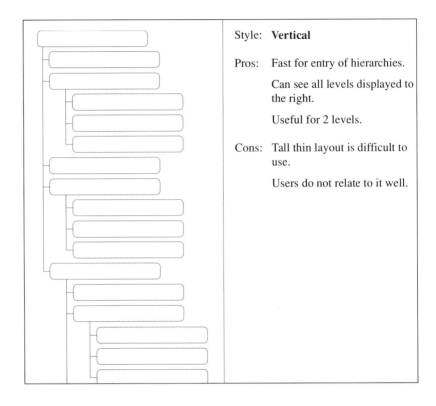

Style: **Vertical**

Pros: Fast for entry of hierarchies.

Can see all levels displayed to the right.

Useful for 2 levels.

Cons: Tall thin layout is difficult to use.

Users do not relate to it well.

Figure 5-9
Horizontal Layout

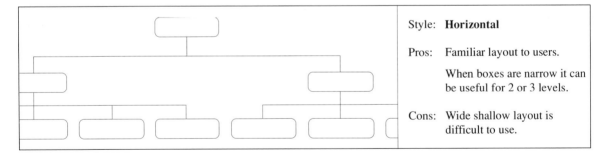

Style: **Horizontal**

Pros: Familiar layout to users.

When boxes are narrow it can be useful for 2 or 3 levels.

Cons: Wide shallow layout is difficult to use.

Recommended Layout

The hybrid style (Figure 5-10) is the recommended normal layout, with boxes to give about twenty characters across and a maximum of five or six lines deep for function names. Two variants on the standard horizontal and vertical layouts are also illustrated (Figures 5-11 and 5-12).

Figure 5-10
Hybrid Layout

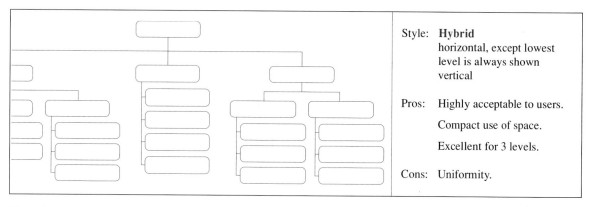

Style: **Hybrid**
horizontal, except lowest
level is always shown
vertical

Pros: Highly acceptable to users.

Compact use of space.

Excellent for 3 levels.

Cons: Uniformity.

Figure 5-11
Specialized Layouts

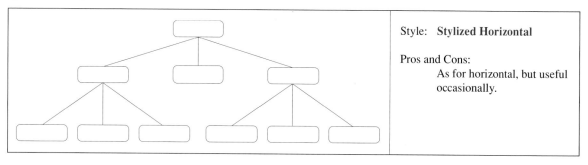

Style: **Stylized Horizontal**

Pros and Cons:
As for horizontal, but useful
occasionally.

Figure 5-12
Specialized Layouts

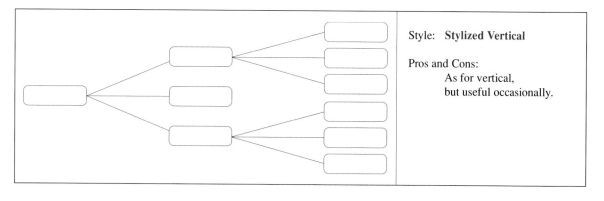

Style: **Stylized Vertical**

Pros and Cons:
As for vertical,
but useful occasionally.

Making Your
Models Memorable

All of the layout patterns so far have used identically sized functions. In each one the structure of the hierarchy is shown unambiguously, allowing checking to be done. But none of these patterns is memorable. People tend to recognize and remember unusual patterns and shapes, and as you can see the problem with hierarchies is that they tend to look the same. When you get to the tenth, apparently identical leg in the model it starts to get difficult to concentrate on the job of checking it.

Where the analyst wants to provide special emphasis, or bring something very specific to the reader's attention, or take advantage of our ability to remember patterns and their context, other tactics can be employed. Some of these are shown in the next set of diagrams, Figures 5-13 to 5-17.

Figure 5-13
Make Key Boxes Bigger

Figure 5-14
Use Shadow and/or Colour

Figure 5-15
Subset the Information

Show omissions by some means.

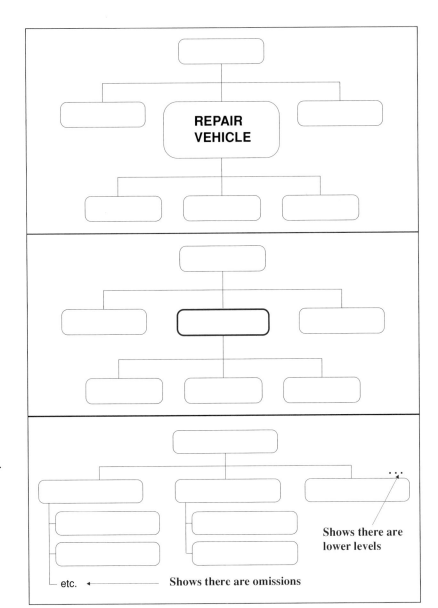

Figure 5-16
Add Something Extra

Use graphics, icons, arrows, illustrations or some other annotation to add something extra to an otherwise conventional layout.

Figure 5-17
Use Extended Lines to Create Patterns, and Mix Styles

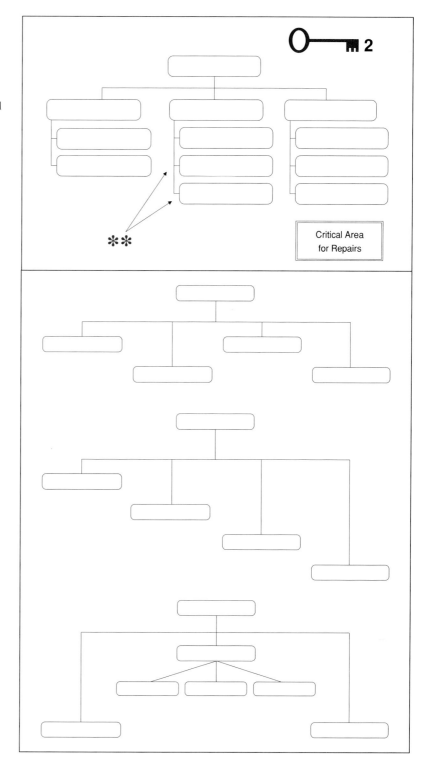

In other words, use your imagination to make it interesting, but remember that each memorable shape should be used only once to avoid ambiguity. Some CASE tools allow this approach, either within their capability or by outputting a diagram into a drawing tool for subsequent manipulation. Although the illustrations only cover hierarchies, the same principles can be applied to the other diagram types shown in this book.

**System and Program/
Procedure Level**

This technique of arranging functions is equally applicable at a system level, for creating an easy way of finding all the system functionality, and at a program/procedure level. In both cases, it is often a useful source from which to construct computer menu systems or arrange clerical procedures.

CASE Tools

Any good CASE tool will have a hierarchy diagrammer. It is a good idea to produce a rough hierarchy before using the tool, as seeing the whole thing in a readable form can be a problem on even the highest resolution graphics screen. The CASE tool will, typically, enable you to:

- rearrange sequence
- re-parent functions
- view different legs, to different numbers of levels
- manipulate or produce hardcopy output of the model to different layout standards.

Summary

We have examined the techniques for building a function hierarchy and testing it for quality, consistency and completeness. To construct a hierarchy from scratch, we start with initial interview notes and known business objectives and build a framework showing the essence of the business top down. The hierarchy is cross-checked and completed bottom up by taking detailed functions from the sources mentioned above and fitting them into an appropriate place in the hierarchy, which will grow, evolve and change shape as the exercise proceeds. A number of procedures for testing the hierarchy were explored and, finally, we looked at ways of presenting a hierarchy to check that its meaning represents a real business requirement.

Of the six interrogative words, who, what, when, where, how and why, only the what and why should appear in a function model; the **what** is an operation the business does, or needs to do, and the **why** is the objective it is trying to achieve by doing it. Of the others: **who** is extracted with the removal of jobs and roles; **when** does not appear because functions have no implicit sequence or timing in the hierarchy; **where** is removed when references to parts of the organization are taken out; and **how** is separated out with the removal of the mechanisms.

6 INTRODUCING FUNCTION DEPENDENCY

In the first few chapters we have concentrated on an airline example. Let us now look at a different example to introduce a new concept – **function dependency**. Modelling function dependencies is a useful technique to show that the completion of one function may trigger the start of another or, conversely, that one function may be dependent on another; that is, it cannot be activated until another function has been completed. Many real-world situations require this sort of modelling to ensure their essence is captured and correct design decisions are made. In Chapter 5 we briefly discussed the sequence in which functions are carried out, but avoided specifying this while constructing a hierarchy. A dependency prevents a function being carried out until another one has finished; a collection of dependencies determines the sequence in which a set of functions **can** be done to meet the business need sensibly. Dependency modelling can be used at the business ⬭, system ⬭ and program/procedure ⬭ level.

The Second Example

The automobile has become an integral part of western society for both private and commercial use. Unfortunately (except for garages*), they require service and maintenance work that demands skills beyond the capability, or available time, of many individuals. This example is based on a business that consists of several garages that maintain and service privately owned and commercial vehicles.

(*Garage, as used here, is equivalent to an automobile repair shop in the US.)

A company called 'On the Road Garages' has twelve garages in eight towns and cities in a small locality. Each garage has its own manager, skilled engineers and fully equipped workshop. Spare parts are stocked at each garage for all the commonly required parts, and a larger stock is held at the central garage (which has more space than the others).

Customers call to book their cars in for servicing and repairs. Each garage operates a scheduling system to ensure that the best use is made of its mechanics' time and that a predictable turnround of work can be achieved. The order in which things are done has evolved over the years to combat a problem that the company used to face: customers would book, say, a 10.00 a.m. service and then deliver the car late. Locating a vehicle left by a customer could also cause significant loss of time. This was even more noticeable when a vehicle broke down and had to be repaired on the roadside, or towed back to the garage for further work. As a result, it has become company policy that until a vehicle has been located a mechanic is not allocated to work on it.

Once a vehicle has been located and a mechanic allocated, problems and faults are diagnosed by inspection, spare parts are found and the vehicle is repaired and tested. Standard prices are quoted for many routine jobs, but customers are contacted and their approval obtained if additional work is necessary. (A booking for standard-priced work implies customer agreement on the price.) All costs are logged by the mechanic on a costing form, which is then used as the basis for invoicing the customer. Occasionally, work is contracted out to third parties.

The management of the group has decided to position the business at the 'quality end' of the market, and many extra services are to be introduced which are commensurate with this. These will include:

- *a loan car whilst the customer's car is being repaired*
- *a courtesy service to drive customers between garage and home or work while their own cars are unavailable*
- *valeting the interior and exterior of the car prior to its return*
- *comfortable areas for customers to wait in*
- *up-to-the-minute information on new cars and related technology.*

The management believes the need for repair and servicing will gradually decline over the next decade, owing to more reliable vehicles, improved public transport infrastructure and a declared government intention to reduce the number of vehicles that use hydrocarbon fuels. Management is, therefore, acutely aware of the need to retain a competitive edge and 'add value' in what is expected to become a highly competitive market.

Function Hierarchy

Before you study the next page, you might like to produce your own hierarchy for the current activities of 'On the Road Garages'. As an extension to the exercise, you could model the future requirements to allow the company to cater for the quality end of the market.

Figure 6-1
Function Hierarchy for 'On the Road Garages'

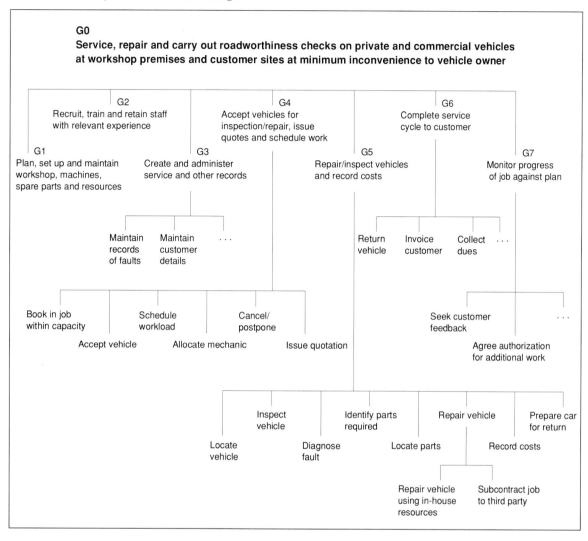

Many more functions (and a larger sheet of paper) would be needed to produce a full model, and in some places we have simply used ellipses to indicate omissions. The function names are also somewhat cryptic, but are sufficient for this exercise to allow us to explore the dependencies between functions.

Function Dependency

You may have noticed that there is a sense of a 'flow' through the business functions. There is some implied sequence in which things must be done to be sensible as a whole, although in the early stages of function modelling the essential thing is to identify and record the functions without specifying the sequence.

Take the function G5 of repairing a vehicle, for instance: the components of this, shown in the next level below in the hierarchy, are likely to be done in sequence as shown in Figure 6-2. In fact, it is not possible to complete some of the functions unless others have already been completed.

Figure 6-2
A Simple Function Dependency Diagram

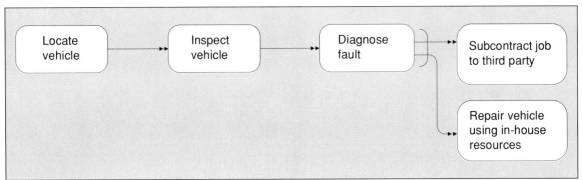

A vehicle cannot be inspected until it has been located, cannot be repaired until the fault has been found, and so on. Towards the end of the above sequence, following diagnosis of the fault, the vehicle is **either** repaired at the garage where it has been inspected **or** the job is subcontracted to a third party, usually another garage. The either/or is shown on the diagram by the arc across the two lines leading from the 'diagnose fault' box.

A diagram like this is called a Function Dependency Diagram. The most important aspect of it is the lines that join the functions: each line shows a business dependency. The function at the arrowhead of the line cannot be started until the one at the other end has been completed. The function at the arrowhead is said to be 'dependent' on the one at the other end.

Extending the Dependency Diagram

After a vehicle has been located something else has to be done before it can be inspected – a mechanic must be allocated to the vehicle and, even before that can be done, the workload must be scheduled.

So now 'inspect vehicle' is dependent on both locating the vehicle **and** allocating a mechanic to inspect it, shown by the dependency lines joining together (see Figure 6-3). Notice that the functions in the diagram do not all come from the same parent function but are spread throughout the hierarchy; the dependency chain is completely independent of the position of functions in the hierarchy. If a function in a dependency chain can be decomposed further, this means that some, or all, of the functions in the decomposition have a dependency on the functions earlier in the chain.

Figure 6-3
Another Dependency for 'Inspect vehicle'

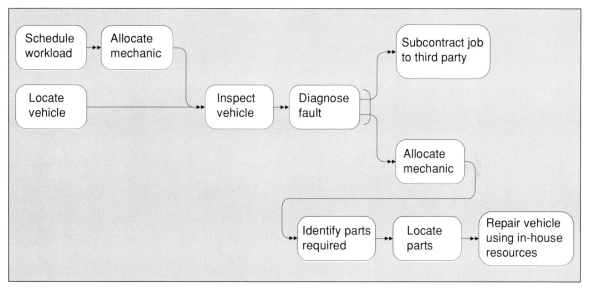

You will notice that the function 'allocate mechanic' appears in two places. This is an example of an apparently common function. In one case we need to allocate a mechanic to do the inspection; and if the repair is to be done in-house we also need one or more mechanics to carry out the repair. Functions may frequently reappear in different dependency diagrams, reflecting different ways in which the business is carried out.

Unnecessary Dependencies

As a matter of company policy, mechanics are only allocated to a task once the vehicle had been located. If this dependency is added to our diagram, the existing dependency between locating a vehicle and inspecting it is no longer required. Since inspecting a vehicle is dependent upon allocating a mechanic, which itself is dependent upon locating that vehicle, this implies the dependency between locating a vehicle and inspecting it – this dependency is therefore redundant.

Figure 6-4
Removing Unnecessary
Dependencies

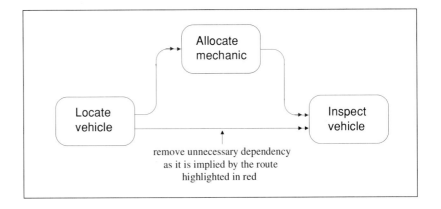

But beware of policy changes! If the company policy changes to allow the allocation of mechanics, whether or not the vehicle has been located, it is important to re-establish the lower dependency chain.

Deriving a Systems Development Strategy

As you can imagine, producing and, more to the point, maintaining function dependency diagrams can be a time-consuming exercise. So let us look at the value of dependency diagrams to the process of deciding a systems development strategy.

A systems development strategy includes a definition of:

– what systems will be developed
– what each one will do for the business
– what order they will be developed in.

When a system is to be developed to carry out or support a selection of business functions, many decisions need to be made, including:

- What scope should the system cover? (i.e. what functions does it support?)

- Which functions can be carried out by each component of the system?

- What is the most sensible way to present the system components to its users?
  – what sequence?
  – what menu structures?
  – what should happen when a component fails?

- What sequence of components would:
  – be the simplest to use?
  – get the job done most quickly?

– be the most relevant to the 'normal' case?

 – give us an 'edge' over our competitors?

Many of these questions demand an understanding of what **could** be done first, so that when we design the system we can make an informed decision on what order things **will** be done. Let us look at an example and see what choices would have to be made when a system is scoped and designed.

System Support

Firstly, let us look at the implications of the function dependency diagram on possible systems for supporting the business by examining the first dependency in this chain.

Figure 6-5
The Link between
Schedule and Allocate

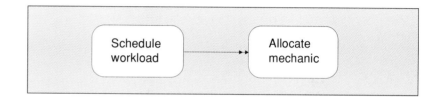

The allocation of the mechanic must be done after scheduling the workload (company policy). When it comes to choosing systems to support these business functions there are a number of choices.

Figure 6-6
Areas where System
Support may be Provided

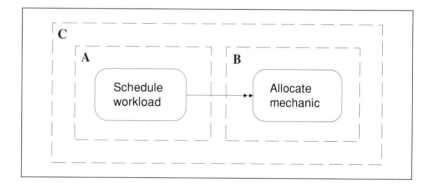

Option A

System support is only provided for 'Schedule workload'. This means that 'Allocate mechanic' must be considered external to the system, since it is not supported by the system. At the very least, an inquiry mechanism should be provided, so that the dependency can be resolved (e.g. list schedule of jobs to be carried out). Functions outside the scope of a system which are dependent upon functions within the scope of that system typically require 'feeding' with information.

Option B

Support is only provided for 'Allocate mechanic'. This means there needs to be some means of establishing the results of scheduling the workload prior to carrying out this allocation, and this will come from outside the system. Functions within the scope of a system which are dependent upon functions outside the scope of that system typically need 'feeding' with information.

Option C

Support is provided for both functions. This means that there is only one order in which to carry out the functions in our system, because of the dependency. 'Allocate mechanic' must be done after 'Schedule workload'. One of the checks the system should make before allowing the allocation of a mechanic is that a schedule has been produced.

The choices in system definition come when there are no dependencies. In the following example, a system has been chosen to support four functions. The dependencies between these functions limit us to three options for the sequence in which they can be supported.

Figure 6-7
A System to Support
Four Functions

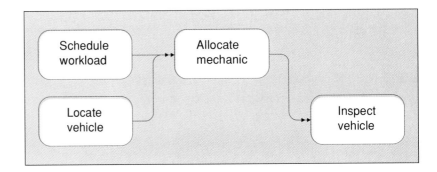

Vehicles may be located before, after, or at the same time as scheduling workloads (since there is no dependency between them).

Dependencies can be used to help decide a sensible grouping of functions for system support. The more dependencies that are across boundaries between systems, the more complex and error prone the systems are likely to be at their interfaces. And conversely, the fewer dependencies there are within a system, the more choice there is for sequencing functions and having functions run concurrently.

Presenting
Function Dependencies

A complete function hierarchy, showing the dependencies as well, might look like the next diagram – a mess! As you can see, this is getting complicated: more like a street map than a system definition. This diagram is **not** intended for presentation; it is simply to give you, the reader of this book, a feeling for how everything fits together.

Figure 6-8
Function Hierarchy with the Dependencies Added

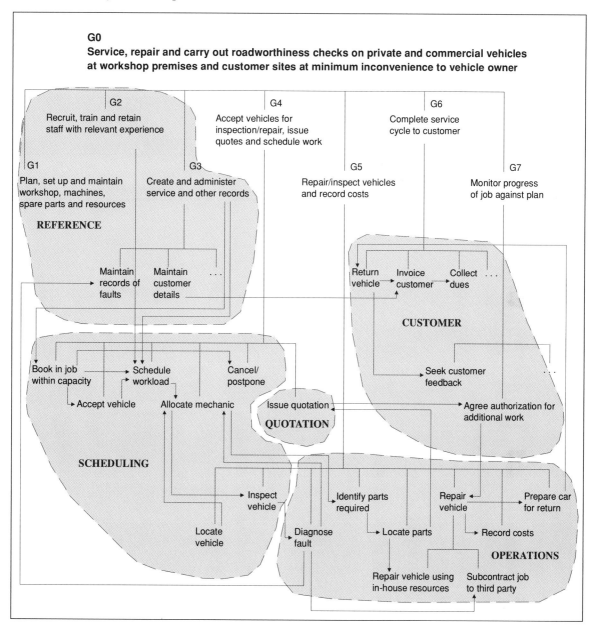

The black text and lines represent the original function hierarchy. The dependencies have been added in red (notice that they cut across the 'legs' of the hierarchy, which is a reflection of the way we chose to group the higher levels of the hierarchy). Finally, the shaded areas indicate collections of functions which we intend to provide system support for.

Notice the dependencies across the boundaries between these systems – these are the ones that will determine the order in which we can develop entire systems.

For presentation, especially to senior management, the suggested systems (the shaded areas on the hierarchy) are represented as shown in Figure 6-9.

Figure 6-9
Dependency Chain between Suggested Systems

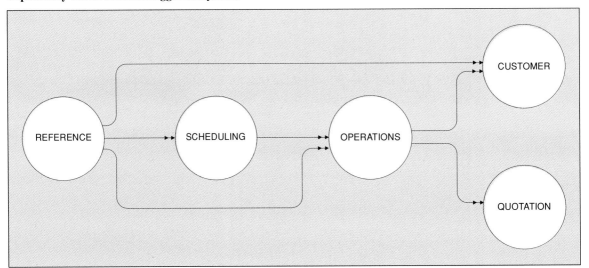

At this level, a line represents at least one dependency from a function in one system to a function in another. This kind of presentation diagram can be used to gain commitment and consensus from senior management for:

- what systems to develop
- the scope each should cover
- the order they should be developed in.

This diagram is simply a very high-level summary of the detailed hierarchy and dependency diagrams. It is not necessarily definitive, but it illustrates the options and can therefore be very useful in helping some decision-making process.

For each system on the diagram it is simple to show:

- a detailed listing of its functional support (its scope)
- the extent to which it helps to achieve the objectives of the business (its relevance)
- a set of interface dependencies with other systems (its dependencies)
- the options for where it could appear in a development cycle
- the information needed to support the functions in it.

These named systems or sub-systems can then be thought of as a unit of work. They can be estimated and costed. From the diagram showing the dependencies between systems the order in which to develop systems can be decided, based on the highest value to the business and the estimated cost. In some cases this may be a formal cost/benefit analysis or some other analysis of return on investment. The scope of each system can be modified to change dependencies, implementation sequences and costs. Presenting information in this way exposes the (very complex) process of deciding on a system development strategy.

Summary

We have examined a second example and used it to introduce the concept of a function dependency. This recognizes that a function may have to wait on the completion of one or more other functions before it can be carried out itself. We have seen how this dependency information can help us make decisions on such things as:

- the scope of a system
- the order in which systems can be developed
- the order in which functions within a system can be presented to the users of that system.

We will now look at the formal definition of a function dependency in Chapter 7.

7

FUNCTION DEPENDENCY DIAGRAMS

In this chapter we look in detail at two concepts: the function dependency (introduced in Chapter 6) and the key result. These are useful and even essential modelling concepts for defining the requirement or design for complex interrelated systems. When an event occurs, it may trigger a sequence of functions to achieve some desired outcome (a key result) for the business. The completion of a function can also trigger the start of another function – one can consider that the end of every function is an implicit event. A function dependency diagram shows the sequence of functions that occur when a business responds to an event and the outcome that is a result of that sequence. Function dependency diagrams help to focus attention on important sequences of functions so that relevant systems can be designed to support them.

Function dependency diagramming is a generally applicable technique; whilst only illustrated at the business level ⬭, it is also applicable at the system ⬭ and program/procedure level ⬭.

Function Dependency

Function Dependency Definition

A dependency of one business function, B, on another, A, means that B cannot start until A has finished.

There are a number of reasons why dependencies arise, varying from rigorous rules to whim. They are:

Data   – Function A produces information required by function B.

| Legislation | – | It is a legal constraint that the business must first do function A before starting function B. |
| Corporate Policy | – | That is the way executives want it to be done and, as such, can often help to differentiate a company from its competitors. |

Data Dependency

Data dependencies are common, the easiest to understand and most useful of the three types of dependency. A data dependency arises when data produced by one function is operated on by a dependent function. Because of this, the dependent function cannot start until the data on which it operates has been produced. For example, the function 'assign seat to passenger' will produce some new information: it will create an instance of an individual booking for a seat on a flight. As a consequence of this, another function may be triggered which results in a boarding pass being issued for that particular seat and passenger.

Legislative Dependency

This is a dependency required of the business by law. Such dependencies constrain the way a business is **allowed** to operate. For example, in an international freight haulage company, imported goods must clear customs prior to being put in a bonded store.

Policy Dependency

Business policy may dictate that one function must follow another even though there is no **inherent** reason why. This, by the way, is part of what gives a business its characteristic 'culture'. A passenger may report, "*I like travelling on Atlantis Island Flights: they always serve drinks before take-off.*" Policy and executive whim are fairly common reasons for a function dependency. Another example is a company that will not satisfy any orders until all orders for the day and the stock available are known; available stock can then be allocated on some weighted priority basis.

Figure 7-1
A Function Dependency

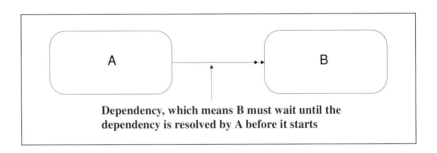

Dependency, which means B must wait until the
dependency is resolved by A before it starts

Function Dependency Representation

Dependencies of all types are shown as a double-headed arrow between two function boxes. The function at the arrowhead (B) is dependent on the function at the other end (A), as on many flow-style diagrams you may be familiar with.

Key Result

Key Result Definition

A key result is the outcome the business is trying to achieve upon receipt of an event. From the example of On the Road Garages (Chapter 6) 'customer delivery of vehicle for service' is an event. There are two key results that the business is aiming to achieve upon receipt of this event:

'successful service of vehicle', and
'return of vehicle to customer'.

A key result is, in fact, just another event and is represented in the usual way by a hollow arrow with the name of the event inside it. The result 'successful service of vehicle' may itself trigger further functions.

Figure 7-2
A Key Result

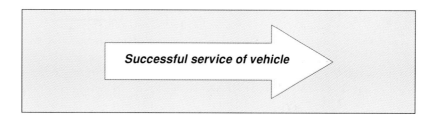

Detailed Function Dependency Diagram

One or more events, with one or more key results, provide the scope for a detailed function dependency diagram.

Figure 7-3
A Detailed Function Dependency Diagram

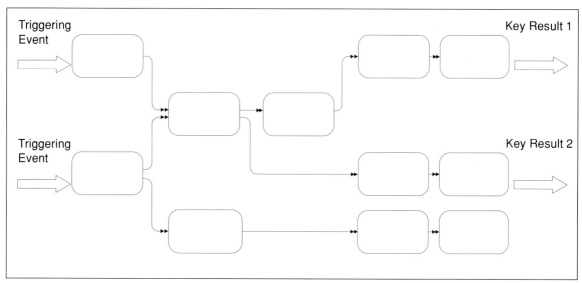

A detailed function dependency diagram is a diagram showing a subset of the business function hierarchy with its interdependencies. The detailed diagram identifies all possible 'routes' or sequences through the subset of functions. Such a diagram may show how we arrive at a key result following some predetermined types of event.

Using Function Dependency Diagrams

The High-level Function Dependency Diagram

As a presentation aid, the function dependency diagram can be used at a very high level (i.e. the functions on it are aggregates of more detailed functions from the hierarchy). In this case, the triggering events and key results are often not shown, and the dependencies are derived from the many detailed dependencies between lower-level functions. This form of the diagram is, typically, produced very early in the development cycle as part of the presentation material, describing what has been found during an analysis exercise. The dependencies in this case are usually derived from your knowledge of the business at the time; they will not necessarily be verifiable to a detailed and definitive level. Do not worry about this –

Figure 7-4
Two Levels of Function Dependency Diagram

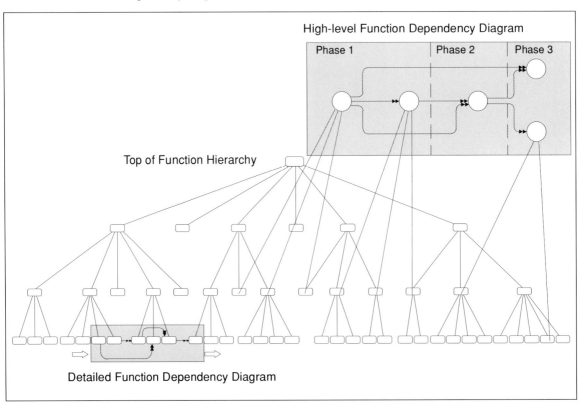

the high-level dependency diagram is still a good visual aid to understanding, especially with executives. The function groupings on the diagram can be drawn as circles to differentiate them from the 'real' functions.

Presenting High-level Dependency Diagrams

The high-level function dependency diagram is a presentation aid. Detailed function definitions may not yet have been produced for the functions that it references, and when they are produced they may prove that the original dependency diagram is wrong in some detail (in which case the alterations necessary can be used to control changes in the scope of an analysis or design exercise). It can be used as a way of exposing your understanding of a business, as a way of proposing outline systems that support the functional requirement of the business, or simply as a way of grouping functions so they can be talked about more easily.

A typical use might be to present a high-level diagram as a proposal for phasing the development of a computer system.

Figure 7-5
High-level Dependency Diagram (illustrating phasing)

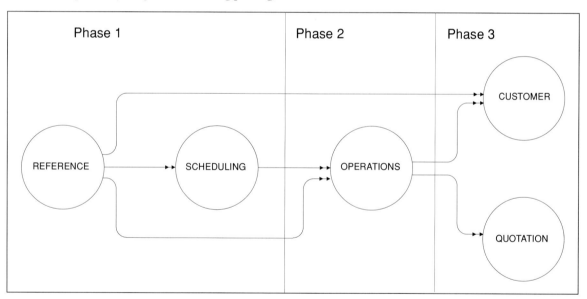

A Feedback Scenario

A possible scenario for feedback of this diagram to users might be:

> *"Before we can do anything we need some reference information (REFERENCE). This includes records of what machines we have, which workshops they are at, our employees and outline customer details. This can be kept to a minimum and be very simple. As this is*

useful, but not critical to the business if mistakes are made, we will use this as a training exercise to introduce our computer specialists to some new database software and tools at the same time. Once the reference information for machines and employees is available, we can support the scheduling functions, which includes booking in jobs and vehicle inspection activities.

"Once we have the result of an inspection we can consider support for OPERATIONS, which start with fault diagnosis, but we suggest leaving that until Phase 2. Phase 3 would then consist of CUSTOMER and QUOTATION systems: since neither of these provides quite as much support for the business objectives as OPERATIONS, we suggest leaving them until this final stage."

Question *What would be the effect of including 'fault diagnosis' and 'locate spare parts' in Phase 1?*

Answer *Well, we could separate the diagnostic component from the scheduling and operations parts we showed you so that it contains the vehicle inspection and then fault diagnosis, identifying spare parts required and locating them from the Operations system. That would clearly make Phase 1 much bigger and it would look something like this.*

Figure 7-6
Alternative System Phasing

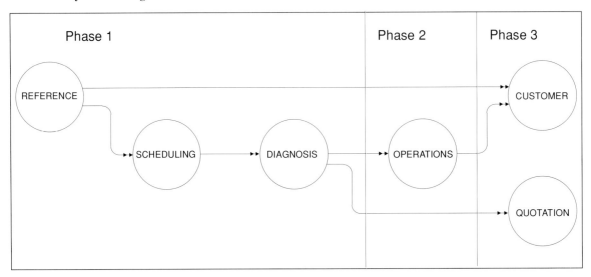

Question *Yes, but could we not leave the scheduling until Phase 2 and put Operations into Phase 1?*

Answer   *No, we cannot do that because we need some of the results of scheduling before we can inspect the vehicle and do the other parts of Operations.*

"Okay, let us draw the line at the end of the new scheduling system and leave that as Phase 1."

As you can see, the diagram provides quite a good focus for talking about the very complex issues of deciding what the system should support, whilst controlling the interdependencies between systems, via another level of detail, so that decisions can be made on a sensible basis. The high-level dependency diagram is a good communication aid, enabling complex issues, such as system scoping, to be discussed rationally. The value of a system in business terms, however, should be judged by those people who know the business.

Such important decisions can often be made by the executives, with the help of the strategists and analysts, without the need for detailed cost/benefit analysis or an investigation of return on investment. This is because this decision point will have been just a part of a strategy study, feasibility study, or other analysis that has helped the parties involved get a clear and objective view of the business and alternatives. More often than not this knowledge plus existing knowledge of priorities, issues, objectives to be met, and so on, leads to a quick, sound decision agreed by all. It is, however, important that the strategists and analysts have a more detailed knowledge to back up their advice. They should also be experienced enough to know the consequence and feasibility of any decisions. In some circumstances more detail is required. When such conflicts of priorities, resources or other critical issues dictate, these systems or sub-systems can then be estimated, costed, set against a time plan and associated with tangible and intangible benefits to help the decision-making process come to a sensible conclusion.

The Detailed Function Dependency Diagram

Although essentially the same type of diagram, the detailed function dependency diagram is used for completely different purposes. The detailed diagrams are based on events that trigger functions and the key results the business is trying to produce. This type of diagram can be produced for any functions that are key or critical in business terms.

Creating a function dependency diagram can be done with no detailed knowledge of **how** any system is to be implemented (leave the intricacies of specific types of computer and so on out at this stage), but dependencies other than data dependencies are, in fact, high-level system design decisions and ought to be recorded as such with a reason to justify them. It is also useful to record assumptions made for critical or controversial decisions. This task is frequently referred to as 'logical system design' and, in the strictest form of system design, deals with processes or mechanisms (which we will examine fully in Chapter 10 on system design) as opposed to business functions.

The detailed function dependency diagram directs the system designer to a more precise definition of what needs to be done so that relevant, useful and usable systems can be developed to support the business.

Identifying and Modelling Dependencies

Let us look at how to identify dependencies from an interview and then how to build up a dependency diagram. Whenever an event occurs which triggers a sequence of functions, there is some outcome or result in mind – the business is trying to achieve something in response to the event. (People carrying out business activity from day to day will recognize this, although they may not use the terms event, trigger, result, and so on.) Interview and observation techniques can be used to establish this structure in detail. For instance, take the following extract from an interview with a booking clerk at Atlantis Island Flights:

". . . so the most common thing that kicks the whole process off is a passenger making a reservation request."

Question *So what are you trying to achieve when you get a reservation request?*

Answer *Well, ideally, **booking the passenger on an AIF flight that he is happy with**, although we do sometimes have to book people in with another airline if we can't satisfy their requirements.*

Question *Are there any other possible outcomes?*

Answer *Yes, it is possible that we just **can't find any way to satisfy the requirements** at all and we have to turn someone away – although, of course, we might **put the person on a waiting list** in case a cancellation arises.*

Summary *So, there are four possible results that could be outcomes following a reservation request:*
– an AIF booking
– a booking on another airline
– a waitlisting on an AIF flight
– an unhappy passenger!

Question *Are there any others?*

Answer *We do occasionally waitlist people with other airlines.*

Question *Let us look at the process of turning a reservation request into an AIF booking. What would normally happen to achieve this?*

Answer	Well, first we have to establish what the passenger needs, when he wants to travel, where to and so on, then we identify AIF flights that meet these requirements and check them with the passenger before we check availability of seats on a particular flight. Assuming there are seats available, we attempt to make a reservation for the passenger. If this works, then we have achieved our goal.
Question	You said "if this works". What do you do if it doesn't work?
Answer	I curse quietly and then see if I can't find some requirement that the passenger is prepared to change – perhaps travelling business class instead of first class or maybe on an earlier or later flight.
Summary	OK, as I understand it, the reservation request causes you to establish the passenger's requirements, find an AIF flight that suits these requirements, check availability on the flight and book a seat. If this fails, you check with the passenger to see if he is prepared to change any of his requirements.

The first questions establish the results that are relevant to the event (what the business is trying to achieve) and the second set of questions pursues the sequence of functions that take place in order to achieve this result. A function dependency diagram of the sequence of functions to get from a reservation request to an AIF booking might look like Figure 7-7 and illustrates a number of points.

Repetition

Notice that the failure to reserve a seat causes the cycle of identifying flights, checking availability and reserving a seat to start again, and that this cycle will continue over and over until either a reservation is made (our result is achieved) or the passenger is no longer prepared to change his requirements and we have failed to satisfy the booking request.

Aside

Events can be used as a very powerful interviewing technique as shown by the following example. On a project in the electricity supply industry, following formal structured interviews of two power station managers, the third manager was approached in a different way. The analysts arrived at half-past eight on a Monday morning so that they could identify all the incoming electronic and normal mail that had arrived over the weekend. The manager's secretary was asked to put telephone calls through to the manager, as she normally would if he was not too busy. The analysts then spent three hours with the manager asking questions such as:

– what is this?
– what would you do with that?
– what would happen next?

– why did you pass that on to . . .?

– what would they do with it?

This is a very simple but effective way of identifying events and what happens as a consequence. However, beware: only some of what you learn will have direct relevance to your project – the remainder is very useful background knowledge, which may have surprising benefits later.

Figure 7-7
Initial Function Dependency Diagram

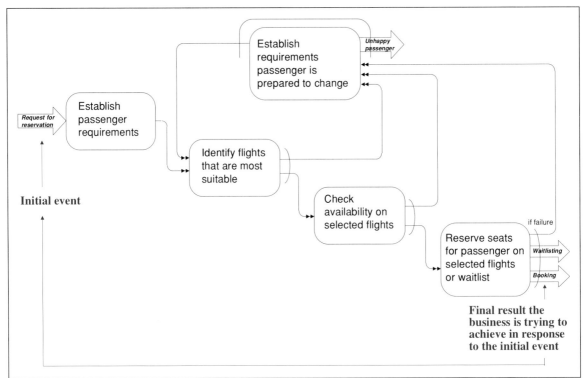

Exclusivity

Sometimes, a function may be capable of producing a number of different results or resolving a number of different dependencies, or a mixture of these. When the outcome is either **one result OR** the resolution of **one dependency** this is shown as an arc on the diagram. (See Figure 7-8.)

The arc means that **one** (and only one) of the enclosed dependencies or results will be resolved or produced each time the function is carried out. The absence of an arc, when more than one dependency or result may be resolved or produced by a function, means that **all** the dependencies will be resolved and all the results will be produced (although not necessarily all at the same time).

Figure 7-8
Exclusive Results and
Dependencies

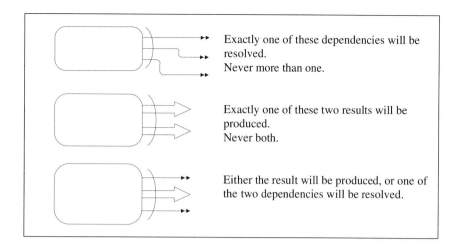

Exactly one of these dependencies will be resolved.
Never more than one.

Exactly one of these two results will be produced.
Never both.

Either the result will be produced, or one of the two dependencies will be resolved.

Figure 7-9
Producing Multiple Results

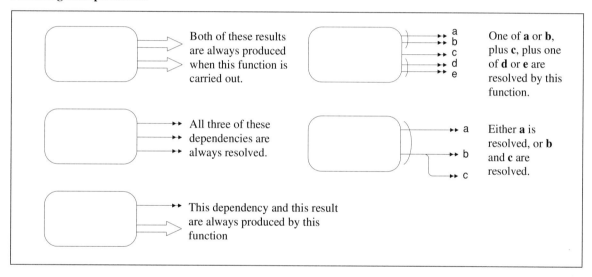

Both of these results are always produced when this function is carried out.

One of **a** or **b**, plus **c**, plus one of **d** or **e** are resolved by this function.

All three of these dependencies are always resolved.

Either **a** is resolved, or **b** and **c** are resolved.

This dependency and this result are always produced by this function

So far, what we have described here is very similar to a flowchart, which is often used to describe the sequential flow of control in some process or another. Where function dependency diagrams differ from these becomes apparent when we start to consider the effect of multiple dependencies. Where a function resolves two (or more) dependencies, the functions that are triggered may be carried out together (i.e. at the same time).

Figure 7-10
Parallel Functions

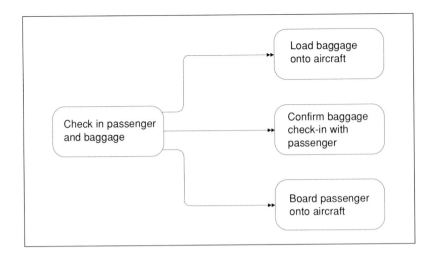

From the diagram above, it is not possible to:

- *load baggage onto aircraft*
- *confirm baggage check-in with passenger, or*
- *board passenger onto aircraft*

until the function 'check in passenger and baggage' has been completed. However, once this function has been completed (thus resolving the three dependencies) the three dependent functions could be carried out together (at the same time) or in any order (i.e. at any point in time relative to one another). It is quite likely there will be a normal or even preferable sequence for some of these functions. For example, we might normally want to confirm the baggage check-in before the passenger is boarded on the plane, but there is no inherent reason why this **must** be the case. In this example, we can certainly load a passenger's baggage onto the plane independently of whether the passenger has boarded or not (which could raise important security issues). Function dependency diagramming can be used in this way to isolate exceptions or rare occurrences that might nevertheless be important to the business.

We might pursue our understanding further by questions based on the initial function dependency diagram.

Question   *You have said that before you can reserve a seat for a passenger you need to check availability on the flight – is there anything else you must do?*

Answer   *Yes, we usually check how the passenger will pay and give him all the other payment details before we actually book the seat.*

Question Alright, that implies to me that once you have identified the flight that meets his requirement most closely, you would check this with the passenger each time you go through the cycle.

Answer Oh no! This usually happens only once – at the beginning of the cycle. Typically, when we come up with alternatives, we are talking about the same flight, but a different time or day, or possibly a different flight to an airport that is very close to the original, and these things don't affect the price too much. So we only tend to go back to the passenger if there is a big difference in price.

This piece of interview has revealed two new points: firstly, there is a missing function and dependency to check the payment details with the passenger before we can reserve a seat; and, secondly, this function is not always carried out, but is at the discretion of the person handling the reservation. So, let us extend the dependency diagram to incorporate this.

Figure 7-11
Extended Function Dependency Diagram

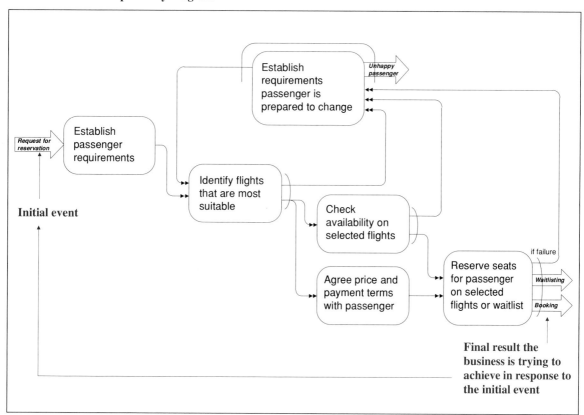

Notice that this diagram (Figure 7-11) allows the 'determine availability' function and the 'agree price and payment details' function to proceed in parallel, or for either to be done first. If these functions are carried out by a trained reservations clerk, then the clerk can decide whether to agree payment first, check availability first, or even agree payment with the passenger whilst checking availability. If Atlantis Island Flights were to standardize its reservations procedure, then a dependency might be added to ensure that payment was agreed before checking seat availability on a flight – this would be a matter of business policy. In general, it is better to model only dependencies that are absolutely essential: wherever a choice is **possible**, create a model that allows it. This includes exceptions as well as the usual cases.

Take care to ensure that a dependency means that:

- **every** time the function is carried out the dependency is resolved

- it is not possible **under any circumstances** to start this function until one of its dependencies has been resolved.

This will encourage the construction of flexible systems, wherever possible: systems that will be capable of dealing with exceptional conditions as well as the norm, and also capable of dealing with changes in business practice and style. Later on, when the system is implemented, you can add a few rules to ensure that the system is used in the manner required by your executives' whim.

Let us now check what we have just modelled. The function 'reserve seats for passenger on selected flights' has two dependencies, and either creates a result or resolves a dependency that starts us round the loop again.

Figure 7-12
Reserving the Seat

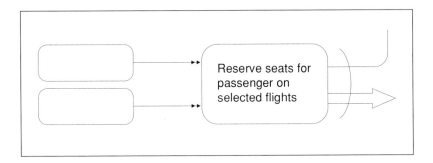

This model shows that the function is triggered by one of two dependencies being resolved, that is:

On **either** a seat being available **or** agreeing price and payment terms with passenger, reserve seat for passenger . . .

This may be what is required. However, we might mean:

> On **both** a seat being available **and** agreeing price and payment terms with passenger, reserve seat for passenger . . .

The latter can be modelled as follows:

Figure 7-13
Two or More Dependencies

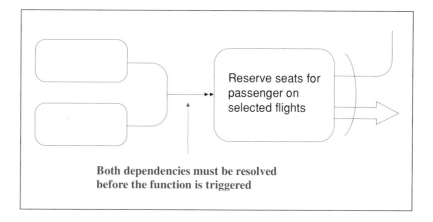

Reserve seats for passenger on selected flights

Both dependencies must be resolved before the function is triggered

which shows that both (or, in the general case, all) dependencies that 'merge' prior to triggering the function must be resolved before the trigger actually takes effect.

Decomposing Functions with Dependencies

During the process of defining dependencies between functions, it will frequently become necessary to further decompose a function (*"This has become more complicated than I imagined it would", "I missed something important", "I don't understand this any more",* and so on). In further decomposing a function, however, a number of anomalies arise. For example, what does a dependency going into a parent function mean? Does it mean a dependency on all the children? on just one? on at least one? As a result, dependencies should only be considered rigorous and valid when modelled between atomic functions. When decomposing a function with dependencies to or from it, you should consider which of the children these dependencies should be 'moved down' to.

If you study the diagram shown in Figure 7-14 closely, you can see that there are some complex relationships between various triggers which we could not see from the diagram prior to decomposition. For instance, if 'a' and 'b' are resolved, then prior to decomposition, we would get either 'x' and 'y' or the key result 'R' **plus** the dependency marked 'z'. After decomposition, however, 'z' can **only** be resolved if the dependency marked 'c' is resolved as well. The decomposition **is different** from what

Figure 7-14
Decomposing a Function with Dependencies

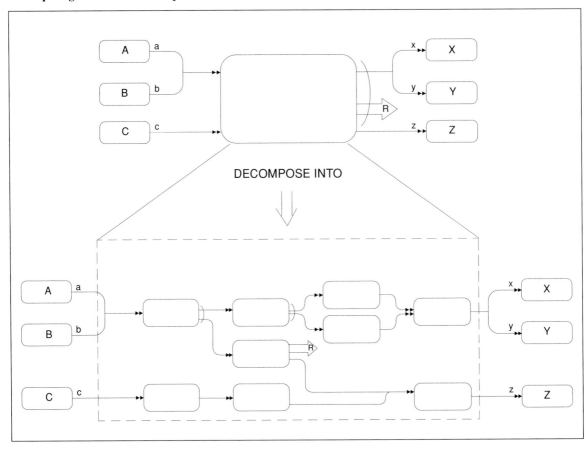

we started with. This is typical of decomposition – we learn more as we uncover detail. When modelling function dependencies, it is usually better to wait until there is a high level of detail known before starting and always keep dependencies modelled at the lowest level of detail.

How to Read a Function Dependency Diagram

It is useful to be able to read these diagrams simply to check that you can understand them. It is even more useful if the users can not only read the diagrams but can also help you check and correct them. The normal procedure is to read the diagrams in a top-to-bottom and left-to-right manner, following the arrows, using the syntax below. It is also a good idea to check some parts from the other end or to start at some function in the middle and look at the whole diagram from that context: the more aggressive the questioning style the more effective the use of inverted syntax.

Event Syntax

Events and the functions they trigger can be recorded using the syntax:

*On the **event-name** event, the **business-function-name** function is triggered.*

For instance:

On the 'request for reservation' event, the 'establish passenger requirements' function is triggered.

To be really rigorous you can use an apparently simpler syntax, which forces you to take great care with the wording of event names:

*On/at **event-name**, **function-name**.*

Our example would now read:

On request for reservation, establish passenger requirements.

Inverted Syntax

*The **business-function-name** function will only ever be triggered after the **event-name** event, is that true?*

Quality Checking the Diagram

For each function in a function dependency diagram, check that it satisfies the following conditions:

– Is this function always needed to achieve the required result?
– What other event could trigger this process?
– Is it true that the only events or dependencies that are needed to trigger this function are shown?
– Are there any events or dependencies for this process that are not **really** needed?

And for each dependency:

– Must this dependency always be satisfied before the next function can start?
– Could the functions on each end of the dependency ever be done simultaneously or the other way around?
– Is this dependency always resolved when the function is carried out? If not then it should be in an exclusive arc with some other dependency or result.

And, finally, for the whole diagram:

– Are all key results shown? Are any missing?
– Can every loop be terminated?
– Are there any other events that could cause these key results to be produced?

A summary diagram of these checks is given on the next page.

Figure 7-15
Quality Checking Your Diagram

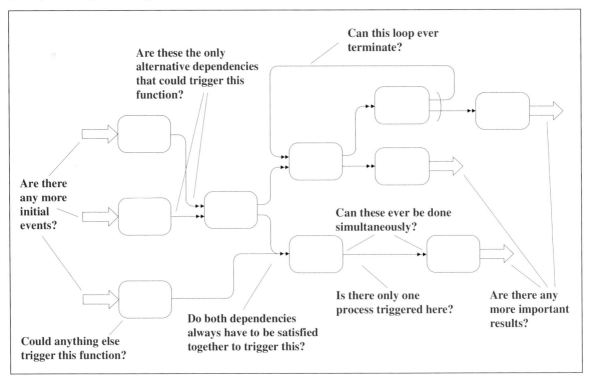

Feedback

An important part of any modelling exercise is to check the accuracy and acceptability of the model with the eventual users of any system produced and other experts. A function dependency diagram is a tremendous aid in this process. When checking models with experts, however, do remember that **they** are the experts, and the purpose of checking the model with them is to find the faults in it, not to display how good you are at producing diagrams! People will think more highly of you if you are prepared to change and evolve your model than if you defend your original model when it is wrong. Deal with any flaws that are revealed or worries expressed by the experts, and incorporate suggested improvements and amendments. Get into the habit of recording, sketching and amending on the actual model, rather than on separate notepads; this allows everyone to see all the information and it can, therefore, be checked again and again quickly and effectively.

In particular, function dependency diagramming is a useful technique for dealing with the tremendous complexities of system scoping and system interdependencies. A fairly simple, overview dependency diagram can be produced and discussed during feedback to users; this should have enough supporting detail to answer questions such as *"Why can't the Customer system be produced before the Operations system?"*. For most changes of scope, with the exception of wholesale reorganization, boundaries for systems can be redrawn fairly easily, thus changing their scope and, of course, the implied interdependencies, costs, development time, and so on.

Some Words of Warning

These models should never be used in isolation as they only give one view of the world. Examples, pictures, lists of business objectives and other types of models help to ensure that the full picture is covered. Remember also that other factors always contribute to the cost and development times of producing a system. For example:

- technology being used or considered
- skills of existing staff
- complexity
- accuracy of existing systems
- data dependencies
- availability of staff
- availability of training
- unforeseen interruptions (e.g. illness) etc.

The outline systems and their dependencies will give enough information upon which to base a reasonably accurate system development plan, but it is not normally practical to assume costs, time, skills and other development issues during a presentation, when the scope of systems is being changed to this extent. Function dependency diagramming is very useful, but it is not a panacea.

Beware also of system professionals who spend weeks and months 'perfecting' the models before they are shown to the users. Early, repeated and quick feedback of all such models is undoubtedly the fastest way of getting good models that can be used to advance system development.

Detailed Feedback

A detailed function dependency diagram is often useful with people aware of the interdependencies of business functions in their day-to-day jobs. It can serve as a kind of route map to talk through what needs to happen with detailed business experts, and can also be used to check the dependency model, using some of the following constructs.

Hidden Dependency

For two apparently independent functions A and B, you can check that they are **really** independent by asking the question:

"Would it make any difference whether we chose to do A then B, or B then A, or both at the same time?"

| Is It Really a Dependency? | If a dependency has been identified between two functions A and B, where B is dependent on A, test whether the dependency really exists by asking the question: |

"What would it mean if we did B before A?"

Common sense and judgement need to be exercised in the use of this question. For policy or legislative dependencies, it will improve your understanding of why they are important if they have been tested in this way; but applied to **every** dependency it quickly loses impact and your own credibility will probably fall.

Missing Dependencies

These are often the hardest to find, but it is surprising how quickly people will discover new dependencies when a business function is tested from two directions by asking:

"What needs to have been done before this function can be carried out?" and
"When this function has been carried out, what does that enable you to do next?"

Or, alternatively,
"What cannot be done until this function has been carried out?"

Choosing which business functions to test is an exercise of judgement and common sense, but there is more benefit to be gained from checking the key, and critical, functions that are the essence of a business than from checking functions that are supportive or less critical. Bite the bullet: check the ones you are **least** sure of or most concerned about. From experience, the main factors governing when to stop are time and budget!

Summary

Businesses everywhere spend much of their time reacting to external stimuli. Function dependency diagrams are an easy-to-understand way of modelling what happens on receipt of an event, what functions are triggered and what key results are eventually achieved. The diagrams can be used for rigorously defining sequence, interdependency and functions that can be carried out in parallel at a business, system or program/ procedure level. We have found that diagrams at the high level are very good for agreeing the scope and sequencing of new systems with management. At the detailed level we have found that they must be used on leaf (lowest level) functions to maintain accuracy and are a useful modelling technique for functions that are oriented towards key results following external stimulation.

Function dependency diagramming is another excellent technique to learn to help model the business requirement, communicate with users and build appropriate systems.

Chapter

8 RELATED AND FURTHER CONCEPTS

In this chapter we look at some further concepts that may be required from time to time and additional detail that may be needed. Some related concepts and how they should be handled are also considered. These are all applicable at the business level ⬭ and the system level ⬭.

The **common business function** is a further concept for functions that appear at more than one point in a hierarchy. **Function detail and frequencies** complete function definition; in particular, how often functions are carried out, their urgency and profiles of their use. **Roles and business units** are related concepts used when modelling what type of person or department or business unit carries out each function and how that might influence design. **Geography** is part of the essential analysis needed for any business that is distributed geographically. **Mechanisms** can be critical when a certain way of doing things is so fundamental to the business that it needs to be examined in special detail. **Entities, attributes and relationships** must obviously be considered when examining how details on an information model relate to functions; in particular, which functions **create, retrieve, update** or **delete** information (**CRUD**). And finally **volumetrics** cover how the combination of function frequency information and the structure of an entity model can help to predict volumetric information.

Each of these concepts may be an important consideration in different circumstances, especially prior to looking at system design from the aspects of reusability, performance, access rights, distributed processing and distributed data. We start off by examining common functions.

Common Business Function	Common functions occur because it is often necessary to carry out the same processing in order to achieve two or more different results. An example would be a function to substitute one crew member for another. This might be part of a function to 'assemble the crew for a scheduled flight' and also part of a function to 'handle unpredictable staff events, such as sickness or injury'.

If you have been doing some modelling whilst reading the earlier parts of this book, you may already have found that you want to use the same function in more than one place in a hierarchy; for example, 'allocate mechanic' in the garage example in Chapter 6. |
| **Common Business
Function Definition** | A business function that appears in more than one place in a hierarchy is known as a common business function.

We try to avoid common functions as much as possible during the early stages of a modelling exercise because this helps us to produce a more generic solution. In the latter stages, however, common functions are found quite frequently. A common function should be thought of as the same function appearing at more than one place in the hierarchy, rather than two functions with the same definition. |
| **What Difference
Do They Make?** | Identifying common functions is an important activity for two reasons. Firstly, it identifies where different parts of the business integrate and share common information and processing. The very act of discussing this commonality helps different parts of an organization to realize how similar they are (and may even help to rationalize the business itself). One way of saving costs in a business is to streamline how things are done, sharing processing wherever possible between departments. This becomes much easier to spot when we remove organizational constraints from our functional analysis. Furthermore, the presence of common functions encourages the development of generic and reusable systems, which can be used to satisfy more than one requirement.

The second reason for identifying common functions is purely an administrative one – there will be fewer definitions to maintain if the common functions have been identified because the information only needs to be held once. The resulting smaller model will also tend to be simpler and more generic. |
| **Representation** | A common business function is shown by the same symbol as a business function, but with a vertical bar at each end of the box. It is usual to cross-reference a common function back to the first place where it occurs (called the **master** function) using a label on the top-right of the box. |

Figure 8-1
Common
Business Function
Representation

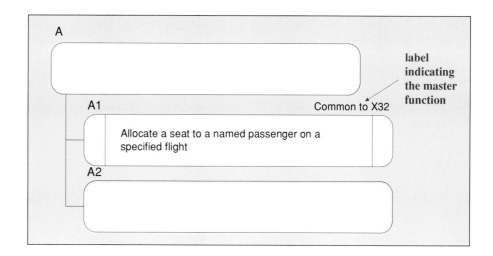

The two vertical bars may also be used at the system ⬭ and program/ procedure ⬛ level to denote commonality.

When function modelling 'manually' or using paper to record the function definition, take great care to control references to the master function; and if you change the definition of the master function, make sure to check that the change is relevant to **all** places where the function is referenced.

Analysis recorded on paper suffers from the distinct drawback that if a change is needed to a common function the change must be propagated through all places where that function occurs. Often, the description of the function is written out manually at each place where the function occurs, rather than simply referencing the master. (This means sorting through the functions to find it each time you need to read it.) A CASE tool can make life a lot easier by automatically carrying out all the cross-referencing and enabling a single change to be propagated to all the necessary places.

**Removing
Common Functions**

In the early stages of business function modelling it is sometimes possible to remove common functions by using the following process, illustrated in Figure 8-2:

- take the functions that are the same (shown by common-function boxes)
- trace the route back up from each one (shown by the heavy lines) to a point where they have the same parent function
- replace the common functions with a single function at the level immediately below the parent.

Figure 8-2
Removing Common Functions

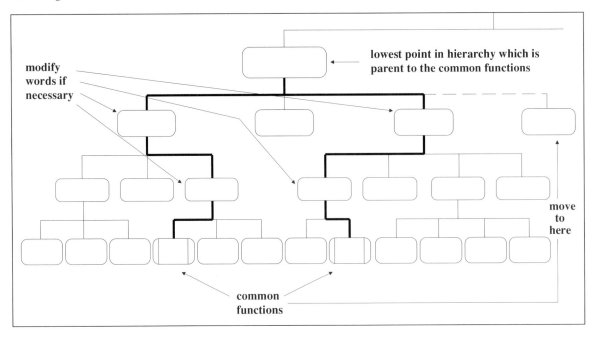

It may be necessary to modify the words in a number of the business functions between the common parent and the positions the common functions started from to change their scope, so that they no longer include the function that has been moved.

This process is a little bit like escalating a problem to the executive who is above **all** of the people in a dispute – and sorting the problem out at that level. Where this cannot be done (because the words cannot be changed without them becoming cumbersome or unreadable), test to see if the functions really are common (see next section). If they are, select one as the master and cross-reference it from all the others.

Are They Really Common?

There is nothing wrong with common functions, but a test is needed to determine whether two functions really are common.

Are they **identical**? Under all circumstances do the two functions:

- carry out the same functional processing?
- manipulate the same information: use the same entities, attributes and relationships in the same way?
- have exactly the same decomposition (structure) and detailed definition?

When you compare the detailed definitions of the functions you may find that although they are not identical they are so similar that it is sensible to make them identical and thereby common functions. At this time, all of the detail is put against the master function and held there once and only once for all the functions common to this master, and the common functions are cross-referenced to it.

Quite frequently, it turns out that something thought at first to be identical is different in one case or another. When this happens, the functions may be very similar, but they are **not** common. If there is any doubt whether two functions are common or not, it is safer to assume they are not. It is more difficult to change a system built to satisfy one common function when there are really two **different** functions than it is to build a system to satisfy two business functions that are the same. The worst that can happen in the latter case is that there is duplicated effort.

Generic Functions

In the computer industry we have been striving for years to produce generic computer software. A generic piece of software is one that can be used to satisfy more than a single requirement. With careful design two things that are similar can be satisfied completely by a single solution.

Take an example from the mechanical engineering world – a nut and bolt can be used to fix two pieces of a bridge together, secure an engine to the chassis of a car, or hold together the frame of a timber building. The nut and bolt is a generic design solution to the requirement of holding two things together (which happens to be a requirement in bridge building, car manufacture, the construction of buildings, and lots of other things). The more primitive or detailed the requirement, the more likely there is to be a generic solution to it, so there tend to be more common functions the lower you get in a hierarchy. Remember, common functions are really a single function that appears in two or more places in the hierarchy, rather than different functions that happen to have the same definition.

It is more likely for two functions that are really common functions to have **different** descriptions, so you fail to notice that they are common. This is often the case with functions that operate on two or more different items of information, so that functions can be written from the different viewpoints. For instance, in a university or college, the function:

Allocate a class to a specified room for a regular slot during a term

might appear under a function to produce a schedule for a class; whereas:

Allocate a room for use by a class at a regular time each week throughout a period

might appear under a function to manage the resources of the college.

Although the viewpoint and words differ, this may be the same function in practice: each manipulates the same information in the same way. In rationalizing the two functions to a common place in the hierarchy, it might be an opportune time to reword the function to reflect the symmetry between scheduling a class and managing resources and also to cater for a more general case of room allocation at the same time. For example:

Allocate a class to one or more rooms, or parts thereof, for regular use at a specified time interval and slot (e.g. weekly on Monday mornings) during a specified period (e.g. the summer term).

Elementary Function and Common Function

Very occasionally an elementary function is further decomposed though the components must not be elementary themselves (see Chapter 9, "Detailed Function Definition"). It is possible that a function appearing as part of this decomposition, where it is not elementary, may also appear elsewhere in the hierarchy as an elementary function (see Figure 8-3). This is because the term elementary applies to a position in a function hierarchy rather than a function, although it is often spoken about as though it is a property of the function.

Figure 8-3
Elementary Functions and Common Functions

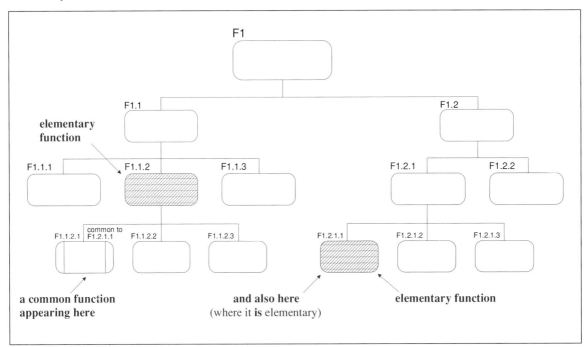

Whether for a normal business function or a common function we often need extra detail and, in particular, details about how functions are carried out. So let us move on to look at these aspects.

Function Detail and Frequencies

How do you make sure you record the **right** level of detail about a function? Analysis is an exercise to establish an understanding of a business and to provide a firm foundation on which to build systems to support that business. There are important details of a business function which cannot be shown using the techniques of function decomposition, function dependency modelling and function logic alone. But this detail is often expensive to collect, complicated to manage, and is certainly expensive to maintain when things change. On the other hand, the details of functions that are critical to the success of the business often need to be known before successful systems can be built.

So the ideal objective is to provide precisely the right amount of detail in **only** those cases where it is necessary. A dilemma arises because at the outset it is not possible to tell **which** cases are necessary! Sometimes you will not know until a system has been running for some time. What follows are some general guidelines we have found useful in practice. The challenge is to determine which are appropriate in a specific situation. Almost certainly they will not all apply, so make your choice wisely.

How frequently a function occurs is of interest, both as a cross-check during business analysis and also as information for a designer working on a system, as the system must have sufficient capacity to handle the volume required for the size of business. In the section on function frequencies, we look at the issues involved in measuring the required frequency and some sensible precautions to prevent this becoming a major drain on our business analysis resources.

Simple Function Frequencies

The frequency of a function is the number of times the function will be carried out in any one period of time. For example, if the function frequency were quoted as being one hundred times per day, this would mean that, in any one working day, the function would be carried out about one hundred times. The deviation from this frequency will usually either be small (perhaps varying between ninety and one hundred and ten times per day) or considered unimportant. In about eighty percent of cases a simple, absolute numeric value for a frequency is sufficient.

You need to choose an appropriate time period to record the frequency for each function. For instance, one function might need to be recorded as one hundred times per day (rather than three thousand times per month) while another might be carried out once per year (rather than 0.0028 times per day!). You can imagine the guidance that this offers a system designer: a function that is carried out once per year allows a different set of design options from one that has to be carried out five thousand times per day! A standard form for documenting function frequencies can be found in Appendix C.

Coupled with function frequency is another value, known as the **urgency** or the **response required** for the function. This is a measure of how tolerant the business can afford to be over the time that it actually takes to carry out the function. The urgency of the business function is the length of time that is acceptable, in business terms, for the business function to take. (This is **not** the same as the response time on a computer.) In most cases it is perfectly adequate to record the urgency of the function as 'immediate', 'overnight', 'the next day', 'the next accounting period', or some other such description of a time period. It might be part of the culture, or even a specific objective of a business, to specify an absolute time for the urgency; for example, a business may set out to 'provide customer with quotation for services to be provided' in not more than five minutes. Objectives like this are becoming quite common in service-oriented businesses, where one of the very tangible business objectives is to improve services from the customers' perspective. A prompt turn round of quotation, ordering, customer enquiries and so on forms a big part of how the customer sees the business.

Common Functions and Frequency Information

Where the function being discussed appears more than once in a hierarchy, the frequency and urgency information is usually recorded for the place where the function occurs. A function that appears in three places might have quite different frequencies at each; for instance, a frequency of ten per day in the first place, one per year in the second and one hundred per month in the third.

Once in a while a function that is **key** to the business appears during an analysis exercise with an unusual frequency and/or urgency. It is particularly useful in these cases to highlight that function and provide an accurate documentation of its requirements. For example, in a manufacturing organization operating a 'just in time' purchasing policy, functions to do with the supply of purchased parts and raw materials from the suppliers are critical, so the urgency for the delivery of an order might be defined as 'not greater than two hours'. (The philosophy of 'just in time' is that stock arrives just in time for you to work on it, reducing the cost of holding stock within the organization.)

More Detailed Definitions

The following function details are only rarely required; in other words, they account for the twenty percent or so of functions that cannot adequately be documented by a simple description of their urgency or frequency, as described above.

Details over Time

Some functions have a highly variable frequency, notably in seasonal businesses. For example, tour operators in Western Europe would have a business function to:

accept a booking for a holiday

but they recognize a custom of European holiday-makers to book their holidays early in February (after the excitement of Christmas and the New Year has worn off). This custom leads to a February panic in which most Europeans book their holidays in the same three-week period!

**Figure 8-4
Profiles of
Bookings
by Month**

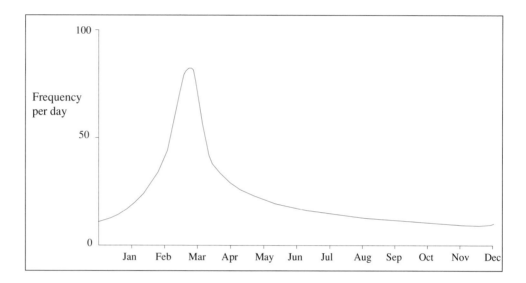

If you are trying to design a system for this business, you certainly need to know where the peaks and troughs are to do a good job, otherwise there will be some very frustrated holiday-makers!

Another aspect of frequency of functions over time is that of growth or decline. Businesses themselves may change rapidly, and as a result the frequency of carrying out an individual function may change. To be useful in supporting the business requirement, the system must be designed to cater for change, in particular for known or planned change. For instance, if a freight haulage company set itself an objective of increasing the amount of freight carried by air by twenty percent each year for the next three years, you would expect all business functions peculiar to haulage by air to rise by a corresponding or consequential amount. Conversely, if this were to be in place of freight currently carried by road, a decline in those functions peculiar to haulage by road would be expected. In these special cases, a graph or table of values is needed to document frequency information accurately (see Appendix C, Forms 12 and 13).

Functions by Role

Many of the further items of detail required for a function are to do with related concepts. We are now going on to look at the aspects of function detail to do with roles, business units and geography.

Not everyone in an organization will carry out every business function. Typically, people specialize through training, and so on, becoming proficient at carrying out a subset of the functions in the business. This subset is usually determined by job type or role. Occasionally it is peculiar to an individual such as an expert in a particular field or when a company only has a few employees.

In the general case, how often a function is carried out by individuals in a particular role or role type can be recorded. In a retail organization, for example, shop managers carry out the function 'plan the profile of goods to be offered for sale by a particular store', perhaps once a month. This is invaluable information to a designer so long as one or two other pieces of information are also known; in particular, the number of shop managers (current and planned for the future), so that a system designer can work out how often this function is to be carried out and design a mechanism that would best support the requirements of a shop manager. The matrix below shows that the majority of sales are made by sales assistants. This analysis begs the question of whether there is a difference when a shop manager or chief executive handles a sale. You may find that the chief executive negotiates large deals with special customers. This exceptional circumstance may mean that a different function has to be defined.

Figure 8-5
Function by Role

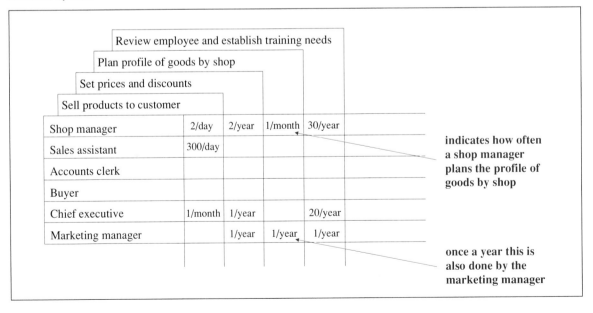

There may additionally be cases where legislative or other policy constraints insist that functions be carried out by a particular role or individual. For instance, government health inspectors could be the only people authorized to inspect a food retailer for conformance to hygiene regulations.

As you have seen, a matrix of functions against job type (or role) provides a good cross-check, and possibly a good planning tool in some cases. You can record if a given function is performed by people with a given job type (or role), the frequency with which that function is carried out and, possibly, the urgency required of that function in that role as well.

Functions by Business Unit

Whole collections of people are organized into units by most businesses. These business units, often called divisions, subsidiaries, departments, teams, and so on, are responsible for carrying out defined business functions, so recording frequency and urgency by business unit is another, possibly essential, means of cross-checking the results of an analysis exercise. The level of detail used to define the organization can be chosen appropriately, so that in one case individual departments may be listed and cross-referenced to business functions, while in another case it may be sufficient to record business functions by type of department (e.g. a sales department, a research department, a manufacturing department). The latter is useful in big multinational, multi-company organizations, where each company has a similar structure but perhaps operates in different countries to meet slightly different market needs. Matrices of function against both role and business unit will often help to determine the computer programs made available on menu systems at a later stage in development.

Figure 8-6
Function by Business Unit

	Sell products to customer	Set prices and discounts	Plan profile of goods by shop	Review employee and establish training needs
SALES	10000/month		100/year	
ACCOUNTS				
PERSONNEL				100/year
RESEARCH & DEVELOPMENT				
MARKETING		3/year	100/year	

Immediate business benefit can sometimes be gained by this simple additional modelling process of creating a matrix of function by business unit. The objective, remember, is to find out who does what and where.

When this exercise was carried out at a retail company the team noticed a number of things. Several departments apparently did not **do** anything! This meant that either there were missing functions (a good quality check) or that some rationalization could probably be carried out. They also found that the split of functions was not what they expected. There was far more duplication of effort than expected and the focus of some departments was wrong. Corrective action followed. Finally they were also able to use the distribution data they had collected to test various ideas about a possible new distributed processing system.

This particular company took an interesting additional step and checked all job definitions against the function list. Some jobs disappeared; others were redefined; and all were subsequently reissued to include the function definitions to which the jobs related. It is interesting to carry out this exercise with the computer department and their jobs. It is also revealing to repeat the exercise but replacing the business functions with business objectives on the matrix.

An interesting question to ask in any company is what does the computer department do and what does it contribute towards corporate goals?

Functions by Geographic Location

Finally, one further way of recording frequency and urgency information for business functions is by geographic location. All businesses are spread over some geographic area. Some are local in the sense that the area is very small: perhaps just a single town or a single retail outlet. But even these businesses usually have customers and suppliers spread over a wider area, and the nature of the geographic location of the parts of a business may also be important information to the system designer. In some cases, such as an airline, a geographic spread is fundamental to the very nature of the business and the area may be a continental unit or the whole world.

In a big multinational organization, a business function may be carried out a hundred times a year in Germany, a thousand times a year in the USA, twelve times a year in Singapore, and four hundred times a year in Australia. For a small organization, recording frequency information by city, country or state may be more appropriate. Occasionally, more detail still may be required (e.g. by site) where an organization is highly localized but, nevertheless, the split of functions by site is a characteristic of the business.

In summary, volumetric information can usually be recorded on the function itself, but in some circumstances key functions may need volumetric information in relation to:

- time
- role/job type/organization
- geographic location, or
- some combination of the above.

Figure 8-7
Volume and Urgency Measurement

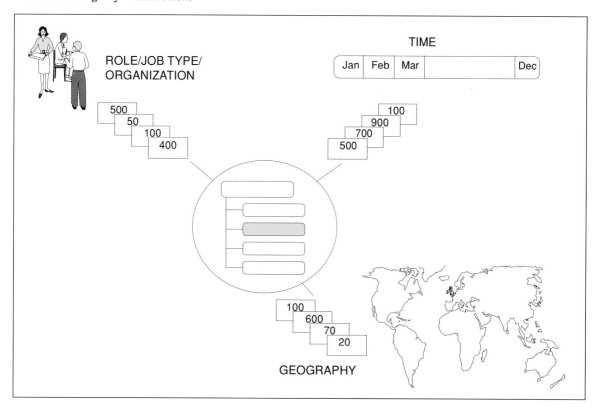

Mechanisms

When performing analysis and design for business systems, a balance must be struck between available technology, cost, and what is culturally acceptable to the business. Analyzing the technologies applicable to each function can give an important insight into what is acceptable. For example, in the retail food business a high-volume supplier, such as a hypermarket, would probably demand that customer transactions be carried out using point-of-sale computer technology like laser bar-code readers. In contrast, a low-volume, specialist supplier, such as a health food chain, would consider laser bar-code readers inappropriate and want a manual implementation (with the personal touch) such as the use of an older mechanical cash register. Indeed, an organization may have invested massively in technology and existing mechanisms in order to carry out its current business and this may constrain later development of systems. The cost of decommissioning the currently used technology may be so high that to use an alternative technology would be prohibitive. This happens with large engineering establishments where the cost of changing from, say, one energy source to another may be huge.

Given an indication of what technology (or choice of technologies) is acceptable or expected for each function, a designer is in a much stronger position to make decisions about the nature of a system to support the business.

All of the frequency and urgency information discussed above can be recorded quickly and accurately using a matrix, with business function on one of the axes. (There may be cases where you need to design your own specialized type of matrix which we have not discussed here.) One final use that appears from time to time is to record the responsibility and authority for business functions by role on a matrix (i.e. who is able, or expected, to do each business function). Authority, in particular, is something that appears in many government, defence, financial and other 'secure' businesses.

How Functions Use Entities, Attributes and Relationships

Up to now we have been concentrating on business functions in their own right, but the other most used way of modelling a business prior to designing a system is based on the information needs. This is typically modelled using an entity relationship model, a related concept that must therefore be examined in some detail.

We spoke briefly in Chapter 3 of how business functions manipulate information documented as an entity relationship model. The information a given function uses acts as a strong cross-checking mechanism, both for completeness and consistency of functions and information in the entity relationship model. An additional level of detail, however, may be needed to document which particular information is manipulated and in what manner each time a function is carried out.

It may be that the function exists to create an instance of an entity. In the example shown in Figure 8-8, if a tour operator carries out the function 'accept booking for a holiday' we would probably expect this to create one instance of the entity BOOKING. But what would be the effect of accepting a booking for a whole family or a bulk booking for a school skiing group or a photography club? How many instances of the entity would be created from a single occurrence of this function?

Figure 8-8
Holiday Booking

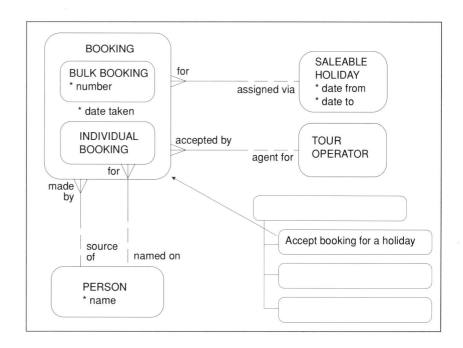

The situation can vary dramatically when the profile of the bookings of a large tour operator is considered. Possibly ninety percent of all bookings are INDIVIDUAL BOOKINGs, that is, for specific named people. Others might be BULK BOOKINGs where there is a specific number of expected people, but none explicitly known yet. The function will create a single instance of the entity BULK BOOKING, but this time the attribute 'number' becomes significant as this will supply the value for the number of instances of certain related entities, such as the number of seats to be allocated on an aircraft for the journey.

Bookings for families may reveal interesting variations in how functions use information. If each member of a family results in a separate instance of an INDIVIDUAL BOOKING the number of instances of the entity created by the function could be anywhere from two to ten or more, reflecting regional, cultural and sociological factors. These factors would be relevant to many organizations; for example, the food retail sector where there may be marked differences in the profile of products sold in different outlets and at different times of the year (although the creation of instances of the PRODUCT named 'burger and french fries' seems to transcend most boundaries).

Cancellation of a holiday booking would result in deletion of instances of an entity, while changes to the people travelling with a group would require retrieval and updating of the attributes of an instance of an entity. As the date for the holiday approaches the tour operator will insist on knowing the names of the holiday-makers and a BULK BOOKING may be replaced by the relevant number of INDIVIDUAL BOOKINGs. This involves modification and possible deletion of the instance of BULK BOOKING and the creation of instances of INDIVIDUAL BOOKINGs.

To be complete, the following details can be defined for the usage of an entity by a function:

- method of use – create, update, delete or retrieve instances
- number of instances affected – the number of instances affected each time the function is carried out (average and peak)

and, if the function does not always affect the entity (i.e. sometimes the function creates instances of the entity and sometimes it does not):

- percentage of times affected
- conditions that affect the entity.

Figure 8-9
Function Detail for 'Allocate Stock for Delivery to Branch'

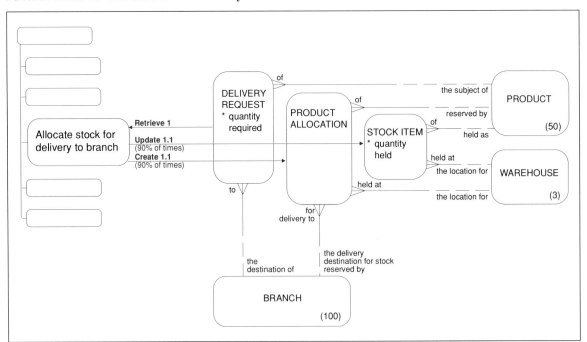

For example, in Figure 8-9 above, the function detail for 'allocate stock for delivery to branch' shows that the function retrieves a delivery request, and ninety percent of the times the function is carried out it updates the stock items and creates an allocation of the product for delivery to the required branch. The condition for doing this is that the quantity required on the delivery request is less than, or equal to, the quantity held of the stock item of the requested product. (Detailed function definition for this kind of description is covered in Chapter 9.)

An analysis of function to entity will normally be adequate for most purposes. However, in large, complex, performance-critical situations, it can be useful to analyze business function to attribute and relationship selectively. For attribute the fine detail would be:

- set value
- reset value
- nullify

and for relationship:

- connect or make the relationship
- disconnect or unmake the relationship
- the transfer or simultaneous disconnection and reconnection of a relationship.

In all of the cases above, take to heart the warning about cost. Limit yourself to those cases which reward you for the time you put into them. These will, typically, be functions that are critical to the business. Exceptions often seem to catch us out; systems that do not cater for peak volumes and so on. Where critical functions are not adequately dealt with, the cost to the business will be high; but do not get caught in the trap of religiously filling in every square of every matrix – this is a guarantee that you will never finish the project!

Finding Volumetric Information

The urgency of a function is largely executive whim; that is, a subjective judgement of what is acceptable. We are almost always limited to interviewing as a means of determining this. Function frequency information, on the other hand, can be found by interview or by deriving it from other frequency information.

Let us examine the overview of the business model shown in Figure 8-10. All the concepts may have volumetric information recorded against them:

Event	–	how often this event occurs
Function	–	how often this function is carried out
Entity	–	how many instances of this entity there are and the growth rate
Relationship	–	how many instances of one entity are associated with an instance of the entity at the other end of the relationship.

**Figure 8-10
Overview of
Business Model**

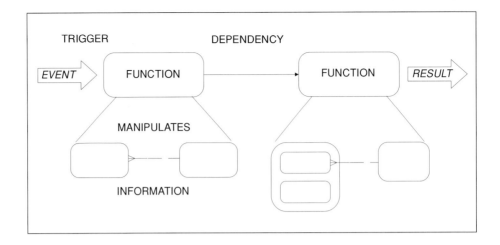

Actually calculating the frequency of a function can be an involved and complex process. The calculation has to take into account the frequencies of all the events that trigger it and the frequencies of all the functions upon which it is dependent. The frequency of a function is ultimately limited by the least frequent event or least frequent function upon which it is dependent, and this figure can be used as a rule-of-thumb value for the maximum frequency for this function.

When a function is triggered by the completion of one or more alternative functions or events, the frequency of that function is the sum of their frequencies.

The entity volume should be the number of instances that exist initially, plus the number of instances created by functions that create it, less the number of instances deleted by functions that delete it. Factors such as growth (or decline) over time, and volumes and frequencies recorded by role, business unit, location, and so on, serve to make the picture a very complicated one. However, in general, we will be dealing with aggregate figures that are approximations; a high level of accuracy is **not** required in most cases so acceptable approximations can be made.

As a cross-check, volumetric analysis can show some interesting results (and identify possible problems in advance). For example, the event 'request for booking' occurs say one hundred times per day at Atlantis Island Flights. Sometimes the request is made on behalf of a single passenger, sometimes more, and on average there are 1.2 passengers per event. Eighty percent of these events trigger the function 'book seat on flight for passenger' successfully, so it would be reasonable to expect:

- a growth pattern in the booking entity volume of 100 x 1.2 x 80 (i.e. 96 per day) and no functions to delete the entity, or

- functions that delete 96 bookings per day on average for bookings made over say 3 years ago and thus no growth rate in the entity volume, or

- some other growth rate and functions to delete some selected instances of the entity BOOKING.

Figure 8-11
Checking Function Frequency with Data Volumes

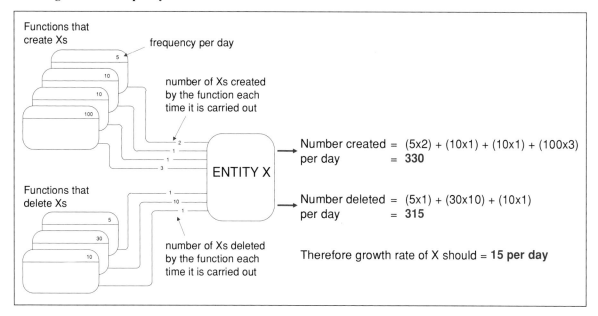

Theoretically, the actual volume of entity instances, their growth or decline, and other volumetric data should match up with the volume predicted by the frequencies of functions that create, delete and otherwise modify data. In reality they rarely do first time because:

- many figures may have been guessed, because there was no (economic) way of getting the required numbers

- the event frequency has not allowed for a seasonal pattern

- there are missing functions that create or delete entity instances

- exceptional cases may be so abnormal that they skew the figures and may invalidate a subsequent design

- archiving and/or destruction of data have not been considered.

Warning! Calculation of frequencies and volumes as described above can be complex and time consuming. It needs to be done for critical functions; that is, the most frequent, most urgent, most important and most complex.

In most cases all we need to do is get the values to balance approximately but be reasonably accurate for these functions, which tend to be used in system sizing or performance predictions – in other words, the functions needed for design.

Use of CASE Tools

Several times in this chapter we have discussed analyzing functions against some other factor, such as business unit. A good CASE tool should have a sophisticated matrix diagrammer that can help you here to capture, analyze and manipulate the information. It needs to be able to handle the scale of your business, perhaps manipulating thousands of entries on each of two axes. Useful features of such a tool include:

- selection of information to be displayed; for example, urgency

- sorting of the axes, to focus attention on the more critical; for example, functions (sorted by frequency) versus entities (sorted by volume)

- filters, to subset the functions to only those in which you are currently interested

- clustering algorithms, to give insight into various natural or useful groupings of information.

Useful matrices include function to:

- business objective
- business unit or business unit type
- role or person
- time
- entity
- attribute of entity
- job definition location or site
- event
- program or module.

An integrated CASE tool will often have populated this sort of matrix as a side effect of some other action. For example, creating a dataflow diagram and identifying the attributes and data items on the flows should implicitly populate a matrix of function to attribute, relationship **and** function to entity.

Computerized matrices can also be of inestimable value when trying to determine the impact of change by analyzing, for example, what programs might be affected if these functions were changed. Working at this level of detail on a large problem does not make any economic sense these days, unless it is supported by a 'no-limit' CASE tool with sophisticated matrices and reporting capabilities.

Figure 8-12
Summary of Function Details

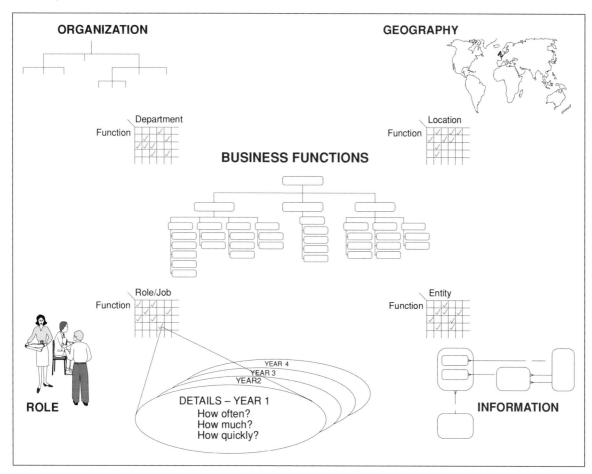

System Design

Later on in the system development life-cycle it may be useful or necessary to estimate the size and performance of a new system. During this process, which can be as simple as a good designer getting a feel for it or as complex as running a full system simulation exercise, the detail that has been recorded will be very useful. In particular, systems designers are interested in the:

- m most frequent
- n most urgent
- o most complex

- p most geographically dispersed and
- q otherwise subjectively or randomly selected processes

where m, n, o, p and q are numbers that are chosen to give a sufficiently representative set of processes to ensure a good design.

Special consideration may be necessary for other functions, such as those that have a peak load. A retail credit company, for example, has around forty percent of its transactions on the five or six Saturdays before Christmas, **and** between ten in the morning and two in the afternoon.

Summary

We have looked at common functions – when the same function appears in more than one place in a function hierarchy – and how they can be removed by escalating to a common parent, or recorded and cross-referenced by choosing one as a master. We have also examined how the frequency and urgency of a function can be recorded against each of organization, role, geography and time period to guide a system designer towards sensible options for supporting the business in question.

We have also looked at the interaction between business functions and the information model, paying particular notice to whether a function creates, retrieves, updates or deletes information. And we have seen that a CASE tool is becoming more and more essential to handle the vast scale of important cross-related information.

9 DETAILED FUNCTION DEFINITION

Introduction

When using these techniques to define the business requirement for a new system, the goal is to produce definitions of elementary functions and function logic which may then be used to define some new system. An elementary function ensures that the information it manipulates remains consistent and coherent, and that other functions going on at the same time do not have access to inconsistent interim results. It is as though the function 'publishes' the results of its processing all in one go, as the last thing it does. Function logic is a technique for specifying, in full detail, the precise nature of the processing being carried out by a function. It is applicable to the business ⬭ and system ⬭ level. As it can be quite complex to use effectively, function logic is typically limited to a few really key functions rather than applied generally. These two topics are dealt with together because elementary functions are normally prime candidates for the application of function logic.

Elementary Business Function

Elementary business functions are those business functions which must be completed successfully or, where this is not possible, actions carried out to the point of failure must be wholly undone. An elementary function, therefore, always terminates successfully, leaving the business with additional information **or** has no observable effect at all on the information known to the business. For those of you familiar with database technology, it is analogous to a commit unit or success unit, but at the business level.

A good illustration of why the concept of an elementary function is important to a business is shown by the function 'transfer funds from one bank account to another'. The function has two parts to it: taking the money from one account (a debit) and putting it into another (a credit). If the debit succeeds but, for some reason, the credit fails, then the bank's business is in an inconsistent state: it has lost some money – not in the sense of profit and loss, but in the sense of mislaid. Very specifically, this only matters to someone, or some other business function, trying to establish the status of one or both accounts. If the result of the debit is in some way made available to any other business function **before** the credit has succeeded, then an anomaly arises. Because of this, the transfer should be marked as an elementary function. So, an elementary function is one that ensures that **all** changes to information representing the state of the business are correct and coherent before **any** of them are made available to another function.

There are really two aspects to an elementary business function. Firstly, there is the issue of when information becomes available to other business functions. In our example, the debit occurs first, but must not be apparent to any other function until the credit has also been made.* In general, any changes to the information known by the business must remain wholly local to a function declared as elementary until completion, at which time **all** the changes made become available instantaneously.

The second aspect is that of failure of the function. Failure occurs if completion of the function would violate some business rule, policy or constraint. For example, a bank may have a business rule or constraint that 'transfers into closed accounts are not allowed'. Imagine you pay a monthly allowance to a daughter by transfer from your bank account to hers. When she starts a university course she closes her old account and opens a special student account but neglects to tell you and your bank, having assumed **her** bank will somehow make all the necessary changes. The function 'transfer funds from one bank account to another' may succeed in the debit, but the function as a whole will fail and, by our definition, the debit must be undone as though it had never happened. (And you get a telephone call from a penniless student!)

You might like to think of an elementary function** as one that behaves as though a copy were taken of all the information to be changed, leaving

<hr />

*   There is, of course, no reason why the credit shouldn't be done first, but our nature doesn't seem to allow us to think of it the other way round!

** The term elementary should strictly be applied to an event, the sequence of dependent functions it triggers and the outcome of this sequence. However, for simplicity, functions are frequently modelled so that dependent sequences all have the same parent in the hierarchy (or the sequence is so simple that it can be defined as a single function) so it is common practice to refer to an elementary function.

the original for other functions to access. Changes are then made to the copy, and the copy is used to replace the original if the function is successful, or discarded if it is unsuccessful. Obviously, if it is critical that the original information is not used whilst the elementary function is being attempted some form of business locking mechanism must be used.

Elementary Functions and Business Systems

So what effect do elementary functions have on the development of systems to support a business? The most important thing is for a system to keep any interim results that a function might produce during its processing and then 'publish' those results in a single action. There are numerous ways in which systems do this; one common way is to use a special status to represent interim results. Typically, this is an item of information that indicates that something is part-way through and therefore cannot be used for a short period of time – that is, an elementary function has not yet been successfully completed.

Take the example of the head of a school amending the timetable because a classroom has been taken out of use. The head takes a copy of the timetable and works on this copy, switching rooms, classes and teachers to accommodate the loss of the room; leaving the original on the noticeboard for everyone to use, with a note on the bottom stating that it is being amended. The copy has a 'provisional' or 'work in progress' status and, until it is completed, it must not be used by anyone who wants to know where he or she should be. If one teacher looks at the copy and sees that she is due to teach in Room 3 tomorrow afternoon, but then the head juggles the schedule to put a different class in this room and this is seen by another teacher, the result will be pandemonium.

In computer systems the status approach is often used to achieve much the same result, by marking records in a file or rows in a database table as temporary or provisional and making sure that other programs avoid these records when processing. This is typically achieved by the use of database locks of, say, rows of data, in combination with a recovery file that can roll back incomplete work. Of course, the most common way that computer systems tackle the issue of elementary functions is for a program to read data from a file or database into local memory, process the data in memory (where it is not accessible to other programs) and then put the results back on the file when they are complete. Anyone used to a wordprocessor or desktop publishing package will recognize this as loading up a file, editing it and then saving it again. It is important to be able to 'undo' changes, if for some reason something fails. For example, if you discover you have made a mistake amending a file (such as accidentally deleting a section of text), the amended file can be abandoned and the original reloaded. In the case of the school timetable, if the new schedule is not working out, the head can throw away the amended copy, take a fresh copy of the original, and start again.

Atomic Function

The term **leaf** functions is applied to functions that are found at the bottom of a hierarchy (by analogy with trees). Functions may appear to be at the bottom of the hierarchy because the analysis is still incomplete and further decomposition can occur. Where analysis is complete, these leaf functions are called **atomic** functions (considered to be indivisible at this level of working).

Figure 9-1
Different Categories of Functions

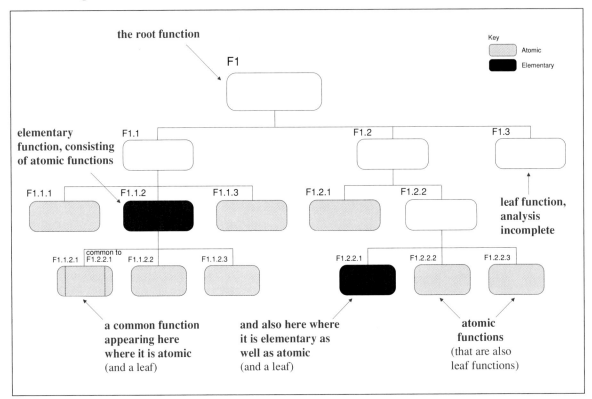

The whole purpose of creating a function hierarchy is to identify all the elementary functions the business actually carries out. The hierarchy can be considered as a means to an end, a good way of grouping elementary functions, an excellent cross-check for completeness and consistency; but when actually considering the development of a new system it is the elementary functions that are implemented. It is, however, useful to maintain the function hierarchy to assist in change management and to provide guidance in the natural grouping of functions in system design; for example, computer menu systems.

When you have completed your analysis, the functions at the bottom of the hierarchy should be atomic and/or elementary. If we were to look at a candidate elementary function we would probably find that it manipulates a small, well-defined portion of the information model. It is now the job of the elementary function definition (function logic) to define precisely how the information in that portion of the model is to be used or transformed by a business function.

Function Logic

Function logic is a detailed specification of the processing carried out by a business function. It exists to define precisely and unambiguously what the function does, especially in those cases where the function is complex or involves arbitrary business algorithms. It is time consuming to define a function in terms of function logic and also to verify and maintain that definition. As a result, we try to limit the number of functions which are subjected to this level of specification.

Selective Definition

Choosing with care those functions that require the full specification of logic is a valuable precaution. To be a candidate, a business function must be atomic, will probably be elementary, and will typically be complex or critical.

Transforming Information

When a function manipulates the information known by the business a variety of things can happen:

- information can be retrieved
- instances of entities can be created
- values of attributes can be modified
- relationships between instances of entities can be forged, transferred, or removed
- instances of entities can be deleted
- other functions can be triggered
- some physical or mechanical action can be carried out.

The action of a function changes the information known to the business at that time. This transformation will be done according to some business algorithm or rule governing its precise nature.

Let us focus first on one specific example from one company we worked with where it was critical to use the correct fee rates for consultants when they were allocated to different jobs.

The function 'quote a consultant's fee rate for a contract' involved a business algorithm specifying that the following should be done to derive the rate:

> *take by preference the fee rate used for that consultant on a previous contract with the client or shown in a master agreement*

or

> *use the standard fee rate quoted for the consultant when carrying out that type of job, working with that job title or at that grade*

or

> *use the personal fee rate for this consultant; or use some default value applicable to any consultant.*

The starting rate derived from this algorithm in this order of preference may then, of course, be changed by negotiation.

Figure 9-2
Navigating the
Information Model

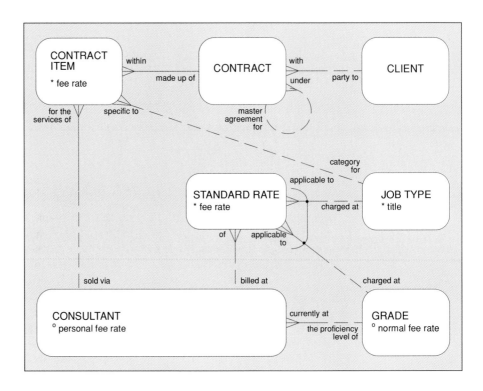

As you can see, what we are doing here is creating a specification of how information from the entity relationship model is to be gathered. Function logic identifies a number of attributes and entities in the information model which should be visited when looking for a specific piece of information. In this example we have additionally expressed a precedence (i.e. that one item of information should be used in preference to another if possible). Navigating around the model is one aspect of function logic.

When specifying function logic, we try to avoid giving any indication of the **sequence** in which the entities and attributes need to be visited. Often two sequences can yield the same result, but one may be much faster or more efficient than another. This speed and efficiency is dependent on the implementation mechanism and should, therefore, be considered during a physical design activity: it should not be done as part of the analysis of a function. Rather than saying 'if there is a rate A then use it, otherwise go to the rate B and use that instead, otherwise go to the rate C and use that instead', it is better to say 'use A, B or C in order of preference'.

Another aspect of function logic is the derivation of new values. For example, 'determine regular customer payment to cover estimated quarterly usage' might be something that a company supplying electricity would do if it offered customers the chance to pay a regular monthly sum as an alternative to quarterly or annual bills. Given that electricity consumption follows a pattern that repeats itself annually, the function logic might include an algorithm that will:

take the sum of the previous year's actual payments,
and
multiply it by a factor based on an estimated growth in electricity consumption for a category of customer and by the estimated annual rate for inflation,
and
divide the result by twelve to yield a monthly payment.

This kind of algorithm is sometimes a complex mathematical or computational exercise, generally expressed using an appropriate mathematical formula. Beware of building such formulae into function logic if they are subject to frequent change. It is often better to have a named formula that can be replaced when necessary to reflect different circumstances, rules, policies or legislation. For complex systems like multinational payroll systems, the formulae and their conditions for use may be modelled as entities, and then stored as data that can be invoked from a database.

A third aspect is the scope (the set of instances of entities, attributes and relationships from the information model) which will be affected by a particular function. The function:

substitute an alternative runway for nominated flights (e.g. in response to a normal service runway becoming unavailable)

may include a statement in its function logic to determine precisely which flights are to be rerouted; perhaps those which are scheduled for take-off on a nominated runway for a nominated period of time. A particular execution of that business function might substitute Runway 5 for all flights scheduled to take off or land on Runway 3 for the next twenty-four hours. A different execution of the same function under different circumstances might substitute Runway 1 for all flights on Runway 2 for only twelve hours.

Typically, the scope affected by a business function is determined by loose and relatively ambiguous phrases in our descriptive wording of the function. Until now, this has not been a problem; in fact, this slight ambiguity has helped to improve the quality and completeness of the model when using the various completeness checking techniques, such as *"what else might this function apply to?"*. At an early stage, minor ambiguities flush out those exceptions and problems that could cause serious trouble at a later date if undiscovered. Small ambiguities, however, can lead to embarrassingly large differences in results and may have dangerous consequences. For instance, in the airline example the term 'scheduled to take off or land' was used to 'scope' those flights to be changed. But what precisely constitutes a flight that is scheduled to take off or land? Are there **unscheduled** flights, such as emergency, ad hoc or training flights, which might take off or land on the runway in question? Are there other uses of the runway apart from take-off and landing? Do these things matter or not to the business? Function logic specifies unambiguously how information is to be used – we do not want aircraft using a runway at the same time as someone is painting a white line down the middle of it!

Function logic is a means of specifying usage of information, business algorithms and the scope that changes should apply to.

When to Do It

The precise proportion of functions which requires function logic will vary from one exercise to another. Where a highly trained team of experienced designers with good knowledge of the business are to design a system, few functions will require such detail. If the system designers are less experienced or working in a team that might suffer regular changes of staff, more functions may need this detailed treatment. Another factor that has to be considered is the importance of a business function. For relatively unimportant cases the accuracy of natural language will suffice, but in many cases the precise detail of the function is key to the success of the business. For example, rescheduling the wrong aircraft would be a very costly error in an airport. As a guide, somewhere between five and twenty-five percent of business functions that require further system support are typically subject to this treatment in commercial data processing systems developments.

Many languages and other techniques for specifying function logic have appeared over the last decade, with varying degrees of success, ease of use and relevance. They differ tremendously. The formal mathematical languages, such as VDM[4] and Z[5], are at one extreme. Functions specified using these languages can be mathematically proven consistent and correct; whether they do what the business wants is still a matter for good analysis. And there is no way that they can be used as a communication vehicle with users. The more subjective, individual, natural languages (English, German, Japanese, and so on) lie at the other extreme. With these natural languages there are often many ways to say the same thing but, unfortunately, more than one interpretation of the same sentence, hence an inevitable ambiguity. As a consequence, most practitioners have chosen a middle course, which does not require the full rigour, training and intellectual finesse of the formal languages, but nevertheless affords some degree of definitive specification. Many such languages resemble computer programming languages; the diagram below illustrates how practitioners of information engineering would show how to 'create a delivery schedule to satisfy customer orders'. You can see here the aspects of navigation, business algorithms and the scope of the effect. This example is used again later in the chapter, where it is defined more fully (see Figure 9-13).

Figure 9-3
Information Engineering Diagram

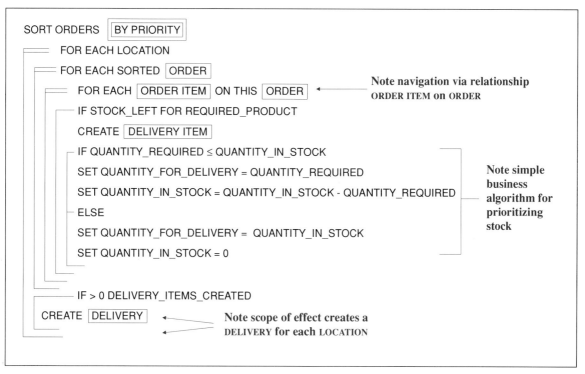

In this chapter, we introduce an informal technique that has been used successfully to model many business functions. It is not, however, mathematically rigorous, and this means that some function definitions will need to be supplemented with annotations in a natural language (e.g. Spanish) or a more formal or mathematical notation (e.g. a definition for a set of linear equations) as appropriate. The careful use of terms appearing on an entity model can improve the rigour with which a function is defined.

Much research is still being carried out in an effort to find a way of expressing complex detail unambiguously, in a way that is easily read by business people without the need for formal training. The use of these pseudo-languages can be simplified and minimized if we take full advantage of logic for navigation, validation, derivation and other rules that are implied in a well-constructed entity relationship diagram.

Focusing Your Effort

Our function logic language is based on structured English and tries to retain a grammatical structure that is close to other western national languages, such as French. It encompasses many of the business terms that have been found during an analysis exercise, thus keeping the communication lines open. When a very complex business function has to be defined, it becomes even more important to feed that understanding back to business people for verification, so aim to reduce your definition to its simplest possible form. Do not be tempted to use the opportunity to show off this marvellous new sophisticated definitive language: instead, aim to use it as little as possible; and, where it is used, respect the fact that anyone being asked to verify it is also being asked to learn a new language before verification can be done.

Imagine discussing putting an ornamental pond in your garden with a gardener who asked you to verify the plans for this, but produced details with the cost of the scheme in barter terms (9 sheep and 5 pigs), time for building and stocking the pond in nanoseconds (1.2096×10^{15}ns), the building materials measured in cubic light years (2.36×10^{-49} light years), and the plant stock in terms of *Myriophyllum spicatum, Ranunculus aquatilis*, or even mollybobs, maids a milking, and so on! How would you feel? In a few circumstances, the business itself will be a highly technical or mathematical one, such as a statistical forecasting business, in which case a more formal mathematical language may be appropriate. **But in general, remember the expression 'KISS': keep it simple, clear and in terms your users can understand and react to.** (If not, the second S will apply!)

The next example illustrates the aspects of navigation and scope of effect.

Let us look at the function logic for the function to create details about a new scheduled regular flight of an airline route, and how it could be defined in a very simple way by implying data-dependent functionality. The entity relationship model for booking seats and flights is shown in Figure 9-4 below. Using this model directly gives the business function:

> *On demand, create an instance of a FLIGHT on a specified **date of departure** of an AIRLINE ROUTE identified by a supplied **flight number** from an AIRPORT with a supplied **name** to an AIRPORT with a supplied **name**, operated by an AIRLINE identified by a **code**, where the **name** of the AIRPORT that is the source of the AIRLINE ROUTE is not equal to the **name** of the AIRPORT that is the destination of the AIRLINE ROUTE.*

You will notice that this logic is a little formal and includes a business constraint – that the airline route must be from one airport to a different one.

Figure 9-4
Entity Relationship Model for Bookings and Flights

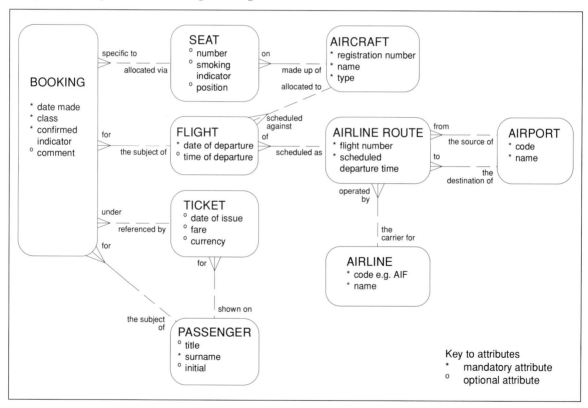

Now let us examine how this same logic can be simplified by using a predefined business view on the basis that users often talk about the concept of regular flights.* (A business view is a frequently used subset of information derived from an entity model.[6]) Using the REGULAR FLIGHT business view (see Figure 9-5), this definition is simplified to:

On demand, create an instance of a REGULAR FLIGHT using supplied date scheduled, flight number, departure time, airline, destination and origin, where the destination is not equal to the origin.

The business view REGULAR FLIGHT is a named concept, based on the subject entity FLIGHT. It consists of a usual working set of attributes from the entities FLIGHT, AIRLINE ROUTE, AIRLINE and AIRPORT (via both relationships). These attributes have been renamed to their normal business terms as follows:

date scheduled	from	date of departure of FLIGHT
flight number	from	flight number of AIRLINE ROUTE
departure time	from	scheduled departure time of AIRLINE ROUTE
airline	from	code of AIRLINE
destination	from	name of AIRPORT via the relationship 'the destination of'
origin	from	name of AIRPORT via the relationship 'the source of'

Figure 9-5
The Business View
REGULAR FLIGHT

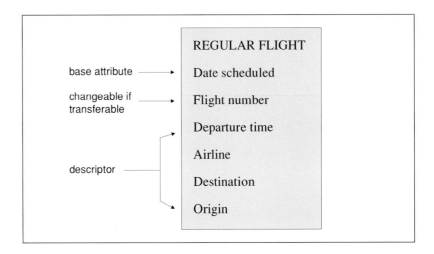

* Business views are also very useful concepts to use in dataflows and datastores (see Chapter 11).

The simplified business definition is much easier for a user to understand, and the relationship links used in the original definition are completely implied when using the business view. However, we can go even further. The business view (and for that matter any entity definition) also implies the normal integrity constraints for attribute optionality and values. For example, if an attribute is mandatory and a date, it is implicit that a value must be supplied and this value must be a valid date.

In this particular example as all the attributes of REGULAR FLIGHT are mandatory we can simplify the business definition even further to:

> *On demand, create an instance of a REGULAR FLIGHT where the* **destination** *is not equal to the* **origin**.

With a sophisticated entity model and/or business view the additional implied logic can be further extended. So far we have used implied navigation around the model, optionality, format and the implication that any value quoted must be valid (e.g. a known airline). We can easily add further data concepts such as values or ranges, integrity constraints and so on. A particularly useful addition is the concept of the derived attribute. When derived attributes, such as **number of bookings for flight** or **profit on ticket**, have been defined, the derivation clause can be defined once for the attribute and then inherited by all the functions that use it; thus simplifying the function logic definition by another large factor.

When defining functions it is useful to think in terms of business views. Simple functions tend to operate on a single business view, often on an entity between two or more other entities (an intersection entity); for example, BOOKING on a ticket for a flight. Other functions tend to operate on perhaps two or more business views, which then need to be correlated by reference to identical, derived attributes in their business views.

All the attributes in the business view may be used in the business function for **conditions**, **where clauses** or to otherwise **identify** the target instances. In general, only the attributes of the subject or base entity of the business view can be the subject of modification actions. The only exception is when a modification attempts to change the attribute values that unambiguously correspond to a unique identifier of an entity that is directly related to the subject entity. This would represent an attempt to change the relationship. For example, on the business view for BOOKING (Figure 9-6), changing the flight number (an attribute of AIRLINE ROUTE) and date of departure (an attribute of FLIGHT) would be an attempt to change the BOOKING to enable you to catch a different FLIGHT on a different day.

You can see again that a simple logic statement such as *"On demand, create an instance of a booking"* on the business view BOOKING can imply all of the data and integrity rules required for this function – that is, valid passenger details, valid flight details, request for seat number, smoking preference, and so on.

Figure 9-6
The Business View
BOOKING

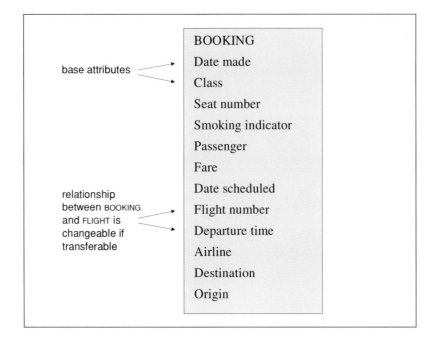

We shall come back to detailed function logic later in this chapter, but let us first look at data dependence and annotation of these useful entity models and business views.

Data Dependence

At the end of a strategy study or during any subsequent stage of development it is useful to know what other data and related business functions must be implemented in a system to enable you to implement some really key item of data. In our airline business, let us assume that the original paper system for knowing when flights were scheduled can no longer cope with the increase in air traffic, so we need to computerize it very quickly. From the entity relationship model we know we cannot implement booking details without first implementing details about flights. We will add details later for tracking the tickets and coupons.

Data Dependence Rules

From the model in Figure 9-4 we can see that to implement details of FLIGHT we must also supply appropriate details of AIRLINE ROUTE. This data dependence is easily identified if you look at the relationship definitions and obey the 'must be' rules (that is, there is a solid relationship line going away from the entity FLIGHT); in this case, a FLIGHT **must be** of an AIRLINE ROUTE.

We also add in any entity that is unambiguously related to the subject entity by a many (or one) to one relationship; for example, a FLIGHT may be allocated to an AIRCRAFT. Both mandatory and optional relationships are considered.

Details of entities further removed, as identified by the above two rules, must also be supplied, which adds AIRLINE and AIRPORT to the list of dependent data. You will notice that AIRPORT is required twice, once in the role of destination and once in the role of source. Thus to implement details of a FLIGHT you must have already implemented AIRLINE ROUTE, AIRPORT (source and destination) and AIRLINE, and you may also need details of AIRCRAFT.

More Complex
Data Dependence

In this more complex example about orders we have introduced the concepts of entity sub-types (shown by boxes within boxes) and exclusive relationships (arcs) and applied the **must be** rule to a one-to-many relationship as well.

Figure 9-7
A Model of an Order
and its Order Lines

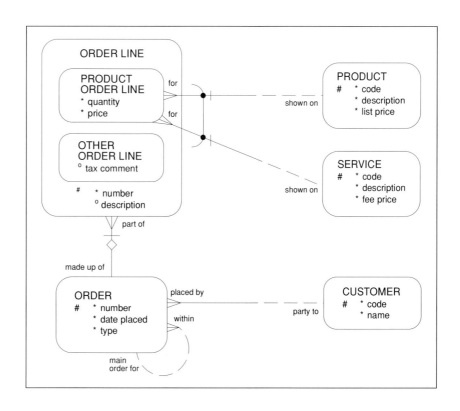

The business view of ORDER consists of all the details of:

ORDER	the subject entity
CUSTOMER	
ORDER(s)	recursively, because of the optional, many-to-one **within** relationship
ORDER LINE(s)	because each ORDER **must be made of** one or more order lines

For each ORDER LINE, the business view extends to include both its sub-types, PRODUCT ORDER LINE and OTHER ORDER LINE. And because PRODUCT ORDER LINE has relationships, we also pick up either PRODUCT or SERVICE for any instance of a PRODUCT ORDER LINE. This gives us the business view of ORDER shown opposite, which can be used to imply logic for each and every function that uses it.

You will see that a business view is a useful way of looking at a complex object, such as an order, and that the function logic can assume a vast amount of implied data-related logic.

Deriving Information

One other complexity in function logic can be moved into the central definition of the business view – that of derived information. In the ORDER business view, you will notice that it defines derived values for ORDER total, ORDER LINE value and CUSTOMER number of orders.

Development Phases

You can then look at all the business functions that act upon these selected entities, or their business views, and select those that collectively make up sensible phases for development to meet the business needs, objectives and priorities.

This data dependence is reaffirmed by consideration of the important business views that need to be implemented.

Benefits of Business Views

Business views provide an elegant and powerful concept for communication with users in their terms, simplifying business function definitions and providing an insight into data dependence. The insight gained can then help with selection of implementation phasing, evaluation of alternative implementation techniques such as packages and with the identification of the likely data that must pass between two or more systems which must coexist.

Figure 9-8
The Business View of ORDER

		Implied Logic
ORDER (the subject entity)	number date placed type total value	Unique ascending number. Default value 'today'. Allowed values 'C', 'R' and 'M'. Derived value is 'sum of value of PRODUCT ORDER LINE'.
└CUSTOMER	code name number of orders	Must already exist. Derived value is 'count of ORDERs the customer is party to'.
└ORDER	number date placed type total value	Recursively finds all parent orders. Normally the immediate parent and the top of the hierarchy are of most use. Default value 'today'. Allowed values 'C', 'R' and 'M'. Derived value is 'sum of value of PRODUCT ORDER LINE'.
──ORDER LINE	number description	Unique, ascending within ORDER.
── either OTHER ORDER LINE	tax comment	
└ or PRODUCT ORDER LINE	quantity price value	Default value is 1. Default value is 'list price of PRODUCT' or 'fee price of SERVICE'. Derived value is 'price × quantity'.
── either PRODUCT	code description list price	
└ or SERVICE	code description fee price	

An excellent way of describing the detail of a function without resorting to full logic is by annotating small sections of the entity model. Navigation and scope, and often derivation, can be shown somewhat informally, by highlighting an entity model. For example, the function:

> *On demand, create an instance of a FLIGHT on a specified **date of departure** of an AIRLINE ROUTE identified by a supplied **flight number** from an AIRPORT with a supplied **name** to an AIRPORT with a supplied **name**, operated by an AIRLINE identified by a **code**, where the **name** of the AIRPORT that is the source of the AIRLINE ROUTE is not equal to the **name** of the AIRPORT that is the destination of the AIRLINE ROUTE*

uses the following subset of the entity diagram.

**Figure 9-9
The Subset Model**

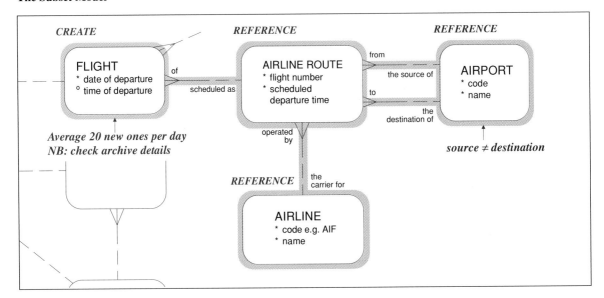

The informal annotation shows:

- which entities are used (use a highlighter pen on paper copies or get a CASE tool to change the box colours)
- how they are used
- a specification of scope
- how the results of the function are to be derived
- additional useful information.

In many circumstances, this is a perfectly adequate description of what the function does and no more is **necessary** to aid understanding.

Exploiting a Powerful Information Model

The richer and more powerful the information model, the simpler that function logic against it becomes. Another simple example illustrates this.

A Simple Example

We are dealing with an entity called EMPLOYEE ASSESSMENT and an attribute called 'date made' (which is the date that the assessment is arrived at). If we want to define the logic for the function 'assess employee for promotion or other change in position', we must explicitly define a value for the date made (see Figure 9-10).

Figure 9-10
Employee Assessment

Figure 9-11
Simple Employee Assessment

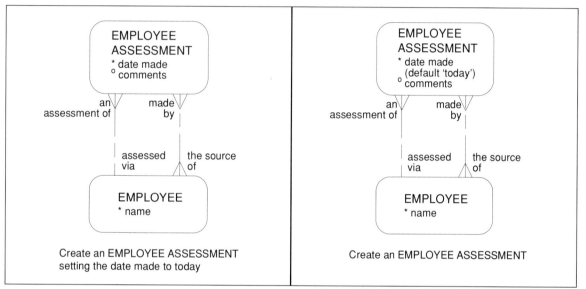

Create an EMPLOYEE ASSESSMENT setting the date made to today

Create an EMPLOYEE ASSESSMENT

If our information model includes a default value for date made (for example, the default might be 'date of creation') then the function logic is immediately made simpler (see Figure 9-11). This becomes especially useful when more than one function manipulates an attribute, because the definition is only needed once (as a default on the information model), instead of being repeated on each function that manipulates it. (You will perhaps have noticed the business view ORDER also had default values for ORDER DATE and PRODUCT ORDER LINE price.)

In particular, the development of accurate function logic is greatly assisted by information modelling techniques that recognize constructs such as:

• Constraints – a definition of what constitutes optional or mandatory constructs, valid or invalid values for entities, attributes and relationships, uniqueness, and so on.

- Defaults – what values are to be adopted if none are otherwise made available.

- Business views – multiple overlapping views of the same information, including derived entities, attributes and relationships, and the subset of information to be used.

From the entity diagram we can also see that any function that creates an EMPLOYEE ASSESSMENT must also acquire details of the EMPLOYEE that is being assessed and of at least one (other?) EMPLOYEE, the source of the EMPLOYEE ASSESSMENT. Notice that as it stands the entity model permits self-assessments – which may be useful in certain circumstances.

Detailed Function Logic

We will now look in some detail at a technique for specifying navigation, business algorithms and scope. This technique can be used to define many business functions unambiguously (although it is not exhaustive). We will start by looking at a statement that retrieves some specified information covering the aspect of navigation around an entity relationship model. Then we will examine a statement used to modify the information, introducing business algorithms and scope.

Figure 9-12 opposite is an extension to the entity relationship model for Atlantic Island Flights used earlier in the chapter, and contains sub-types and some extra entities. The following example of a detailed function logic statement was derived from this model:

Each SCHEDULED FLIGHT, which is of the AIRLINE ROUTE identified, which is for the FLIGHT, which is scheduled against the AIRCRAFT, which is of the AIRCRAFT TYPE, which is manufactured by the ORGANIZATION UNIT, which is the manufacturer of one or more AIRCRAFT TYPEs, each of which is the classification for one or more AIRCRAFT, each of which is allocated to one or more FLIGHTs, each of which is specified on one or more BOOKINGs.

Let us examine how we build it up.

In this technique, navigation is carried out in a series of steps, each step traversing a single relationship. In essence, the steps are linked with the words 'which is', followed by the relationship name and the name of the entity at the other end of the relationship. Navigation along the relationship marked **1** on the diagram:

Each SCHEDULED FLIGHT must be of one and only one AIRLINE ROUTE

is achieved by the clause:

which is of the AIRLINE ROUTE identified.

Where only one case is possible (the relationship has a degree of one), the entity name is prefixed with 'the'. For example, starting at the BOOKING entity and navigating along the relationships marked **2** on the diagram:

> . . . *which is for the FLIGHT, which is scheduled against the AIRCRAFT, which is of the AIRCRAFT TYPE, which is manufactured by the ORGANIZATION UNIT . . .*

Where more than one case is possible (the relationship has a degree of many), the linking words are changed to 'each of which is' and the plural entity name is prefixed with 'one or more'. For example, starting at ORGANIZATION UNIT and navigating in the opposite direction along the relationships marked **2** on the diagram:

> . . . *which is the manufacturer of one or more AIRCRAFT TYPEs, each of which is the classification for one or more AIRCRAFT, each of which is allocated to one or more FLIGHTs, each of which is specified on one or more BOOKINGs . . .*

Figure 9-12
More of the Information Model for Atlantis Island Flights

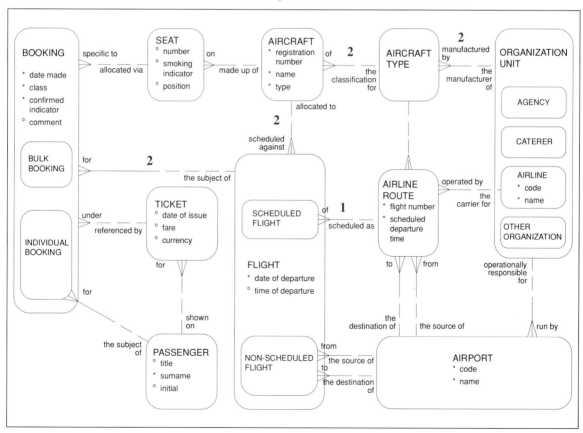

You should be able to define a very precise collection of entities, attributes and relationships now, using as many steps as are needed to navigate around the model. Although the language is written in a sequence, this function logic should not be interpreted as a directive to visit entities in this sequence. The actual sequence chosen should be something decided during a physical design activity, once the implementation technology (the **how**) has been decided.

In this form, the navigation facility restricts the entities to which the rest of the function logic applies. It might be that the route through the model needs to be further refined and qualified. This applies especially when traversing a one-to-many relationship where only some of the instances of the entities at the many end are applicable. For example, we may be interested in flights of a certain type of aircraft which are scheduled to depart over the next two weeks. Perhaps a design fault has been found on that type of aircraft, but only for vehicles over five years old, and we need to assess the impact on our scheduling:

> *Retrieve FLIGHTs which have a departure date within 2 weeks and which are scheduled against an AIRCRAFT which is of a specific AIRCRAFT TYPE and which has a date of commission more than 5 years ago.*

The words 'which is' and 'which are' step down a relationship, and the words 'which has' and 'which have' qualify the instances of the entity at the other end of that relationship by supplying values for the attributes of the entity. You may be tempted to modify this language to make it more rigorous. In the example above the values of the attributes are easily understood, but not expressed with mathematical precision. The value for the attribute 'departure date' is given as 'within 2 weeks'. More exactly, this would be a range of values rather than an absolute value, the set of dates where the value of the date is greater than or equal to the current date and less than or equal to the current date plus two weeks. Obviously, the only simple way to be precise is to use mathematical notation:

$$\{ \text{ current date} \geq \text{departure date} \geq (\text{current date} + 2 \text{ weeks}) \}$$

but bear in mind the reader and the aim of easy, clear communication. This mathematical precision is more appropriate to the specification of business algorithms (or coding programs).

When specifying function logic in this way, it is very rare to find cases in which an absolute number is required. More likely, the actual number will only be known when the function is to be carried out, so these values would be substituted with the word 'supplied'; for example:

> *. . . which have a departure date within the period supplied.*

The Retrieval Statement

The purpose of a retrieval statement is to identify instances of entities for which the values of various attributes are of interest. We could apply the following retrieval statement to the function 'identify alternative flights' from our example in Chapter 2:

Retrieve the date of departure and date of arrival from each SCHEDULED FLIGHT which has a date of departure between the supplied date less 2 days and the supplied date plus 1 day and which is of the AIRLINE ROUTE which has a flight number equal to the flight number supplied.

The structure of this statement is as follows:

Retrieve <list of attributes> from each <entity> which has <qualifying statement>.

The <list of attributes> is a set of named attributes separated by commas or the word 'and'. The <qualifying statement> is a complex 'tour' through the entity model using relationships for navigation and qualifying applicable instances of the entities with clauses that constrain the values of their attributes.

Don't forget that this tour around the entities and the qualifying statement may be simplified in nearly all cases by using a business view instead of a set of entities as the subject of the logic statement.

Business Algorithms

To calculate the value of an expression that is to be used (usually to set the value of an attribute) standard mathematical terminology is used, with the names of attributes and entities as the variables. For example:

Calculate the expected time of arrival as the time of departure plus the flight duration
and
Calculate total flying hours to date as the sum of actual arrival time minus actual departure time, where actual departure time and actual arrival time are obtained from each FLIGHT, which is scheduled against an AIRCRAFT, which is of an AIRCRAFT TYPE identified by the name supplied.

Of course many flights involve crossing time zones or the international date line, and some countries have their own 'summer time'. Full rigorous algorithms would need to include precise logic to cater for these to give the arrival time that would be shown on a clock at the destination.

Notice that almost all function logic statements so far have been operated in the context of a single instance of an entity, which we 'identified' by supplying a value for its unique identifier. This is not necessarily the case, although it frequently is, which introduces the final topic of **scope**.

Scope

Each time a function is carried out it will affect certain instances of one or more entities: by changing the values of their attributes, transferring or creating their relationships, or by creating or deleting instances of the entities themselves:

> *Update INDIVIDUAL BOOKINGs setting the value for the confirmed indicator to 'confirmed' where it is under the TICKET identified by the date of issue and surname of PASSENGER as supplied.*

The scope is determined by a condition, which follows the word 'where'. Only those instances of an entity for which the condition holds true will be affected by the 'setting' clause. The where <condition> can also be used as part of a 'delete' statement to delete instances of entities if information is no longer known to the business.

The verbs we have used thus far are Retrieve, Calculate, Update, Delete and Create, but feel free to use the word Archive for information that has to be kept in a form that is possibly less easily accessible; for example: *Archive FLIGHTs which have a date of departure older than one year.*

Complex Algorithms

The language described so far will cater for many situations in defining business functions, but there are complex cases that cannot be handled by these relatively simple constructs. Consider the following function from a manufacturing company: 'create a delivery schedule to satisfy customer orders'. Some detailed logic to express the elementary function might look like this.

> *Arrange ORDER ITEMs on ORDERs in priority sequence (priority to be determined by customer trading status, amount of money owed to us by the customer, amount of money owed to the customer by us, age of the order and subjective decision) and, working down the list, create a DELIVERY ITEM to satisfy each ORDER ITEM, setting quantity for delivery equal to the greater of quantity required of the order item or remaining stock (when quantity in stock is less than quantity required) until quantity in stock is zero or all the ORDER ITEMs have been satisfied. Also create a planned DELIVERY which is part of the current SCHEDULE and is to this LOCATION and is made up of all DELIVERY ITEMs which are to satisfy ORDER ITEMs which are for delivery to the current LOCATION.*

Notice the importance of defining this as an elementary business function. The effect of doing this means that any other business functions going on at the same time do not interfere with one another (i.e. if this business function fails for some reason, then the deliveries must not become available for other functions to act upon). One other interesting point is the effect of this operation on the attribute 'remaining stock' of entity PRODUCT. This attribute is theoretically always derivable: that is, it can

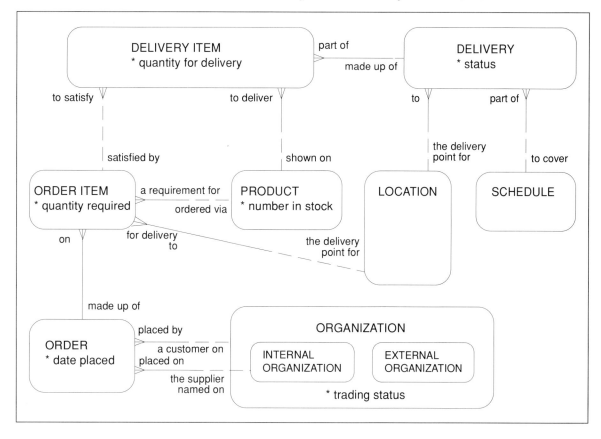

always be worked out from the amount of the product made, minus the amount already allocated to planned deliveries. This means that in our simple example the 'remaining stock' is never updated directly, it only changes implicitly because some component of its derivation has changed – in this case, the planned deliveries. (In reality this is nearly always much more complex. For example, in one company where grain was stored in silos and transferred via overhead pipes from one silo to another, the remaining stock could have gained or lost weight due to wind, moisture, theft, rats, etc.)

Note to Systems Designers

The reason for documenting functions in this form is to **understand** what is going on. It may be (in fact, it is likely) that there are many different ways of designing a system to achieve what is being documented in this function logic. Unfortunately, this logic can look similar to some programming language code – it should **not**, however, be interpreted as a good way of programming a computer application. In the previous example, a direct translation of the function logic into, say, COBOL, with embedded SQL to update data on a relational database, is likely to yield inefficient code because it does not use the set processing capability inherent to a SQL database management system. A better way **might** be to create a delivery with the relevant delivery items for **all** orders and then delete the one that cannot be satisfied from stock! Do not fall into the trap of simply converting a piece of function logic into a piece of procedural code with the same structure. Rather, use the function logic to understand what outcome is required and then **design** for the technology being deployed in the target system.

It is interesting to compare the function logic above with the equivalent information engineering diagram in Figure 9-3. One of the dangers of using the information engineering diagram for defining the logic of the function is that this procedural notation may be inappropriately implemented when using certain mechanisms.

Summary

We have covered the topics of elementary functions and function logic. An elementary function is a function that 'publishes' the results of its actions in one go, or leaves the state of the information known to the business as it was before it started. Function logic is a way of defining precisely the information to be collected from the information model (by navigating around it), the processing to be carried out on that information, and the scope of any modifications to be made. A number of languages, with varying levels of rigour, are available for defining function logic. We introduced our own user-oriented language, an informal syntax for fairly precise definitions, plus some tips for highlighting and annotating subsets of the information model.

Remember, if the systems department is to be an integral part of your business and thus contribute towards its profitability, the exercise of defining functions and building systems **must** be done in a pragmatic and cost-effective way. Too often we have seen **purists** take elapsed years to define the detail requirement unambiguously prior to starting system design, frequently without user involvement. Meanwhile the business requirement may itself have changed! (Don't be like the person who buys an old house and wants it completely restored and perfect before inviting friends to dinner. By the time perfection is achieved your friends may have given up on you, moved house themselves, or even left the country.) In general it is far better to get the balance right and define requirements in sufficient detail to enable the designers and implementors to make a good job of it. Mistakes **will** occur later, but prototyping and iteration based on a good starting point are cost-effective and timely ways of achieving the desired result.

10

LOGICAL SYSTEM DESIGN

Introduction

This chapter discusses the art of designing a system, or suite of systems, that will support the functional needs of a business that has been modelled. These systems would normally be implemented using a combination of computer, mechanical, electronic or manual means. We will concentrate mostly on the design of computer and manual systems.

A number of new concepts such as **process** and **system** are introduced to enable us to record the structure of a system as we design it. These concepts are cross-referenced back to the business functions, which will have been documented using the techniques described in Chapters 1-8 as a record of the decisions made during the design activity and to help subsequent change management.

The most important new concept is the **process**. This is very similar to a business function, except that it models something to be done by a system, rather than something to be done by a business. Processes re-introduce mechanisms (**how** things will be done) by introducing the type of technology (e.g. bar-code reader) that will be used to implement them. The first part of this chapter looks at how we decide what processes there will be in a system. The second half revisits the techniques of decomposition, dependency diagramming and elementary function definition, looking at how they can be applied to processes. The chapter finishes by looking at ways of presenting a design in the form of a system architecture diagram, which summarizes the structure of a system graphically and acts as a framework for subsequent work.

System Design

The job of a business system designer is to design systems that support a defined subset of the known business functions in an effective and usable way within given constraints. In practice, this means we must design a system that is acceptable to users and satisfies the usual constraints of time, cost and available technologies, and other resource constraints. The system must also ultimately perform effectively, be usable, maintainable, reliable and otherwise of a high quality. Some elements of this job call for intuition and creativity, whilst other aspects respond well to the systematic application of techniques such as those presented in this book. Earlier in the book we discussed how dependency diagrams, showing dependencies between business functions, can be used as a tool for scoping systems; that is, deciding **which** subset of a business function model is going to be supported by a system.

Let us look first at definition of the things we will need to deal with when designing systems, then proceed to explore the techniques available to us which can assist in designing a system.

System Definition

A system is a named, defined and interacting collection of real-world facts, procedures and processes, along with the organized deployment of people, machines, various mechanisms and other resources that carry out those procedures and processes.

A system should be designed to provide value to the running of a business. For the most part, the systems in existence in the business world at the moment have grown and evolved as the business and technology have changed over the years. Historically, the vast majority of systems have been built without the benefit of good analysis. Many of those that have followed some formal method have lost sight of their goal and taken too long to implement. The result is often a system that meets some formal methods standard but fails to meet the business need. The optimal solution is a balance between structured methods and business judgement.

A system is, in fact, an **arbitrary** collection of mechanisms, in much the same way that a function in a hierarchy is an arbitrary collection of lower-level functions, and many alternative groupings of mechanisms could, and should, be considered as a system is being designed. **Whether a system is successful or not is nearly always a matter of whether the arbitrary choices are made in a balanced way by skilled practitioners, taking into account both business and technical factors.**

When systems are designed using a top-down method, the approach is, typically, to decide what scope a system should cover in terms of the business functions it will support and then design the components of the system, their components, and so on, until such time as a component can either be satisfied by some existing mechanism or it has been designed in sufficient detail for it to be built. The term **sub-system** is often used for these major components of a system.

A system can be quite large, supporting hundreds, or even thousands, of business functions. Part of the system design activity identifies fundamental building blocks within a system which are smaller and more manageable and which represent sensible units that can be constructed, managed, controlled and, perhaps more importantly, discussed separately. These components are called **processes**. A process may ultimately be implemented as a computer screen or report, a manual procedure or something to be carried out by a machine (a mechanized process). Processes may also be **collections** of screens, reports, procedures, and so on.

Process Definition

A process is a definition of how one or more business functions are to be carried out by a system.

It is a course of action, typically to operate on data within a system; something done by a system in order to satisfy:

- the needs of one or more business functions, or
- the administrative, control or management needs of the system itself.

A process is very similar in concept to a business function – it is something that needs to be done. The difference between a process and a business function is that a process does not model something a **business** does or needs to do; instead it models something a **system** needs to do. Examples of processes might be:

Print invoices for selected customers – a computerized process

Decide which customer will get the remaining stock – a manual process

Take a back-up copy – a computerized and/or manual process required to maintain the system.

Process Representation

A process is represented as a rectangle with clipped corners, often subdivided to give sections for a label and a short name as well as the full name. By convention this second form is used on dataflow diagrams.

Figure 10-1
A Process

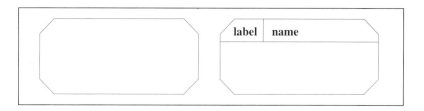

Processes fulfil two purposes. First, and more important, some processes will be necessary to carry out our defined business functions and, secondly, some processes will be necessary to keep a system running smoothly.

A system, then, is a collection of processes, some of which are mechanisms for implementing business functions and others which are mechanisms for implementing the storage of data (such as databases, computer files, manual or paper files).

Business Support Functions

The most important point about any system is that it should do the right thing! So the key thing to identify is which subset of business functions it is to support.

When defining a system we once more use a hierarchy, this time of processes. However, the way we organize a system hierarchy tends to be quite different from the way a function hierarchy is organized – they are, after all, serving different purposes:

- The function hierarchy arranges definition of what the business does or needs to do in a manner that is independent of possible corporate organization structures or implementation techniques.

- A process (system) hierarchy defines the way in which a system will be developed, given knowledge of corporate organization structure, available technology, and so on. If the process hierarchy is done again in a few years time it will inevitably be different as it will be a new best system design for the then relevant organization structure and technologies. In many senses it is this system design that can add real value to a company and differentiate it from its competitors.

The diagram opposite illustrates the mapping between selected business functions in their hierarchy and some newly designed system hierarchy. The system hierarchy has a new top node – this is in effect the scope of the newly defined system. This will be given a generally acceptable name, such as 'Store System' or 'Booking System'. Lower processes in this hierarchy will support one or more elementary business functions or part of one, or simply be required to make the system complete. Some system designers prefer to define this hierarchy in a top-down approach. Others prefer to define processes that can implement the functions, and then group them up into a hierarchy. A combination of both approaches is useful to ensure that the final system definition is complete and coherent; this is analogous to the top-down plus bottom-up technique used when constructing a function hierarchy.

Figure 10-2
The System Hierarchy

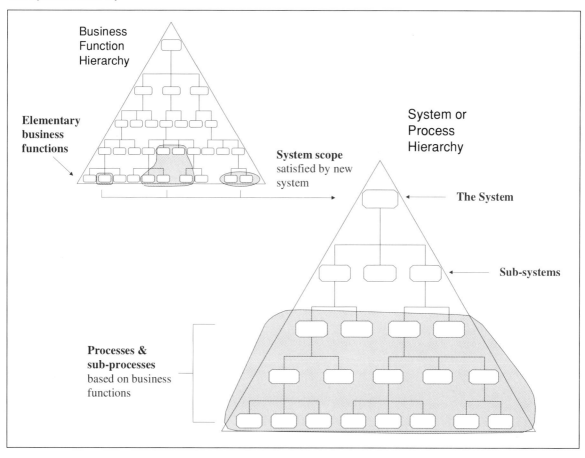

Business Function Hierarchy

Elementary business functions

System or Process Hierarchy

System scope
satisfied by new system

The System

Sub-systems

Processes & sub-processes
based on business functions

Scoping a System

How do you control the size or scale of a system? Without some coherent criteria for deciding whether or not a system should include the capability to carry out a particular function, the decision becomes very similar to a child choosing confectionery:

> *"I'll have one of these, one of those and one of these . . . no, no, put this one back and let me have one of those instead . . . no, one of those and . . . oh, just give me one of each!"*

Of course, in the world of developing business systems, there are some constraints on what we do; cost and time are the two most frequently encountered. So, step one is to establish the parameters that will govern the development of a system. These can be classified in the same way as some of our business analysis parameters such as objectives, priorities and constraints, but applied to the system as opposed to the business.

Objectives	*The system must be operational twenty-four hours per day, every day of the year.*

The system must reduce the number of debts older than ninety days by half.

The first objective is an example of one that addresses the availability of a system; it is not related to the business in any way, other than by assuming that the system will have a beneficial effect on the business and that it is mission critical and will be required all the time. The second is a short-term business objective that has been adopted to give direct focus to the development of a system. Objectives for a system are rarely quite so obvious; more often they are derived from a number of places, such as the business objectives, tempered with the expectation of senior managers and their technical advisers. Ideally, like the business objectives, they are:

- measurable
- achievable
- understood by all.

Constraints

Nothing seems to be free in this world. The cost of providing a system usually constrains what goes into it. In a way this is a blessing in disguise, since it ensures that when we choose our 'confectionery' we are not tempted to choose without thought. We would like to aim for a situation where we can say no to including an extra business function in a system because it would cost too much. To an extent this is rather difficult and even undesirable: difficult, because the complex interacting effects of including a function in a system are difficult to quantify and hard to work out (with all the necessary information requirements, dependent functions and their information requirements, etc.); and undesirable, because a function that costs a lot but provides an even higher value may be worth having, despite exceeding a specified constraint.

Priorities

One way of focusing on the apparent dilemma here is to place a priority on each function. Selecting functions for inclusion in a system in order of priority is an assurance that at least some tangible means of drawing boundaries is available in the process of scoping a system. What we are looking for is a way of understanding the issues involved when a new piece of functionality is added to the scope of a system, so that a decision whether or not to add it can be taken with slightly less emotion.

Presentation

Before we look at the issues involved with adding functionality, let us look briefly at how a system can be presented in terms of what it will do before it has even been designed! This is mostly a question of expectation setting. Whether or not you are **perceived** to be doing a good job is often as important as whether or not you **have actually done** a good job.

Figure 10-3
The Balance of Scope Against Constraints

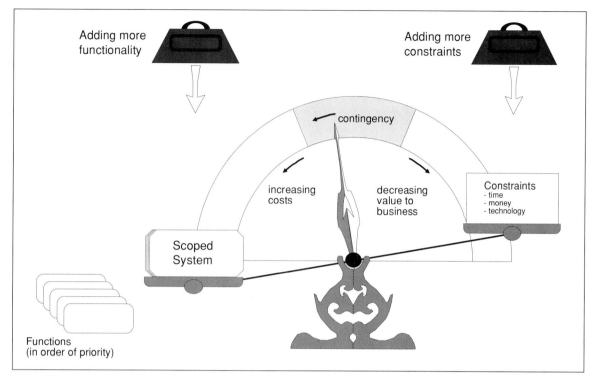

Consider the following:

Which should you do? Trade things in or trade things out?

Scenario 1 – you have completed analysis and during your presentation about the system you are going to commit to twenty major facilities to be delivered within twelve months. Later on, problems arise and you have to do some trade-offs. You actually deliver eighteen facilities two months late. Result – unhappy users.

Scenario 2 – from the same analysis you commit to a system with fifteen major facilities, satisfying priority requirements in a sixteen-month timescale. You actually have a similar plan to Scenario 1. As the project progresses, if things go well you trade in additional facilities. You then notice that the urgency for the system has gone up and therefore deliver the system two months early, with just three extra facilities. Result – happy users, even though what you delivered in the timescale was identical!

A way of presenting the scope of a system to get agreement, and also to measure the completeness of the system when it is actually delivered, is therefore to use a carefully defined scope plus a trade-in list. The scope can be presented as a list of business functions (at a suitable level of detail) that the system must support. This should be viewed, and presented, as the 'minimum that is absolutely necessary' to be acceptable; in other words, less than this will be insufficient to achieve the objectives of the system. A trade-in list is then a list of functions that could be included, if there is time, without compromising either the delivery timescale or the quality of the system. The project manager running a project to deliver a system might present a slightly different view to the team developing the system than to senior user management. Notice that the same functions appear on the senior management's trade-in list and the development team's trade-out list in the diagram below.

Figure 10-4
A Project
Manager's View

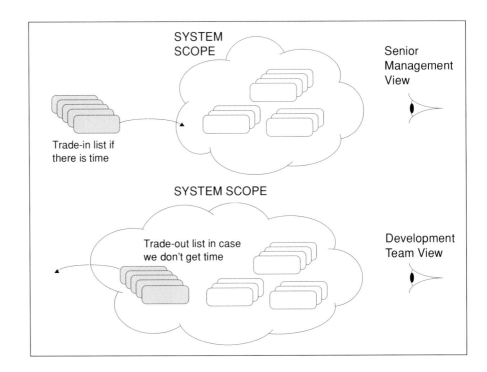

Increasing the Scope of a System

Unfortunately, it is rare to be able to make a system do just **one** more thing without compromising time, quality, or ease of maintainance. A number of interrelated factors are involved in adding a function to a system. Each function manipulates information, expressed as entities, attributes and relationships in an information model; so to include a function we must include the information it manipulates. Each entity in the information model may be related to a number of other entities, without which it makes no sense. For instance, an entity called STOCK HOLDING, which tells us how much of a particular product we are holding in a particular warehouse, is not much use without the entities PRODUCT and WAREHOUSE.

Figure 10-5
Increasing the
Scope of a System

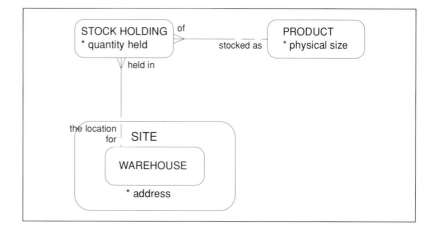

Let us say that the function we are considering updates the stock holding (perhaps it is the function to allocate stock for delivery to a customer) and requires the PRODUCT information to know the physical size of the product, so that it can calculate the loading on a delivery van and the address of the WAREHOUSE in order to produce a sensible collection and delivery route. The function **retrieves** information about PRODUCT and WAREHOUSE and **updates** STOCK HOLDING information. If there are no other functions in the system which **create** instances of the PRODUCT and WAREHOUSE entities (and update them when information about them changes) then our system will not be able to support this function, unless we include the necessary functions to do the maintenance of PRODUCT and WAREHOUSE as well. Of course, if those functions additionally use other information, then the knock-on effect must also be included for them.

Each business function should be weighted by its value in business terms; this must be a balanced judgement, usually carried out with the guidance of business people who know the business well. We can then start to play with a huge spreadsheet of interrelated functions and information, and mould a sensible scope for a system. This balanced view will consider the constraints imposed and be driven by the inclusion of those functions that yield the most business value first, and also the functions needed for maintaining all the information required by these. This is normally done on an iterative basis over a shortish period of time, as it is vital to let the decision makers 'sleep' on ideas and change their minds if necessary.

Strategy Study Scoping

During a strategy study the level of detail known about many functions is scant, so the accuracy with which the exercise can be done is low. The main purpose of carrying out the activity as part of a strategy study is to provide a scope of functions that **need** further analysis and to give reasonably good ball-park estimates of what can be done for how much.

Function dependencies can be very useful in scoping systems, even when modelled at a high level and therefore with a good deal of imprecision. From a strategy study, a small number of **really** important events (say between three and twenty) and their key results will have been identified. The functions that help achieve these key results are candidates for supporting with a well-designed system. At this stage, accurate dependency models are seldom available and the functions are chosen by 'reading between the lines'; the choice is based solely on the strategist's knowledge of the business and of what sort of things can be done. The prime reason for selecting certain functions is to scope subsequent detailed design exercises, thus compartmentalizing costs and focusing on the things that give a high return to the business.

The strategy study of a freight haulage company identified a key result:

competitive, timely, but profitable quotation provided

for the event:

customer request for quotation for haulage services.

The functions necessary to achieve this result included:

Determine options for pick-up, delivery and intermediate transportation.

Cost potential options; for example, add the costs of transport by road, ferry, air and other shipment modes, and the costs of loading, unloading and transferring the freight.

Assess costs, delivery times, margins and other factors for sensible alternative options available.

Produce quotation from chosen option, including standard and special mark-up and other charges.

These functions used information about routes, equipment available and pricing both within the company and from third-party contractors, so other functions (i.e. dependent functions) were necessary to maintain this information. Support for this combined set of functions was christened 'the quotation system' and this name was used as a quick handle in subsequent discussions. In some cultures the choice of name is very important, for example, the quotation system could have been called 'Rapid Quotation System', 'Turbo Quotations' or 'Quality Quotation

Services'. The choice of a good name can often help with the user buy-in and attitude towards the system.

Detailed Analysis Scoping

During detailed analysis the hand-over from analyst to designer is under-way, and the scoping (or rescoping) of the system provides a good check for completeness, as well as sufficient detail for a system to be designed and accurately costed.

More detailed dependencies can be analyzed, especially for the critical business processes, to check the accuracy of the understanding from the strategy stage. In the case of the freight haulage company, detailed analysis showed that some items of equipment could not travel on some routes. For example, certain types of trailer and container are not allowed through some of the tunnels in the Alps between France and Italy, so working out the available routes, times and costs was far more complex than had been realized initially.

System Design Scoping

During design, if a designer finds that there is missing or incorrect analysis, it is often necessary to expand or contract the scope of a system, but **do** remember to involve the relevant decision makers again.

With a clear grasp of what the system must do, we can now design an initial set of processes to do it. In most cases, an organization has existing systems already in place and people employed to operate them. An important new constraint is often that the new system must embrace all of the still-valid facilities provided by an existing system. And, of course, we may require special processes for conversion and reconciliation. In these circumstances, the system designer needs to design new or additional processes for such people to use comfortably.

The key decisions to be made are:

- Which collection of business functions is most sensibly grouped into a single process for somebody in a given job to use?

- What is the best way to present the process so that it is easy to use and effective?

- What is the most suitable technology to use to implement each process?

There are two good starting points from our business analysis to assist us here. The first is the identification of elementary business functions and the second is the business response to an event; that is, what the business is trying to achieve when an event is received and the chain of dependent functions that need to be carried out to achieve it. The objective when designing each process should be to provide complete support for the sequence of functions that is carried out most of the time. For example, consider the dependency diagram:

Figure 10-6
Seat Reservation Dependency

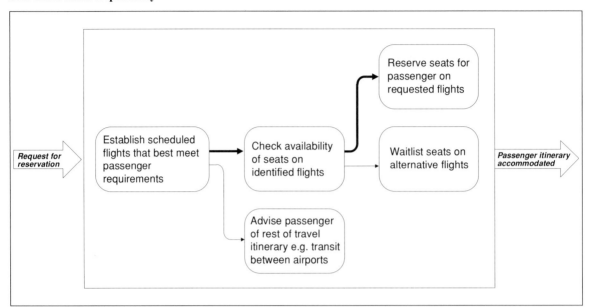

The highlighted route is the normal case (let us say, eighty percent of the reservation requests are satisfied this way) so it makes sense to provide the reservations clerk (the role that will normally carry out this process) with a process that is particularly effective at handling this, the most frequent case. This implies a process to implement the three functions:

Establish scheduled flights that best meet the passenger requirement.

Check availability of seats on identified flights.

Reserve seats for passenger on requested flights.

in the sequence presented by the dependency diagram; this could be a computerized process, a manual one, or a combination of both. In a situation where, say, sixty percent of the reservation requests **also** end with a waitlisting, it will make sense to include support for the waitlist function in the same process. If this is to be done, a decision must be made whether the waitlist should come before the seat reservation, after it, or at the discretion of the reservations clerk. The design should be optimal for the normal case, but also allow for the other less frequent situations in an intuitively obvious way.

Maintaining Elementary Functions

Throughout the process design cycle there is a very important technical requirement to bear in mind – the retention of the concept of the elementary function. An elementary business function is defined as a function that leaves the **business** in a state of consistency; that is, if it fails for some reason, then any effect it has had on the information known to the business must be 'undone'. In the same way, **an elementary process is a process that leaves the system in a state of consistency** and, when a number of business functions have been chosen for implementing in a single process, there may be one or more elementary functions amongst them. Where there is more than one elementary business function to be implemented in the same process, this simply means that having got to a certain stage in the process, the business (and system that supports it) is in a state of consistency and, even if subsequent parts of the process fail, the effects up to that stage are still valid.

Working through the business functions within the scope of a system in this way, a number of processes can be designed, typically around the roles or job types in an organization. These must then be checked for feasibility against the type of technology for implementing them. This rigour is worth some effort as the acceptance of a system by the user community is often improved dramatically, and the attention to detail on the elementary functions and processes may well prevent a subsequent expensive business or system inconsistency.

Precise decisions on how each process is to be implemented are unnecessary; but feasibility can be established, at least to the extent that the designer of the system is satisfied that the process specified could be made to work using a particular chosen technology. In fact, there are likely to be many, and often hundreds, of processes in any one system, and to make a judgement on the feasibility of all processes is both unnecessary and time wasting. Instead, it is usual to select the most important or critical functions and the processes that implement them and test only these for feasibility. Some guidelines about what makes a function critical are:

- its contribution towards achieving a business objective – it is an important function

- the frequency with which it is carried out – it is a major part of business activity

- the urgency with which it must be completed – it is a time-critical function

- its relative importance – it is a competitively vital function

- executive whim – the boss said so!

For these functions, and the processes that implement them, we should spend some time to establish technical feasibility, answering the question: *"Is there a viable technology that we could use to implement this process effectively?"*. Of course, there is rarely a free hand in making this decision; there are constraints on what technology is available:

- existing investments (in computers, machines, people)
- existing skills (both to develop systems and use them)
- what people like and do not like
- the cost of new technology
- the time it would take to change to new technology
- and, conversely, the cost of not changing (and taking advantage of new technology).

System Support Processes

In addition to the processes designed to support business functions directly, we will need some to support the smooth running of the system itself. In particular, processes for:

- system installation
- conversion and coexistence
- collecting statistics
- security
- auditing
- back-up and recovery
- purging unwanted data, and so on.

Producing an Initial System Structure

As a starting point, we have a system scope defined. The system scope is expressed as a collection of business functions that need support and given that all-important, user-acceptable name. In addition, we need to know some other relevant factors that will contribute to the design processes. As mentioned previously, these include technology constraints, time constraints, level of expectation and existing systems. Starting from our system scope, we identify all the business functions within that scope which are elementary. These form a 'shopping list' of functions that need support. Using function dependency diagrams as a guide, we are faced with the challenge of designing components in our system which satisfy collections of functions. These components must respond to events and achieve a desired result in a usable way, within the constraints imposed by the available technology, time, resources, resource capabilities, and so on. There are certainly no hard and fast rules about how to do this. For example, with a simple function dependency diagram with only four functions the possible components include:

- one component per function
- one component for all functions

- one component for the first function and a second component for the other functions
- one component for the first two functions and a second component for last two functions, and so on.

There are eight possible ways of grouping the functions into separate components with this simple case (sixteen ways with five functions, thirty-two ways with six). As a guideline, however, various things affect this grouping activity and the designer should take into account the needs of the eventual users of the system when grouping functions into processes. The process structure should reflect the type of user trying to use it. This is the point at which the role and organization can be re-introduced; or if the enterprise will allow it, the roles and organization units may be modified to more closely map onto the system design!

Imagine, for example, a process to reserve a seat on a flight in response to a reservation request from a passenger. It is the job of reservations clerks to use this process, so we should think of designing something that would be acceptable to them. Group those business functions that represent the most frequent cases, plus those that will be needed periodically to complete the operation, into a process.

You can see how the dependency diagram helps, as it identifies the most frequent cases quite readily. In the example below, this process defines a small subset of functions that can be implemented using the chosen technology; for example, we might choose an interactive computer screen as the technology for our 'Quick Reservations' process.

Figure 10-7
Frequent Case Grouping

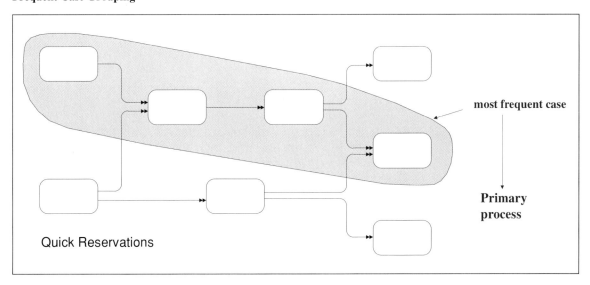

Another major deciding factor (especially in computer systems) is the capability of the technology. There is no point in specifying a process that cannot be built using available technology – often compromises must be made from the ideal, simply to accommodate what the available technology can achieve at a sensible cost.

The more functions that are grouped into a component, the more complex that component will be, but the easier it will be for the user to recognize both the triggering event and what the functions are trying to achieve – the result. On the other hand, the more components there are, the more navigation the users of this system will have to perform to get to the component they need. What is needed is a balance between complexity of the components, ease of understanding of the system for the user, and the ability of the technology to implement a component.

During this initial design phase, you need to focus most of your attention on those (hopefully few) critical aspects of the design. Often these will be critical business functions. On other occasions, the critical aspect of a design is cost, time taken to make a system available, or some other constraining factor. For example, in the late 1980s the Stock Exchange in the United Kingdom went through a business change called deregulation, which allowed individuals, as well as organizations, to trade stocks and shares, where previously only agents could trade. This gave the designers of Stock Exchange systems a challenge: to be able to cope with the expected volume of traffic from a defined point in time, with both system throughput and the time-critical nature of the legislation being crucial aspects of the design.

Good designers often do not know **why** they are good designers. They cannot tell you how they know what components should be in a system – they just know. The thing to be aware of is that there are many alternatives and options and it is important to record the reasons why you chose one particular option, so that if you change your mind or the business or the technology changes you will be able to re-evaluate the system design easily. Most important, always consider alternative structures; do not imagine that the first structure you think of is the best you could possibly achieve.

So we have finished the task of choosing the business functions to be grouped into each process and carried out a cross-check to ensure that all business functions, within the scope of the system, have been catered for at least once (we do not want to miss anything out). The next thing is to consider other essential processes that are necessary to make the system run smoothly, although they do not contribute directly to the functional needs of the business. These may include processes for:

- System back-up and recovery
  - what to do if the computer fails, the chief accountant is ill, the telephone lines are knocked over in a storm, and so on.
- Data purging
  - what to do with insurance policies to stop the disks on the computer getting full, with removal of information about customers who have closed their accounts, and so on.
- Security and access control
  - which users of the system will be allowed to use which processes and what data will they be allowed to manipulate using those processes?
- Audit
  - do we need to make a history available of who actually did what in the system either for legislative reasons (e.g. for tax purposes) or for business integrity (i.e. who to contact when things go wrong)?
- System installation and upgrade
  - what components are needed for installing computer software, making available manual procedures, training and educating the users of the system, and upgrading systems as they change?
- Transition and coexisting
  - what components will be necessary to convert from existing systems and which other systems do we need interfaces to?

Making the System Relevant

When we analyzed the business requirement, we used interviews and other sources to get individual views of the world as a starting point and, as part of our analysis, we came up with a single, integrated function model, which represented a combination of all these individual views. From this integrated model it is relatively easy to design a system that is functionally complete, that is, it does the right thing. But more than that is needed before a design will be acceptable – it must also be relevant to the individual views we started with. Let us examine the things that make a system relevant from the individual viewpoint of various business roles.

Naming

The first, most obvious and, thankfully, the simplest to deal with is the use of different terms by each separate view of the business. Each different view of something, an entity, may have a different name for it. During the analysis phase we should have sought out such generic data concepts and created simpler models which will subsequently be easier to implement and lead to a much more integrated system. However, we must be careful to maintain these synonyms and who uses them, then later on we can provide the appropriately named views of the data to the users – even though they may be actually manipulating a more generic concept. In our example below the entity ORDER has synonyms of CUSTOMER ORDER, CONTRACT, INVOICABLE ORDER and INITIAL SHIPPING REQUEST. A similar situation can arise with functions, although, typically, a function is defined once and the relevant names for the information it manipulates are substituted for the person carrying it out.

Figure 10-8
Business Terminology

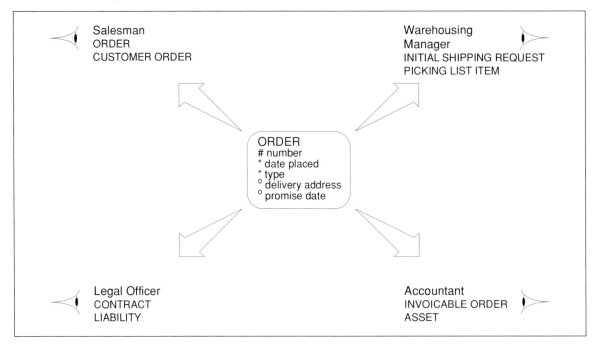

When designing processes, however, we need to make a clear distinction between processes that are to be used by one specific role (e.g. a process for use by an accountant) and processes that are to be used by more than one role. The single-role process can be crafted for a specific view, using all the right terms, whereas a process for more general use will need to adapt to the relevant terms, depending on who is using it. Depending on the technology chosen to implement a process, this can vary from being trivial to impossible. For example, it is very difficult to produce a manual procedure (documented in a book or leaflet) for more than one view: the words would need to change dynamically according to who was reading it! A computerized process, however, can interactively change the titles, prompts, hints and other text presented to the user, depending on his or her role, whilst retaining the same processing internally. Slightly more difficult, but capable of the same treatment, is the case of homonyms, when different people use the same term for **different** things.

Figure 10-9
Homonyms

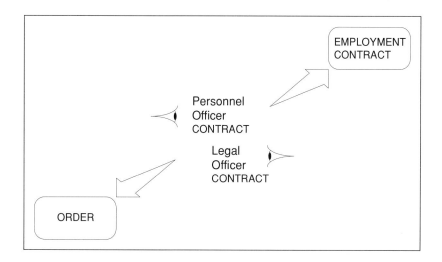

Here the word CONTRACT is being used in personnel to mean EMPLOYMENT CONTRACT, whilst the legal profession is using the word CONTRACT to mean an ORDER (and this could possibly be both a PURCHASE ORDER and a SALES ORDER).

Different Ways of Working

It may be appropriate for different people to perform the same function or sequence of functions in different ways to best fit into their job. A business function or set of interdependent business functions describes **what** must happen to the information in an organization under certain conditions, function dependency diagrams and function logic being used for this description. But **how** the processing is to be done is not described at the business level using these techniques. That is our job as system designers. **We are designing how business functions should be processed as part of a system to meet the differing needs of our users.**

For example, the business function 'reserve seat for passenger on a suitable flight' may be carried out by a reservations clerk talking to a passenger by telephone: a series of enquiries will establish which flight is suitable, whether there are free seats, and so on, followed finally by the reservation of a seat. Whereas an agent making a reservation direct for a regular traveller may simply make the reservation, quoting full details, because four times out of five this succeeds and there is no associated fuss. In these circumstances, it may be sensible to design two processes (perhaps with a common component for making the final reservation); one could be 'streamlined' for fast booking, the other could provide a convenient 'route' to guide the user through a series of smaller processes to establish the information needed to make the reservation. Both would satisfy the same business rules and update the same type of data – it is just the processes that would be different.

Building Relevant Systems

One could argue that the way we have built systems over the last few years has been to take the reality we understood, create normalized models of it that users did not comprehend and then build systems in which we had to work hard to make them intelligible to the users again. A normalized model is a model that conforms to a set of approved or normal guidelines and such a model should be very useful as it is highly generic, flexible to change and independent of implementation techniques. Nowadays the method is similar except that at the half-way house we include the mappings to the business views, as illustrated in Figure 10-10.

Figure 10-10
'Normalized Model' with Mappings to Business Views

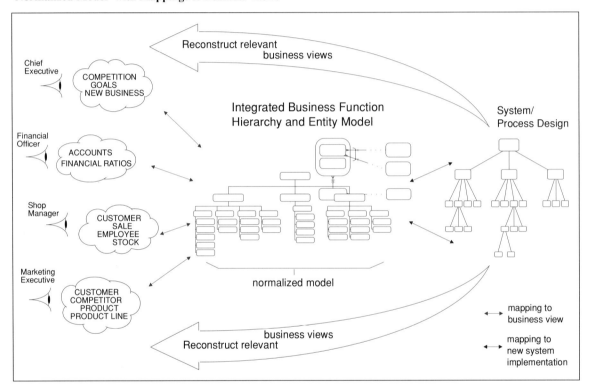

Process Logic

This is analagous to function logic but applied at the system level. Having designed the process structure in some detail, we can then add the process logic, where necessary, to define precisely how a process is to be implemented where this is not obvious from the business function definition. In particular, we may need to specify how we use certain mechanisms such as screens, reports or machinery.

Clearly, much of this logic is dependent on the capabilities of the technology chosen, and it is quite often the case that attempting to design the process logic identifies problems that show that some chosen design is not feasible. For this reason, it is not a good idea to produce process logic religiously for every process, because it often turns out that a decision made later in the design of a system will require changes or even 'rewrites' of many processes defined previously. Designing a system is a highly iterative task that needs focus and willpower for completion in a timely manner.

Good Things to Strive for

Some characteristics of systems that are highly desirable can be used to measure the technical success of a design, assuming the system is acceptable in terms of what it does; that is, it is functionally complete in user terms.

Flexibility

Ideally the processes will incorporate flexibility to changes in either the technology or the business. For example, Atlantis Island Flights may decide to go into the charter business, which would involve renting a whole aeroplane to a single company for a specified flight and then letting that company worry about bookings, reservations, and so on. In order to cope with this business change, how much effort would need to go into designing additional processes and changing existing processes in a system that was not originally designed to do this?

If optical disk storage (cheap, high-volume text and graphics information stored on a laser disk) were introduced, how much effort would be involved in modifying our system to take advantage of the potential cost savings of storing some of our information using this new technology?

Robustness and Resilience

We now have a number of processes in the system, each one satisfying one or more business functions or one or more requirements for making the system run smoothly. Now we must ask ourselves the most crucial question – will it work?

Performance

There are many ways in which a system can be considered inadequate (a bad design). These are often constraints that have not been observed, such as the frequency or urgency of a business function which cannot be achieved based on your knowledge of existing technology. For example, if the required turn-around time for providing a customer with a quotation is two minutes or less and you intend to collect the information needed to give this by using a high-density facsimile machine, if the normal time to dial, redial when busy and transmit the facsimile takes more than two minutes this technology will be inadequate. (Note: we have started to reintroduce mechanisms or at least types of mechanism, such as facsimile, into the process definition.) To make systems perform to the level required by the business, we will frequently have to juggle the definition of components, the types of mechanisms used to implement the process, and the way in which the information is being stored for access. For example, a typical trick used by designers of accounting systems is to keep monthly balances that are derived from all the transactions during the month separately in addition to the transactions themselves, so that references to the monthly balances, which are quite common in an accounting system, can be made without having to add up all the transactions for a month each time.

When considering using computers and networks, performance obviously has a lot to do with the power of the computer that can be afforded and the complexity and bandwidth of the network envisaged. It may be necessary to complete a performance assessment or simulation to ensure that response-time needs and business-throughput peaks can be catered for by the types of hardware envisaged.

Space Utilization

This can also cause a problem if some overall system sizing is not done at this time. A really secure healthcare system could take so many security copies of paper that there is no room left for patients! In one company, where customer service was identified as really important late in the project, it was decided to keep details of transactions for ten years. We sized it and pointed out that regardless of what sort of computer or database system they chose, it would more than quadruple the cost of the computers, which had just been approved in principle by their board of directors. We then asked if two years in detail and ten years at summary level would do instead. Guess what the answer was.

Revisiting the Techniques

So far we have designed a system in outline and made some major decisions about the technology we will use to implement it. This outline is expressed as a number of systems, sub-systems and processes (which themselves form a hierarchical structure). Let us now revisit the techniques of decomposition, dependency diagramming and function logic as they apply to processes, as opposed to business functions.

Decomposition

It is possible to start with a system and decompose it into pieces repetitively, ending up with sub-systems and processes without ever doing any business analysis – this is not recommended, but it can be used to good effect if done carefully. This decomposition technique is highly applicable to processes, and the cross-checking and completeness tests are again very valuable. Some specific points need to be considered.

Completeness

When function modelling, the only aspect we were interested in was **what** was needed in the business. Now that we are talking about systems, and the aspect of **how** we are going to support the business has been introduced, there will be additional processes necessary at each level in the decomposition of a system which would not appear in a business function hierarchy. For instance, processes that are specific to the chosen technology may be needed, such as repair and maintenance of machinery. In a warehousing business, if the technology chosen to carry out the function 'prepare order from stocked items' is to be automated using robotics, it may be necessary to have each robot serviced and repaired regularly and an entire sub-system may be needed just to ensure that the machinery is kept operational with minimum outages. With the business function hierarchy to refer to, it should be clear **why** each process is necessary and it should be easier to spend a reasonable proportion of design time on those things that are most important to the **business**.

Common Processes

We try to avoid common functions when analyzing a business as experience has shown they rarely exist. However, in the case of a system, we are synthesizing (designing or making up) the processes, and there is a significant advantage in trying to **design** common processes. Each process that can be used to satisfy more than one requirement saves implementation, maintenance and enhancement time, so in terms of the good use of system development resources in the form of people, time, money, and so on, striving for common processing is a worthwhile exercise. But remember that individual users of the process will only be comfortable if the process reflects the function **they** are trying to perform, so it is important to ensure that each common process is capable of **appearing** to be specifically for the task that it is being put to.

When to Stop

Do not go too far! Decompose processes only to a point where:

 – you are sure they are feasible (it **will** work this way)
 – they can actually be designed and built.

Each situation will be different, and deciding when sufficient detail for a particular process has been reached is highly subjective. Use decomposition of processes as a test of feasibility and understanding:

"Will it work the way I have designed it?"

"Can those responsible for further designing and building of it understand what I have designed, even if I fell under a bus?"

Process Dependency

We discussed function dependencies, system scoping and, in particular, dependencies between systems earlier. Now that we have embarked on system design, some dependencies between processes will be there because of the technology with which we have chosen to implement them. For example, a machine to price loose goods, such as fruit and vegetables, at a supermarket checkout may insist that the unit price of the goods be entered before the goods are put onto the scales to be weighed. This changes the way in which the user has to operate the process.

Process Logic

Process logic, like function logic, will be needed in a few cases to specify accurately how a process is to be achieved. Processes to support business functions only will probably not require process logic as this will already have been done where necessary as part of the business model. However, processes such as back-up, archive and purge processes that are added to keep a system running smoothly may need the treatment of full process logic if they are complex. The same approach and selectivity described in Chapter 9 for function logic applies to processes that require logic.

System Architecture

In the same way that an architect charged with designing a building uses various modelling techniques to communicate the essence of a design (e.g. plans, scale models, computer simulation), there is usually a need for a system architecture diagram to highlight the essence of a business system design. To continue the analogy, when Sir Christopher Wren designed St Paul's Cathedral in London, precise detail about the materials to be used, the design of the stained glass windows, and so on, was not present on the initial architectural drawings. Instead, these concentrated on the massive domed roof (in its time a new feature), its size, how it could be built, its feasibility, and so on. Similarly, system designers produce system architecture diagrams to emphasize certain key aspects of

**Figure 10-11
Network
Architecture**

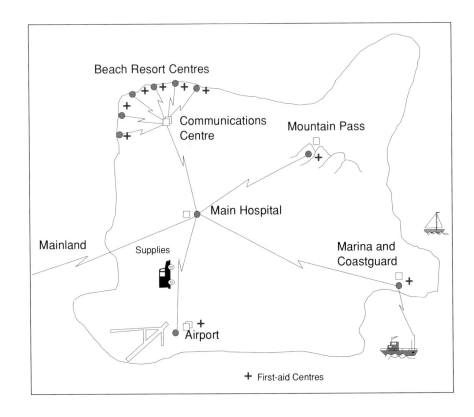

their designs. These diagrams are not definitive (i.e. there are no rules or syntax governing their content or layout), but often name important sub-systems, or collections of processes, and show how they will fit together. A possible architecture for the Atlantis Island Health Authority systems is shown in Figures 10-11 and 10-12.

Figure 10-12
Major Sub-systems

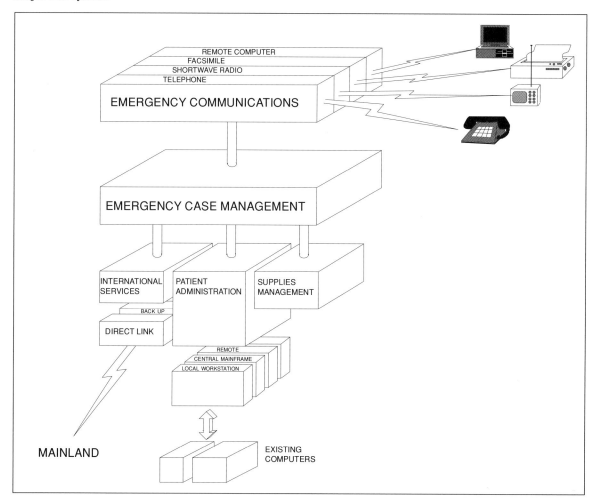

These two architecture diagrams show different aspects of the Atlantis Island Health Authority's system. The network diagram was constructed to give the idea of the scale of the system and to take into account some of the physical (geographical) aspects. Firstly, the system is for an island and the two major sources of emergency activity are from the watersports and holiday beach resorts. Because of this, the authority intends to equip coastguards and major beach resorts with first-aid centres, each having local access to its main hospital computer through an emergency communications sub-system. The mountain activities will be covered by some form of hand-held radio link direct to someone at the hospital. This allows someone dealing with critical accidents to provide advance warning to the hospital of the likely needs of a patient, so that the hospital can prepare for their arrival (allocating emergency resources, bed space, even starting special requests for rare blood types via a link to the international services sub-system). The major sub-systems diagram shows the way that these sub-systems interact or rely upon each other for services.

Why Have an Architecture Diagram?

The system architecture serves little or no **technical** purpose; its main functions are to communicate the structure of a system and to generate senior management commitment. With so much pondering and structured analysis, it is often with the system architecture diagram that things feel 'real' for the very first time.

Imagine you asked an architect to design an extension to **your** house. How would you feel if the design were presented to you as a list of specifications for the bricks, windows, roofing, and so on? An essay describing the extension would be little better – and it takes time and imagination to 'see' what you would be getting. This is why an architect supplies a blueprint of the design (or possibly a mock-up model or an artist's impression of the final appearance) to help check that the design is about right. Unfortunately, systems are not always tangible things that can be drawn realistically like a house, so there can be no standard for their presentation. In some ways, however, this is also an advantage, because it allows greater freedom in the use of shape and style to express the structure and ideas in the design.

Characteristics that Work Well

Although there is no specific syntax or list of rules for diagrams of this type, we include some tips on producing effective diagrams. Remember, the main point of a system architecture is to explain the structure of the system and to generate commitment to the design.

Figure 10-13
Some Three-dimensional Shapes

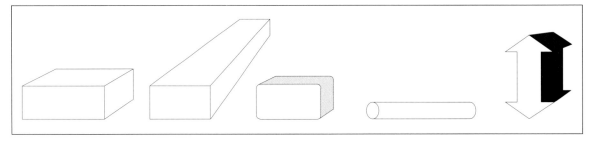

Three-dimensional work

Draw boxes and other symbols in three dimensions, either in true perspective or in a simulated perspective, such as shadowing. This would be overwhelming on a diagram with hundreds of boxes, but can add to the impact of a simple system architecture diagram.

Style

As the boxes and their connectors mean something (e.g. sub-systems and their interfaces), choose a shape that gives the impression you require. For instance, arrows as connectors imply sequence or flow. Interlocking shapes convey the idea of closely coupled or integrated systems, bridges suggest loosely coupled systems, and 'soft' shapes suggest vagueness or flexibility.

Figure 10-14
Interlocking Shapes

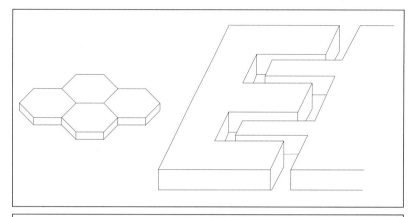

Figure 10-15
Soft Shapes

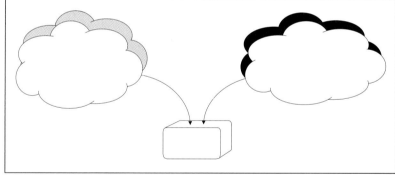

Colour

Use colour, if possible, but use it to mean something. For example, everything in blue will be computerized, everything in green will be done manually, everything in red we have not yet made a decision about! It is best to stick to primary colours, but do not overdo it: three or four colours are probably ample. Also limit the boldness of the colour as a lot of heavy, bright printing especially on white paper can be very tiring to read.

Classifications

Often a system must operate in a number of environments; for example, multiple national languages, multiple computer types, multiple types of user interface. The depth of the shapes can be used to illustrate this.

**Figure 10-16
Classifications**

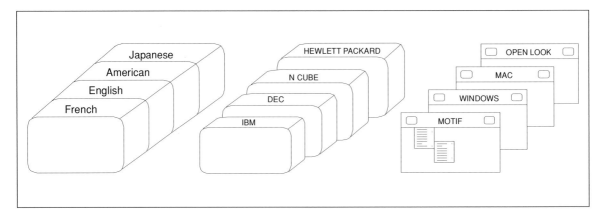

The Main Point

Focus attention on the main point or critical pieces of the architecture, if there are any. Placement at the top, bottom or centre of the page tends to help this focus.

The ultimate goal of this diagram is to implant the concept of the system structure firmly and provide a framework that can be used throughout the system development as a constant reference point. This should be a diagram that the executives must own and want to pin on the wall in their offices.

Producing a System Architecture

There are two main ways in which the system architecture can be derived. Experienced system designers will always use a combination of both; usually in their heads, which can be remarkably frustrating as it is impossible to witness the steps they go through to get to the result – it appears to materialize out of thin air!

Business Function Driven Approach

The starting point for this approach is the function model. Processes are designed from this and then aggregated into sensible sub-systems.

Experience Driven

The second approach is to ask a designer to produce a system architecture 'off the top of his head', using a blank sheet of paper and experience of working on similar systems before. He will use logic and experience to define a sensible and capable system. This technique should not be used in isolation as it rarely satisfies the business requirements – the problem with many 'legacy' systems today.

We all know about a third approach, which is 'let's start coding now and worry about what the users want later'. But this obviously does not apply to you as you are reading this book.

Systems, Sub-systems, Processes and Sub-processes

You will probably have noticed by now that there is not a big difference in definition between the terms system, sub-system, process and sub-process. In fact, the relative scale and size of each component in a system is about the only thing that differentiates them: a process in one organization could be a whole system in another. Furthermore, there is no importance attached to the terms themselves. Clearly, we needed some terms in order to write this book but, if you already have useful terms in your organization, those are the ones to stick with.

For guidance whether something deserves the status of system or sub-system (as opposed to process) use business priorities and importance, as expressed by the senior management in an organization – they are the strongest focusing mechanism we have. Another guide is that when you continually need to give it a group name, it may have become important or big enough to have become a sub-system. It will reinforce the presentation of your understanding of a **business** need if the functions of highest priority to the business are supported by something with the status of system. The accurate naming of the systems themselves in user terms can be used to reinforce this still further.

Summary

We have introduced the concepts of system and process and used these concepts to design something to support a defined functional business need. We introduced alternative ways of approaching the task of systems design and gave some guidance for drawing system architecture diagrams, which can be used to communicate the main focus of a design. We showed that the techniques of decomposition, dependency diagramming and logic definition apply equally to systems and processes as they do to business functions.

In pulling it all together at this level, we have effectively taken the business functions and their related information needs and designed a system architecture and initial process structure. These are a compromise to meet the conflicting aspects of business objectives, organization roles and requirements balanced by available resources and constraints of time and existing systems. This new architecture can now be used to revise project plans and scope future work.

Figure 10-17
Pulling It All Together

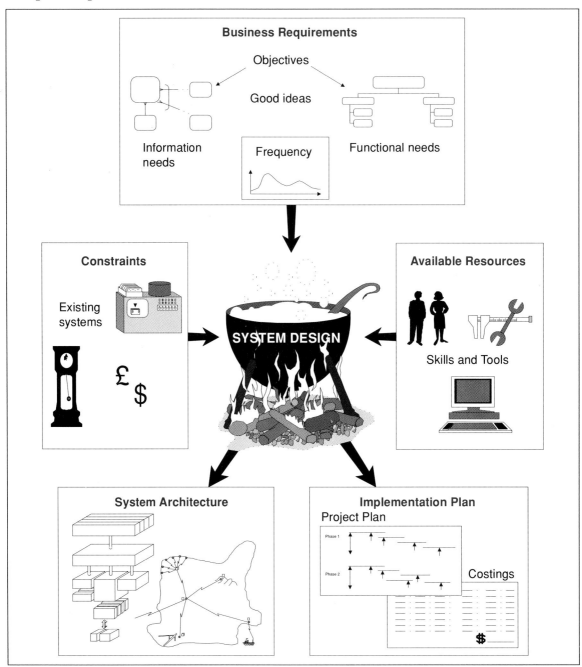

11 DATAFLOW DIAGRAMS

In this chapter we look at dataflow diagramming, a popular technique for modelling systems by describing the movement of data between processes. We introduce two new concepts; the **dataflow** (an exchange of data between two processes) and the **datastore** (a named subset of the data available to be used by a process). A Dataflow Diagram is a special type of dependency diagram, which shows more detail of data dependencies and introduces the additional concept of a datastore.

Dataflow diagrams originally came about to help model the flow of paper into and (hopefully) out of an office, as it progressed through in-trays and out-trays and got stored in filing cabinets. Early computer systems also found these diagrams useful for handling serial computer files, but database technology has reduced their use as the concept of a datastore is less relevant. Dataflow diagrams are generally used at the system level ⬭ and program/procedure level ▭ but are occasionally used at the business level ⬭.

Two Uses of Dataflow Diagrams

Dataflow diagrams show the processes within a system and the data they exchange between them, as well as the way data is moved in and out of the system itself. Where the processes are at a high level of specification, normally shortly after scoping a system, dataflow diagrams help to decide if a process is in need of further decomposition. This is indicated by the number and complexity of the dataflows in and out of it. When the processes are very detailed, the dataflow diagram is used as a specification from which to design and write computer programs, document manual procedures, and design and build machines or electronic equipment. By starting from a dataflow diagram of a system, a detailed specification of all the processes in it can be produced by decomposition.

Dataflow diagrams do not address the processing within each process –
that is left to the function and process logic described in Chapters 9 and
10. Nor do they address the question of **when** a process is invoked – that
is covered by event models, such as those in the next two chapters on
realtime modelling.

Figure 11-1
A Simple Dataflow Diagram

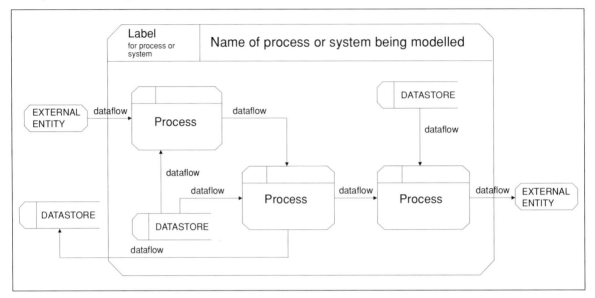

The diagram above shows things that are modelled on dataflow diagrams.
The use of boxes with clipped corners tells us that we are working at the
system level here, dealing with the flow of data to and from processes.
The open-ended boxes represent datastores (see below), the arrows
represent the dataflows (see opposite), and the plain boxes represent
external entities (see page 203). On dataflow diagrams it is conventional
to add two subdivisions at the top of the process or system box for the
label and name.

Datastore
Datastore Definition

A datastore is a named collection of entities, attributes, relationships and
other, as yet unformalized, information (data items) which needs to be
retained over a period of time.

The data is permanent and can only be removed by the specific action of a
process. This is discussed in more detail later in this chapter. An example
of a datastore might be one called AGED DEBTORS which contains

details of all the customers that owe the company money and have not paid within the timescale they agreed to (nothing to do with those customers who are past retirement age!).

Datastore Representation

A datastore is shown as an open-ended box with a label (for quick reference) and a descriptive name describing its content.

Figure 11-2
A Datastore

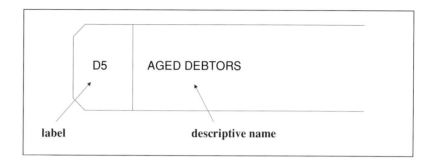

Dataflow

Dataflow Definition

A dataflow is a named collection of entities, attributes, relationships and other, as yet unformalized, information (data items) passing from one place to another, either between two processes or between a process and a datastore.

The existence of a dataflow between two processes means that, when the process at the source of the dataflow is carried out, at some time during its execution it will pass the defined data to the process at the receiving end of the dataflow. A dataflow can be thought of as a description of a pipe or conduit along which the items of data travel. In a physical implementation of a dataflow, such as a telephone line or satellite channel, data will, quite literally, flow in a stream across the communications link.

A dataflow is a transient transfer of data; once it has reached the other end of the flow, it is up to the recipient process to decide what happens to it. If the recipient chooses to ignore it, then the data is lost forever (as frequently happens with unsolicited mail). When a dataflow enters a datastore, this means the contents of the datastore are to be modified using the contents of the dataflow. This might mean addition, modification, or deletion of data already in the datastore. A datastore is there to capture a transient flow of data permanently.

Dataflow Representation

A dataflow is shown as a line with an arrowhead that indicates the direction of flow. It is named to give an indication of the data flowing along it.

Figure 11-3
Dataflow Representation

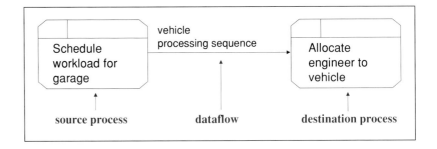

In some dataflow diagrams a double-headed arrow is seen. This is, in fact, a shorthand notation for two dataflows that transfer the same information (hence the same name) in both directions between the processes concerned. It is unusual to find a two-way dataflow between two processes; more often they occur between a process and a datastore.

Figure 11-4
Two-way Dataflows

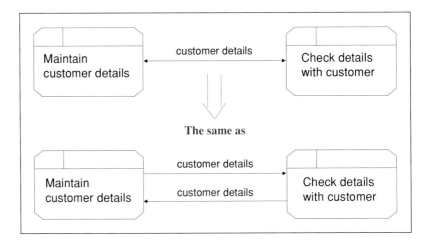

Unlike the dataflow, data in a datastore is not transient and a process must be specified to destroy it if it is no longer required. Destruction of data is actually shown as a dataflow **into** the datastore, carrying the identity of the data to be destroyed. Any dataflow out of a datastore is a non-destructive operation.

At a later stage in the design of a system, we will choose a physical implementation for each datastore; for instance, we might decide to implement five datastores as paper files, one as a computer file and ten more as a computer-managed database using a database management system. On a dataflow diagram at the system level, a datastore does **not** imply any particular physical implementation; its existence simply means that this data must be stored permanently by the system in some way.

The content of both datastores and dataflows is expressed in terms of the instances of entities and their relevant attributes and relationships. An example for the airline booking system is the datastore FLIGHT INFORMATION, defined as 'all attributes and relationships of all instances of the flight entity'; another example is the dataflow 'unconfirmed seats' defined as 'all instances of the booking entity which are not confirmed, plus the tickets they are on if known, the flight they are for and the passenger for whom the booking was made'.

Figure 11-5
Entity Relationship Model for Booking a Seat

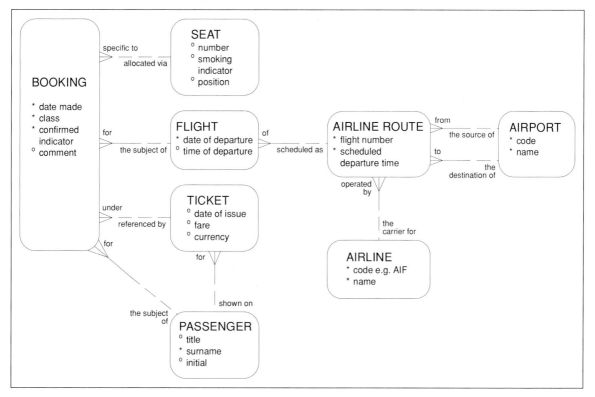

In this latter case, the contents of the datastore would be as follows:

BOOKING
*date made
*class
*confirmed indicator
°comment

SEAT
°number
°smoking indicator
°position

FLIGHT	*date of departure °time of departure
AIRLINE ROUTE	*flight number *scheduled departure time
AIRPORT from	*code *name
AIRPORT to	*code *name
AIRLINE	*code *name
TICKET	°date of issue °fare °currency
PASSENGER	°title *surname °initial

As you can see the content of the datastore corresponds to what a passenger or member of the airline staff would expect to record about a booking. Notice that those attributes marked with an asterisk must be recorded, whilst those marked with an 'o' symbol may or may not be known. Many of the attributes were implied automatically from the entity relationship diagram because of the many-to-one relationships, shown by the $\gg$——— symbol. Alternatively, the attributes can come from one or more business views (see Chapter 9).

Constructing a Dataflow Diagram

To construct an accurate and complete set of dataflow diagrams for a whole system, there are four things we should do in combination. The first is to produce an initial (top-down) architecture and then decompose it into its more detailed definition. At the same time it is good practice to aggregate processes into an internal system – the bottom-up approach. Both approaches are valid: the top-down approach tends to concentrate on the future and new ideas, whilst the bottom-up approach favours existing methods. During this dual process it is important to eliminate the current methods that are no longer relevant, and to temper bright new ideas with the current practical realities. Following these modelling approaches we decompose complex processes (more top-down modelling) and cross-check the result (dataflow balancing). The starting point for a dataflow diagram is usually the system and its key processes, as defined by the system architecture.

The objective of constructing a dataflow diagram is to define the internal structure of a system, its processes and their interaction in terms of the data they pass to one another, and to produce a set of diagrams that make the structure easy to communicate to and check with other designers, users of the system, senior managers who are paying for it, and so on.

Completing the System Architecture

In the chapter on logical system design we covered the development of a system architecture in some detail. In this section we look at the use of dataflow diagrams in controlling that development. Working from the business functions to be supported by the system we are designing, we have to decide on sensible processes that can be expected to satisfy the objectives of the system whilst staying within the constraints identified.

Grouping Functions into Processes

The first step to producing a system architecture or overall system design is to group the business functions within the scope of the system into processes. As an initial guideline:

- Identify **all** the **elementary** business functions to be supported.

- Start by making each one a process.

- Combine the initial processes into a smaller number of more functional processes to reflect the way people will want to use them (check any dependency diagrams for this information).

- Decide what **type** of technology will be used to implement each process and check that this is feasible.

Figure 11-6
Grouping Functions into Processes

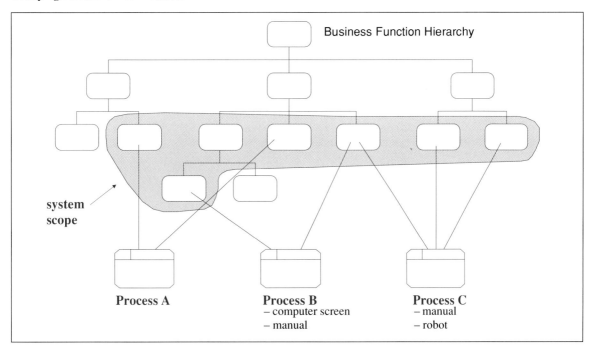

You will remember that when we carried out function decomposition, we explicitly removed all references to role, business unit, organization and mechanism. Now that we are designing a real system for all or part of the current business, taking into account the current reality of organization, geographic location and existing mechanisms, we will tend to have a different grouping of elementary functions into major processes. The design may now even be influenced by the needs of a particular person or role to ensure that the final outcome is acceptable. In the diagram above, process C is designed to carry out three business functions, one of which is also carried out by process B. This happens frequently if the same business function is to be performed by more than one person or role and we have defined a process for each role.

Try to identify a (small) number of types of technology which would be suitable for each process. For example:

- a computer screen
- a computer report
- a bar-code reader
- a manual procedure
- a robot.

It is possible that each process has only one suitable type of technology, in which case there is little or no choice to be made and this job is much easier! Identifying a suitable technology helps you to visualize possible implementations, keeping the expectations of the system designer and the eventual users realistic. Examining **alternative** technologies, however briefly, can lead to a better thought-out design, and occasionally to a cheaper but equally effective solution.

Aggregating Processes

There will usually be a large number of processes to be implemented, all of which need to be agreed and approved by representative users of the system. In a medium system this may run into hundreds, and even in a small system of, say, twenty processes it is hard to assimilate the whole system.

It helps to put a sensible superstructure, in the form of a hierarchy, on top of the processes. This makes navigation around the processes easier and gives us a sub-system structure that can be discussed and used for project planning, handing over responsibility for design and implementation, and so on. In the final delivery of a system this is often presented directly as the main menu structure, which leads the end user to the right place to work in.

Figure 11-7
Process Aggregation

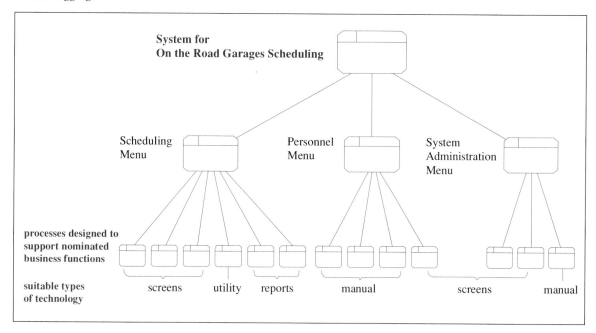

The diagram above shows how the processes for the garage scheduling system have been aggregated. This could then be presented to the users as a menu such as that shown in Figure 11-8. The numbered options on the bottom-level menus directly invoke the processes we started with. Aggregation gives us a number of sub-systems that we can talk about and that reflect the way in which the relevant part of the business will use them. There is no reason why a process should not be aggregated into more than one sub-system at a higher level, and you will notice that general facilities, such as in-context help, may appear anywhere.

Process aggregation is sometimes omitted as a separate exercise and the business function hierarchy is used as the superstructure for the system. This can lead to problems in large organizations where there is a real need for slightly different structures for the processes in different parts of the company.

On the other hand, in many systems departments the business analysis is sometimes omitted altogether and the only hierarchy or decomposition drawn is the process hierarchy for the system. This can be even more of a problem as the system is often overly biased towards pure logical and technical niceties, as opposed to ensuring that it fits in with what is needed.

Figure 11-8
An Example Menu Structure

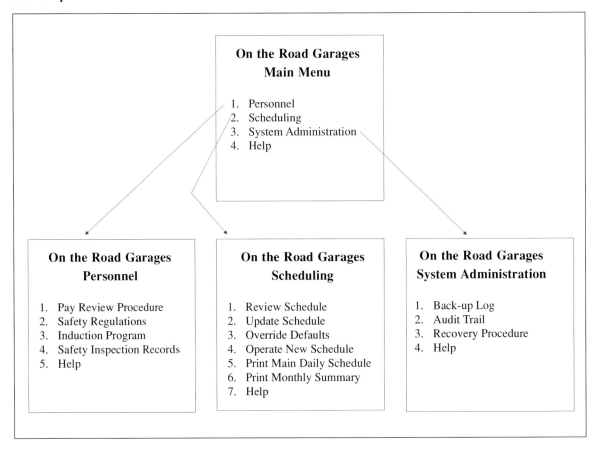

It does not take long to do both processes and experience shows that systems will be more acceptable and less likely to need early change if both are done.

Adding Dataflows

Each of the processes in a system, including the system itself, can be made the subject of a dataflow diagram, and if we were to draw such a diagram of our previous example it would look like Figure 11-9.

This is an alternative representation of a hierarchy, in which the child processes are placed within the surrounding box of the parent process (in this case, the top-level system itself).

Figure 11-9
Dataflow Diagram for
'On the Road Garages'

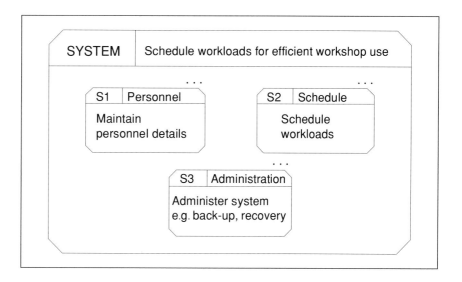

If we were to 'look inside' the process S2 (Schedule), we would find:

Figure 11-10
The Detail of Process
S2 – Schedule

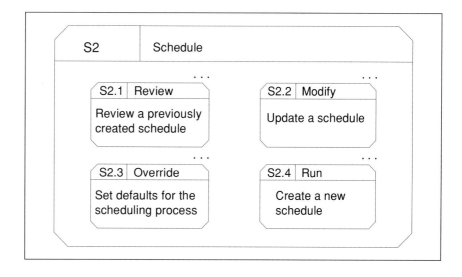

And so on, down the hierarchy. This decomposition can also be drawn as a conventional hierarchy, as shown in Figure 11-11 below.

In our scheduling example here, the children of S2 are the processes we derived by initially grouping together the business functions we started from. To add dataflows to the diagram above, we must return to the dependencies between the original business functions.

Figure 11-11
A Conventional System Hierarchy

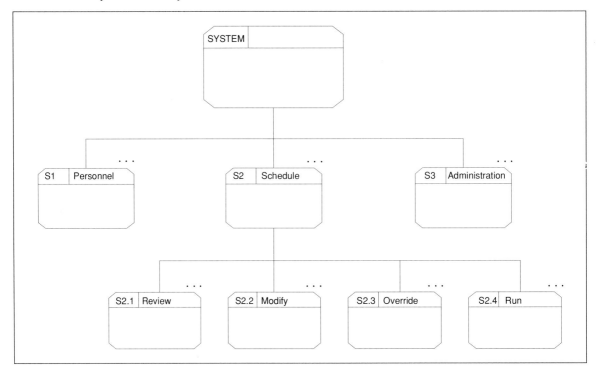

Some of the function dependencies will be data dependencies and these translate directly into dataflows; that is, the data produced by one function, which is required by another, will map onto a dataflow between the two processes that are being designed to implement the two functions.

If a dependency is between two functions that are to be implemented as a single process, then this dependency can be ignored. If, however, the functions are to be implemented as separate processes, then this dependency becomes a dataflow between the two processes.

In the example opposite, A to F represent business functions from the 'On the Road Garages' hierarchy. We have taken a system design decision to implement the three functions B, C and D by a process labelled S2.2. As a consequence, it is the responsibility of the system designer to sort out how to resolve the dependencies between C and B and between C and D which will be handled internally within process S2.2. We have also chosen to implement the functions E and F by a process labelled S2.4. We now need to resolve the dependencies between B and E and between D and F. These will become a dataflow from S2.2 to S2.4. In this way, the dataflow

Figure 11-12
Mapping Functions to
a Process

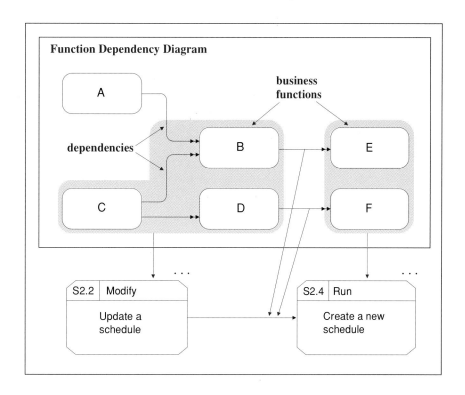

Function Dependency Diagram

diagram can be populated with dataflows based on the function dependencies.

Dealing With Different
Types of Dependency

When the functions at either end of a dependency are to be implemented by the same system, data dependencies are handled quite simply by introducing a dataflow.

But what if one of the business functions is outside the scope of the system being designed? A different symbol is used on the dataflow diagram to represent something external to the system. Somewhat confusingly, this is often called an **external entity**, but it is a completely different concept from the entities we defined at the business level. Admittedly, both concepts represent things of significance, hence the choice of the word entity. Where a dataflow is to or from a function implemented in another system, the external entity is that other system. Where a dependency is to or from a function that is not being implemented in a system that supports our business at all, the external entity is something outside the business altogether – in fact, it is in someone else's system!

Figure 11-13
An External Entity

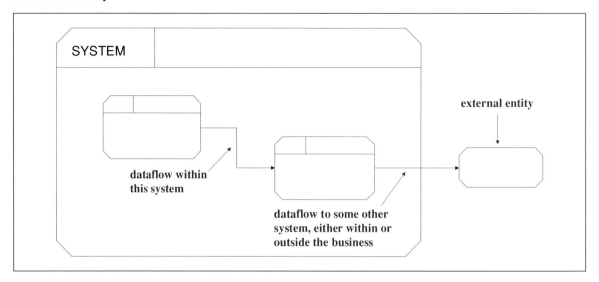

External entities are often given names like 'Customer' when the dataflow passes information out to a customer, or 'Stock Exchange' if the dataflow into a system is the latest stock price for an enterprise.

Other Types of Dependency

Other types of dependency (legislative and policy) also become dataflows, although the data they pass is simply an indication of the fact that the process at the source has got to a point where the destination process can start. If a dataflow diagram is to be used, it is important to include **all** dataflows in this way because, during system design, we will modify dataflows as we progress, and the omission of one dataflow might mean the difference between a process being feasible or not with the chosen technology.

System Dataflows

At the system design stage we will have added processes to carry out the essential functions of system administration. These include processes for:

- menus and other end-user presentation devices
- back-up and recovery of the system
- security and control of access to the system
- purging of data
- removing data from the system and placing it in an archive
- monitoring and controlling the system itself
- system checks for integrity
- auditing, and so on.

None of these processes implements any business functions, therefore there will be no business analysis to call on to derive the process detail or dataflows. In these cases the definition of the necessary dataflows is down to the judgement of the system designer. The dataflows do not provide any direct business benefit – other than the fact that they enable the system to keep operating smoothly!

More often than not these dataflows and the processes that do not implement business functions remain completely separate from any that do. But this is not **necessarily** so. For instance, a dataflow might be added to a process that does support a function in order to carry out a specific piece of auditing, such as recording **who** posted an accounting transaction into a journal in an accounting system. Where little, or no, business analysis has been done, the entire system definition can be done this way. In such cases, the success of the system is dependent on the ability of the individual system designers to 'second guess' what is required. You must judge for yourself if the risk is worth it for this approach (see section on fastpath development in Chapter 15).

Adding Datastores

At first sight there appears to be no need for datastores at all. But on closer examination, the technology chosen to implement a process may demand it; for example, a computerized word processor may require a computer file to work. Another time to introduce a datastore is when the capacity of a process is such that it cannot guarantee to 'keep up' with the data on a dataflow coming into it. Take a telephone sales organization, such as a televised shopping line. A system to dispatch customer orders might be shown as:

Figure 11-14
A Telephone Sales Dispatch System

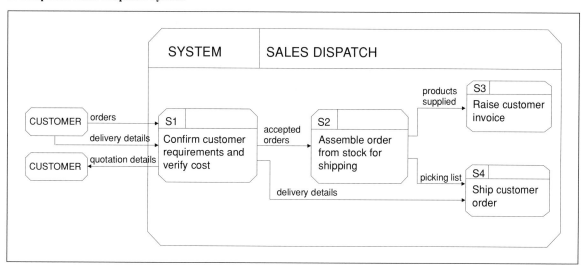

Let us assume that the order assembly (S2) is to be done by automatic, robot stock picking and that the confirmation of requirements (S1) is to be done by a group of telesales operatives using an online computer system. If the robot picking is capable of operating at a constant (maximum) rate of forty orders per hour (for the size of warehouse currently owned) and the customers provide orders at the following rate:

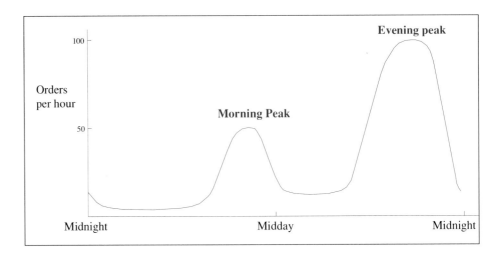

then the two hours of evening television viewing (prior to retiring to bed) and the mid-morning break (for people who are at home in the morning) provide high peaks of business of 100 and 50 orders per hour respectively. The robots will only be able to handle 40 orders an hour (but can continue to do so all day and all night). What happens to all the orders taken which the robots cannot handle immediately?

This is an example of unbalanced processing capacity and the answer (or one of the answers) is simple – we record the order information and save it until the robots **can** handle it. We represent this 'saving up for later' on a dataflow diagram as a datastore. It represents a kind of queuing mechanism that can be used to hold data for a protracted time until it is needed by some other process. We could amend the Sales Dispatch System (Figure 11-14) to add some datastores (Figure 11-16).

The OUTSTANDING ORDERS datastore holds orders until the robots can clear them, and we have added OUTSTANDING DELIVERIES to take account of a similar situation when it comes to the process S4, in which the orders are shipped to the customer (a manual process). To do this, the relative capacity of the two technology types must be known. This is often a constraint on the system design; for example, to use the existing warehousing technology. Where the technologies or their capacities are not known, a designer often **assumes** a capacity mismatch will exist (based on experience or 'gut feeling'). In these cases, the assumption should be recorded against the datastore.

Figure 11-16
Adding Datastores

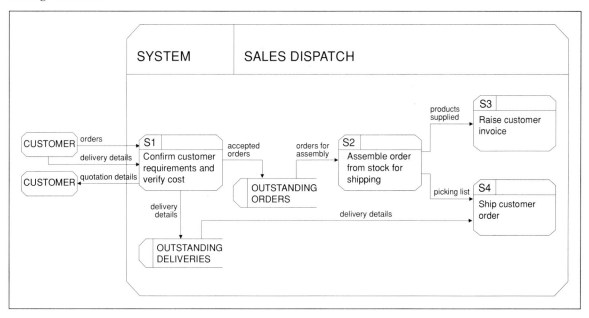

The Basic System Dataflow Diagram

At this point in the system design an initial dataflow diagram exists; produced by grouping business functions into processes, aggregating these processes into sub-systems, adding processes for system administration, converting function dependencies into dataflows and dataflows into datastores, wherever necessary.

Each of the processes in the system will be physically implemented using one or more technologies. Often a whole process can be done manually, by a computer program or by a machine, but under some circumstances a process is split during the design of a system into smaller processes (or sub-processes), and each may be implemented by a different technology.

The choice of which technology to use for each process is a difficult one to make generalizations about. It will be affected by influences such as:

- Applicability – whether or not the technology is appropriate for this part of the system, as illustrated by the use of laser bar-code readers on supermarket checkouts.

- Availability – whether or not the technology can be obtained in sufficient volume and in time.

- Cost – whether or not we can afford this technology.

- Implementation time – the length of time needed to make this technology capable of carrying out the process; for example, training time for manual implementations, programming and testing time for computer solutions, set-up and installation time for mechanical and electrical solutions.

- Development skills – whether we have the ability to implement the system in the technology.

- Maintenance skills – whether we could keep a system running economically in terms of repair, upgrade and administration requirements.

What Level of Detail?

The technology chosen to implement a given process can be expressed in very general or very specific terms (or somewhere in between), as applicable.

Figure 11-17
What Level of Detail?

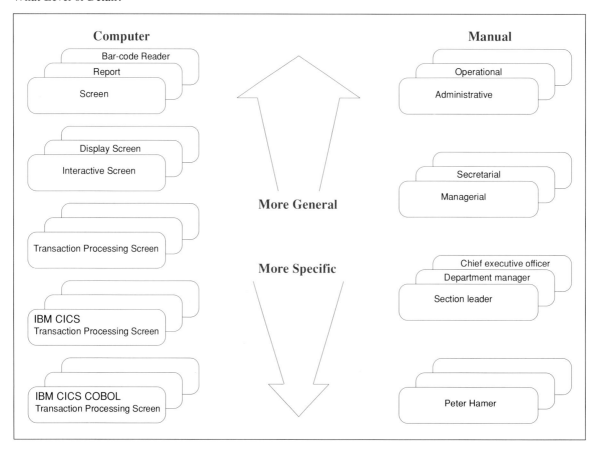

In some cases, particularly those which are critical to the business, a high degree of detail is useful to give a designer confidence that the design is feasible (as the performance characteristics, usability, robustness and other characteristics of the component are known). In other cases, typically non-critical processes, a very general level of detail is acceptable, since there is no **need** for very precise prediction of the performance of the component. As a guide, only provide the level of detail that is adequate to get the job done (i.e. do as little as you possibly can without risking misinterpretation). Over-specification is an unnecessary and costly extra. The chosen technology for each process on the dataflow diagram can be marked at the bottom of the process box.

Process Decomposition

When the decisions have been made to implement each process using a certain type of technology (at the appropriate level of detail) some processes will need to be decomposed further. There are a number of reasons for this.

Mixed Technology

Some processes will be defined as a mixture of more than one technology; these processes may need to be split into sub-processes by decomposition until each sub-process can be defined as being implemented using a single technology. For example:

**Figure 11-18
Decomposing a Process**

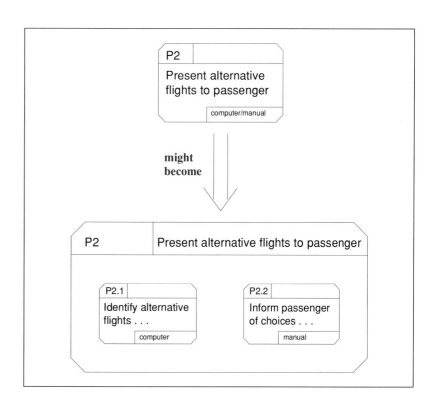

Complexity

A process, particularly a key or critical process, which is complex can benefit from further decomposition (a 'divide and conquer' approach). Each sub-process in the decomposition will be simpler than the parent, since it only carries out a part of it and can, therefore, be designed in detail more easily.

New Datastores

As we introduce new levels of decomposition and further detail of the technologies to be used, it may be necessary to add datastores due to the queuing situation discussed earlier. To form a complete picture of a system, we must also decide which type of technology we will use to implement the datastores and dataflows; for example, a dataflow might be by telephone or satellite communications link; a datastore might be a filing cabinet, or a computer file managed by a database management system.

Balancing Dataflows

When a process is decomposed into sub-processes, each dataflow to or from the original (parent) process should be transferred to one of the sub-processes. This is known as dataflow balancing. In the example below, the process P2.1 is at the bottom (leaf) level in the process decomposition.

Figure 11-19
A Dataflow Diagram of Leaf Processes

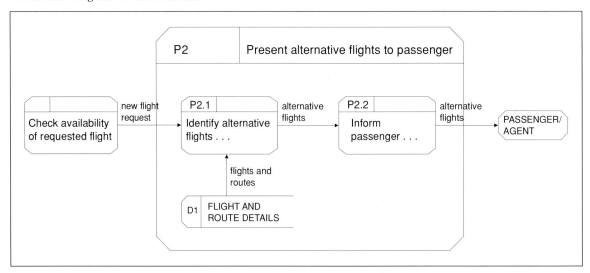

Figure 11-20 shows further process decomposition of P2.1. Notice that the dataflows still go in and out of the process P2.1. Now that we have designed the structure for P2.1 we need to connect these dataflows to the new sub-processes – that is, we need to say which of the parts of P2.1 actually need the information supplied by the dataflow.

Figure 11-20
Additional Decomposition of P2.1

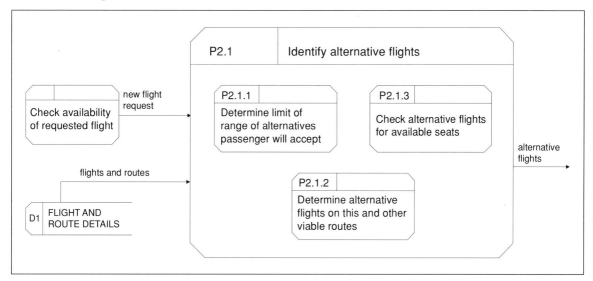

As you can see in Figure 11-21 we have now connected the dataflows into the appropriate sub-processes. Two additional flows have been added to cater for interaction between these sub-processes. The output dataflow has been renamed 'available alternative flights', as the lower level of design has helped us think about the problem in a more focused manner. This is now a **balanced** dataflow diagram in which there are no dataflows in or out of processes that have been or need to be further decomposed.

Figure 11-21
P2.1 Balancing Dataflows

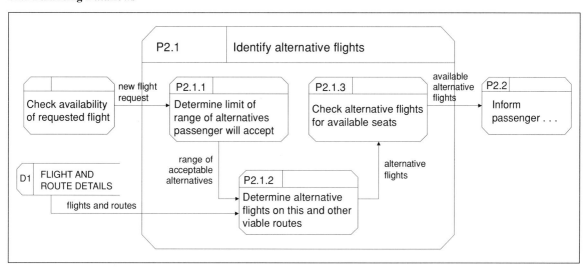

It is sometimes useful at the higher level to continue to show the dataflows in and out of a process that has been further decomposed. This is shown in Figure 11-22 for process P2.1, where you will notice that the dataflows are shown with dotted lines to signify that they actually connect to some sub-process.

Figure 11-22
Unbalanced Dataflows

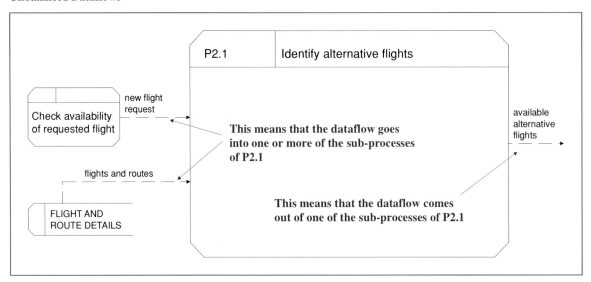

Completeness Checking

In any process, the information coming out must be derivable from the information going in, after applying the algorithms and logic of the process itself. As a final completeness check of P2.1 it is useful to see if the output dataflow and all its details can be derived from some or all of the input flows.

The example below would be incorrect for most payroll systems, as other information (taxation rates, allowances, etc.) is needed to derive net pay from gross pay. The dataflows to supply this information are missing.

Figure 11-23
A Payroll
Gross-to-Net Calculation

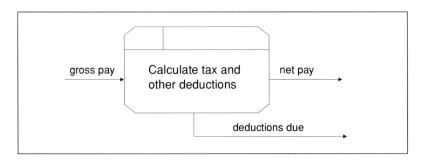

The necessary information could come from datastores, other processes, or external entities; in our case, the tax rates might be supplied by the government (external entities) and the remaining information could come from an EMPLOYEE DETAILS datastore.

Quality Checks

Some things to check on a completed dataflow diagram for each leaf process are:

- There is at least one incoming dataflow (not strictly necessary, but true of virtually all leaf processes).

- There is at least one outgoing dataflow (otherwise the process produces no data of any value).

- The data defined by the output dataflow(s) can be produced by transforming the data on the incoming dataflow(s).

- All the incoming dataflows are necessary (i.e. the outgoing dataflows could not be produced if any of the incoming dataflows were not there).

- All the outgoing dataflows contain data that is used by another process or is fed out of the system.

And for each datastore, the following checks apply:

- There is at least one incoming dataflow to create the contents.

- There is at least one outgoing dataflow which uses the contents.

- There is at least one incoming dataflow to delete the contents – not strictly necessary, but virtually all data needs some means of deletion or systems tend to grow in size forever!

- The outgoing dataflow details can be acquired by data from the incoming dataflows, without any data transformation (as there is no process within a datastore to do the transformation).

Splitting and Merging Dataflows

In practice, life is never quite as simple as the picture painted here. When a process is being decomposed, it is possible (even likely) that a single dataflow in or out of the parent will need to go to or from more than one of its sub-processes. In this case, the dataflow can be replaced by more than one dataflow or, alternatively, the original dataflow can be routed to a datastore and the sub-processes retrieve the data from there when they need it. Wherever two or more dataflows appear between the same two objects, these can be merged into a single dataflow.

Splitting and Merging Datastores

To split a datastore is simple; the only thing to check is that, when one datastore becomes several, no information about the original datastore is lost. The sum of the definitions of the new datastores must add up to the definition of the original one. This can be done to indicate the use of different technology types to implement different parts of the datastore; for example, unconfirmed bookings might be held on a manual file (i.e. paper) and confirmed bookings might be held on a computer database.

Presenting the Dataflow Diagram

The dataflow diagram can be used as a tool to present decisions made during system design and the diagram can be produced at various levels of detail depending on the audience.

Senior Management

For a senior management presentation, details of precisely how a system is designed are largely unnecessary, so an abstraction to a high level can be used. Typically, all dataflows are derived (unless, of course, the system design has not been done at the time of presentation) and few datastores will be evident. The key to success in this kind of presentation is to take the most important external entities and show the dataflows to and from them. For example, the system dataflow diagram for the Atlantis Island Health Authority might be:

Figure 11-24
Atlantis Island Health Authority – System Dataflow Diagram

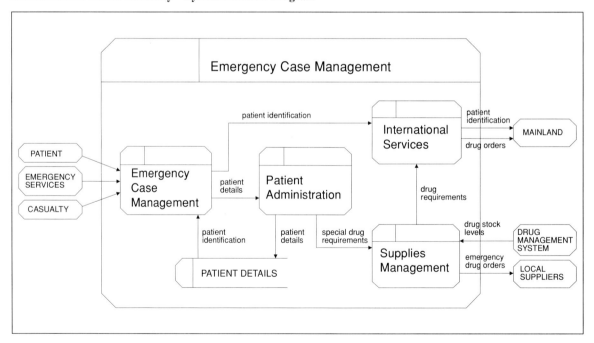

Compare this with the system architecture diagram in the chapter on logical system design in which there is no rigid syntax and the inter-system communications are not named.

Detailed Cross-Checking

In a presentation to operations staff the proposed system might be prototyped on paper. In this case, very detailed (typically leaf-level) dataflow diagrams are used and can be checked by 'walking through' how the system would be used to carry out a certain business function.

Figure 11-25
A Detailed Dataflow Diagram

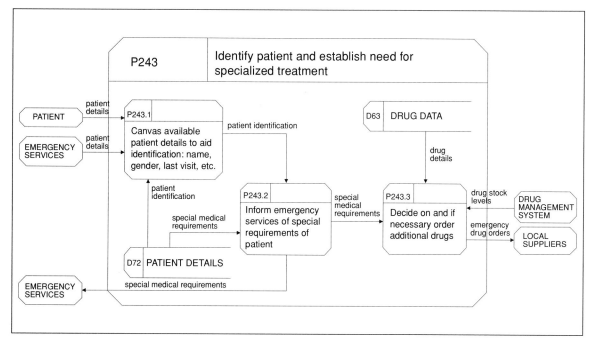

This detailed diagram can be used to highlight sensitive parts of a process. For example:

"When an emergency is reported, the patient is often unable to give us reliable information; if the patient is unconscious, for instance. So we need to be able to identify patients by all sorts of different things, like approximate age, sex, driver's licence number if the emergency service personnel have found a purse or wallet, and so on. It is critical to try to identify the patient accurately and quickly because he or she may be on a course of drugs and need a regular supply, or may be allergic to certain drugs and need alternatives. The key thing is to be able to make the decision and acquire the necessary drugs, so that they are available as soon as the patient arrives, whenever possible."

Summary

We have introduced the concepts of dataflow and datastore. Dataflows, datastores and processes have then been used to model the internal structure of a system. The datastore represents a persistent data storage capability and is expressed in terms of entities, attributes and relationships from the data model of the system. The dataflow shows a movement of data (again in terms of entities, attributes and relationships) between two processes, between a process and a datastore, or between a process and an external entity.

Dataflows are called balanced if they are into and out of processes that are not further decomposed. The task of decomposing a process and balancing its dataflows, by assigning them to its sub-processes, is a top-down design activity which, if taken to a low enough level of detail, can often form an adequate specification of a process from which final construction can take place (using a computer language, manual procedure, electronic circuit, etc.).

Remember, the dataflow diagramming technique is, like many others, an iterative, evolutionary approach to arriving at the final result. Many mistakes will be made and repaired along the way to a completed system definition.

12

REALTIME MODELLING

Introduction

Up to this point we have been considering functions that can be modelled relatively easily. In this chapter we will be considering complex functions that change dynamically as new events occur. These are known as realtime functions or processes and are particularly applicable at the system level ⬭ and program/procedure level ▭.

The techniques already described in this book would require exhaustive analysis of what must happen in response to **all possible combinations of events in any sequence**. For just ten events there are over three million different combinations if they all occurred just once! In addition, it is often a requirement that these processes respond in a timely fashion to some potentially critical event. An autopilot controlling an aeroplane in flight may have only a fraction of a second to respond to a change in air pressure without compromising the course the aircraft is on. Systems that are largely event driven and time critical are called realtime systems and the processes in them are called realtime processes. The term comes from the fact that reaction to events must happen nearly instantly, in **real time**. ("Time and tide wait for no man.") Realtime modelling is predominantly used for system design rather than as a primary business modelling tool.

Realtime processes are often implemented by separate specialist devices (electronic or mechanical), all operating concurrently, designed to perform a critical part of a system, such as a laser bar-code reader in a supermarket check-out. Others are implemented by low-level computer software, often written in languages very close to the computing hardware to take advantage of the speed and control possible at that level of detail (e.g. assembly languages or even hardware control codes in Programmable Read Only Memory chips!). The design of such processes requires an exact and complete understanding of how they must respond to these changing events under all possible conditions. This chapter introduces state diagramming as a technique for modelling the behaviour of realtime processes in an event-driven system (or sub-system).

A state transition diagram defines the conditions under which a process will be invoked in a system. These conditions are expressed as a recognizable state that the system could be in, plus an event that triggers a process; for example, in a domestic heating system the state 'pumping hot water through the radiators' and the event 'required temperature reached' cause the system to invoke the process that turns off the heating. For many people, used to the less stringent demands of commercial data processing, the change of thinking necessary to apply this modelling technique effectively may be quite a challenge. Some system designs, however, would be almost impossible to tackle without it, and, like many techniques, there is often something to be learned by applying it, even if the actual results are discarded afterwards.

State Transition Diagrams

Central to the state transition diagram are two new concepts – the **state** and the **transition**. To introduce these concepts, let us consider a simple example of the domestic television set. In normal operation, this has two states – 'on' and 'off'. (Ours spend far too much time in the 'on' state!) Using state transition diagramming, we would model this as:

Figure 12-1
State Transition Diagram
of the Television

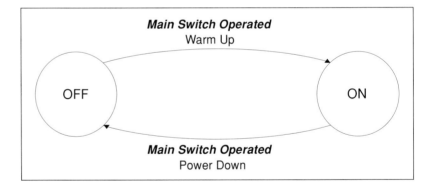

Two states (the circles) and two transitions (the curved arrows) are shown here. The transitions indicate how the television gets from one state to another (in the direction of the arrow). Each transition has two sets of words: uppermost is the name of an event that causes the transition to occur, and below that is the name of a process that is carried out before the television adopts the new state. This diagram has been constructed from the viewpoint of someone designing a television set; that is, the processes are the processes that the television set must perform to make the transition from one state to another, and the events are events external to the television which trigger the transition. The diagram can be read from left to right as:

> *The **television** system will change from the **off** state to the **on** state on the event **main switch operated**, causing the **warm up** process to occur.*

The diagram can also be read from right to left as:

> *The system will change from the **on** state to the **off** state on the event **main switch operated**, causing the **power down** process to occur.*

State

State Definition

A state is a recognizable or definable condition or position of a system.

A system can only ever be in one of a finite number of recognizable conditions or modes, each of which is a state, at any one time. When it is in a particular state a system is completely inactive; it is waiting for an event to occur which will 'fire' a transition out of that state into another. A state is often observable, or detectable, from outside the system. With a television, for example, in the 'on' state you can usually detect this by the sound and picture (in case it is not tuned in to a station, a small red light usually indicates 'on' or 'off' status). However, when a system is in a state for only a very short time before the next event occurs, it may be difficult to recognize or observe this as a separate state. (In many chemical reactions, the reagents form a series of intermediates before reaching the final products. Sometimes these intermediate states are easily detectable (the mixture may change colour), but they may be transient and difficult to detect – a challenge to numerous chemists over the years!)

A system has a single 'current state' at any one point in time. When a system starts up for the very first time its current state at that point is known as the **start state**.

State Representation

A state is shown as a circle, optionally with a name that describes it in upper case. The start state is identified by showing it as a double circle.

Figure 12-2
State Representation

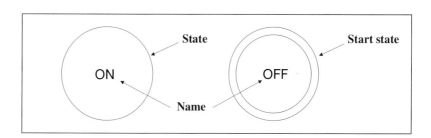

Transition –
A Process Trigger

A transition is a passing or change from one state to another. The system will make such a transition if circumstances defined by the designer and shown on the state diagram occur. The only possible way a system can change its state is via a transition.

A transition is fired by an event and may (or may not) trigger some process.

Thus a transition carries two items of information: the event that causes it and the process that is carried out between leaving one state and reaching another. (Technically, while a process is being carried out, the system is not in a recognized state.) When a system is in a state and a recognized event occurs, the relevant transition is said to be 'fired'. A transition is, in fact, a process trigger, which shows an event triggering a process under defined circumstances (the state of the system).

Transition Representation

A transition is represented by a curved arrow, with the direction of the arrow indicating the direction of the change of state. The event is shown in bold italics with initial capitals. The process is shown below this in normal text in colour, once more with initial capitals. When using a CASE tool, it is normal to show events and processes in different colours to help differentiate between them.

Figure 12-3
Transition Representation

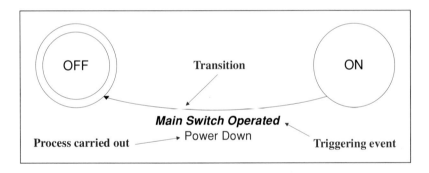

The state transition diagram for the television (Figure 12-3) tells us that if the system is in the 'on' state and a 'main switch operated' event occurs, then the process 'power down' will be carried out and, on completion, the system will be in the 'off' state. Conversely, ...

Extending the Example

There are some interesting questions and cross-checks that can be applied to a diagram which will help us to design the system itself. The following questions help to achieve completeness and consistency in a state transition diagram:

"Are there any states missing?"

"If the system is in a given state, what events should it respond to (and are there transitions to cater for them)?"

"Are there events we know of that do not trigger transitions on the diagram?"

"Are there any states that cannot be reached?"

"Are there any states that the system cannot get out of?"

"Which transitions are reversible or have a corresponding opposite transition?"

In our television example, we might ask what happens if the television experiences a power failure when it is on (or off, for that matter). Perhaps we need to take precautionary measures to protect the internal circuitry so that when power is restored no damage is done, which might extend our diagram as shown in the figure below. We have introduced a third state to indicate that the television is 'on' but the power has failed and, whenever these conditions arise, we want the circuitry to be 'protected' against damage caused by power restoration. Notice that a completeness check caused us to add the transition back to 'off' when the television is in the 'protected' state and the event 'main switch operated' is received.

Figure 12-4
Coping with Power Failure

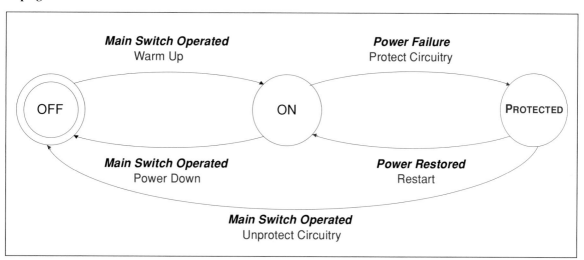

Remember, this is part of a system design. If you were asked to construct a television that exhibited this behaviour, you would either have to design something to 'remember' the current state mechanically or provide some form of power back-up so the television could 'remember' the current state, even if the mains power fails.

There are two further types of transition that we have not yet illustrated. The first is a transition that fires and causes a process to be executed but does not cause a change of state (our television is still on). This type of transition is called a cyclic transition.

Figure 12-5
Cyclic Transition –
a Transition with No
Change of State

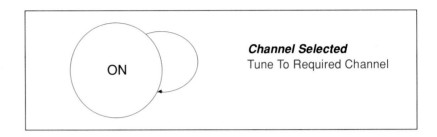

This can be read as:

> *This television system will change from the on state back to the same state on the event channel selected, causing the tune to required channel process to occur.*

Another type of transition has no associated process.

Figure 12-6
Transition with No Process

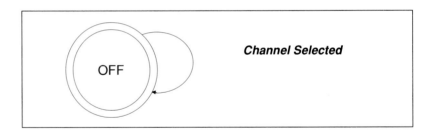

In other words, selecting a different channel has no effect when the television is off. Note how the precise behaviour of the set is now starting to build up – you might like to try modelling a specific television at this point to see how it differs from this example. (If you have a set with lots of gadgets on it, you will find this a much more complex task.) Applying a simple convention for drawing the transition arrows will make your diagram more readable – either all clockwise or all anticlockwise. (Most people find the clockwise direction more readable.) This enables you to read round the diagram easily, giving a feel for the flow of events and processes that take the system from one state to another.

Figure 12-7
Full Model for the Television

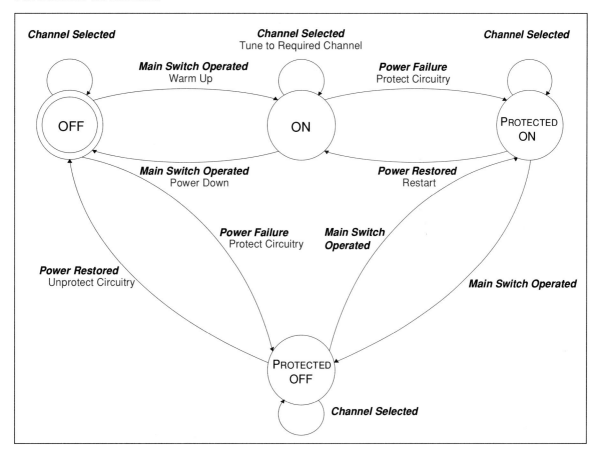

Notice, we have corrected an error in Figure 12-4 (Coping with Power Failure). That model would have failed if the following sequence of events and transitions had occurred:

Main switch operated	–	on
Power failure	–	protected
Main switch operated	–	off
Main switch operated	–	on
Power restored	–	**?**

The earlier diagram does not cater for this event from the 'on' state and the actual behaviour is undefined. It is often these omissions that cause systems to fail or devices like our television to misbehave. And we all know how to fix them – turn them off, kick them, switch back on and hope for the best. Notice another sophistication in the new model: if you press the button on your controller to change channel but inadvertently select the same channel again, the model will still work.

Further State Transition Diagramming

State transition diagrams drawn with large numbers of states and (particularly) large numbers of transitions become unreadable, because it is impossible to draw them without lots of crossing transitions. Two techniques can help to improve the legibility of 'busy' diagrams. The first is the decomposed state, which is covered in the next chapter under advanced conventions; the second is an alternative layout for the diagrams, which show states as vertical lines (the so-called 'fence' notation). The television example would look like this:

Figure 12-8
Full Model for Television (Alternative Representation)

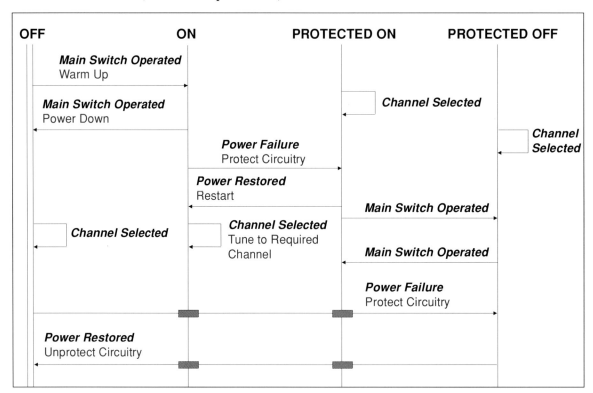

Wherever possible, we prefer the 'bubble' notation used previously because it is more memorable and has a distinctive overall shape (owing to the layout of the states on the page). You may, of course, disagree and we leave the choice of style completely up to you. We will come back to this example in the next chapter, when we look at some more advanced features.

How to Construct a State Transition Diagram

As a state transition diagram shows the states that a system or sub-system can be in, the first thing to do when constructing a diagram is to identify the relevant system or sub-system. But the most difficult judgement to make is whether or not a system will actually benefit from being subjected to the diagramming exercise. As a checklist, the following characteristics often apply to systems that are most likely to benefit:

- the system must deal with many external events
- the sequence of external events defines the behaviour of the system
- it must be capable of existing in multiple, externally observable states
- it should be time critical (i.e. response to events must be within strict limits)
- external events come from more than one source
- it may be one of many systems or sub-systems working together and co-operating or synchronizing with one another.

Two interesting, and common, classes of sub-system that respond to state transition diagramming very readily are graphics user interfaces and process control systems. The graphics user interfaces are supported by interactive applications that respond to events supplied by the user from a mouse or other pointing device. These are becoming far more widespread with the introduction of windowing systems and some fourth-generation languages, in which the designer of an application supplies code (the process) to be invoked whenever a user presses a defined function key on the computer keyboard (i.e. the next process is decided by user action, not the system). Process control systems are the classical realtime systems which monitor and control a production line in a manufacturing plant, the flow of oil in a refinery, the flight path of an aircraft, and so on. These systems have many separate devices that all need to be co-ordinated towards a single goal.

Having chosen a system and defined its scope (in terms of the processes it will perform), there are two places that we can start in creating a state transition diagram of it. First, identify all the events to which the system may need to respond. There may already be a list of events that are completely external to the business, identified by applying the other techniques in this book. Some of these are likely to affect the system chosen (use your judgement initially). In addition, there will be events generated by the various components of this system and other systems which support the various parts of a business. These internally generated (system) events may already be documented by other design efforts, or may be subjectively obvious to you, or (probably most commonly) they will be found during the diagramming process itself.

A Worked Example

Let us illustrate the task of constructing a state transition diagram by using another example. Some automobiles have a facility for locking and unlocking all the doors, including the boot (trunk), at the same time. This is known as central locking and there are many variations of the precise operation on any given model of automobile. In some cars, central locking operates only from the lock in the driver's door; in others, it can be operated from any lock on the car; while others can send a coded signal on an infra-red beam from a button on the key to operate the locks. The many variants of what might happen under certain circumstances easily complicate what is essentially quite straightforward. For instance, where central locking operates only from the driver's door, if we unlock the driver's door and then lock the passenger's door, only one door will be locked; if we lock the driver's door then unlock the passenger's door, only one door will be unlocked. In the simple example of a two-door car with a boot controlled by central locking on the driver's door a limited number of events could happen in any order. They are:

Driver's door locked with key	DL
Driver's door unlocked with key	DU
Passenger's door locked with key	PL
Passenger's door unlocked with key	PU
Boot locked	BL
Boot unlocked	BU
Driver's door opened from inside	DO
Passenger's door opened from inside	PO

These abbreviated short names will be used on the diagram

(In this example there is no means of opening the boot from the inside!)

As a result of responding to a series of events, the vehicle will have a number of possible states it could be in. The second part of constructing a state transition diagram is to list all the externally observable states required. The possible states for the car we modelled are shown below; an open door on the diagram means that the door is actually unlocked.

Figure 12-9
List of States

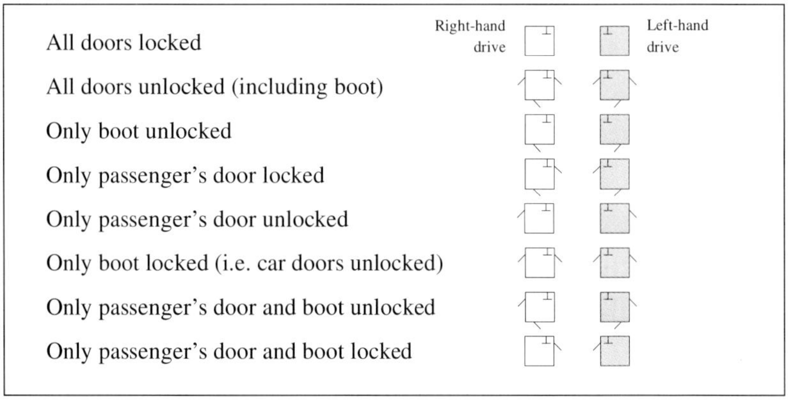

All doors locked

All doors unlocked (including boot)

Only boot unlocked

Only passenger's door locked

Only passenger's door unlocked

Only boot locked (i.e. car doors unlocked)

Only passenger's door and boot unlocked

Only passenger's door and boot locked

Right-hand drive   Left-hand drive

The State Transition Diagram

We can now create a diagram showing which events cause transitions out of each state and the processes performed when these transitions occur. Although quite complex, this is a relatively simple and effective way of showing how **all** the possible states are reachable.

Figure 12-10
Central Locking State Diagram

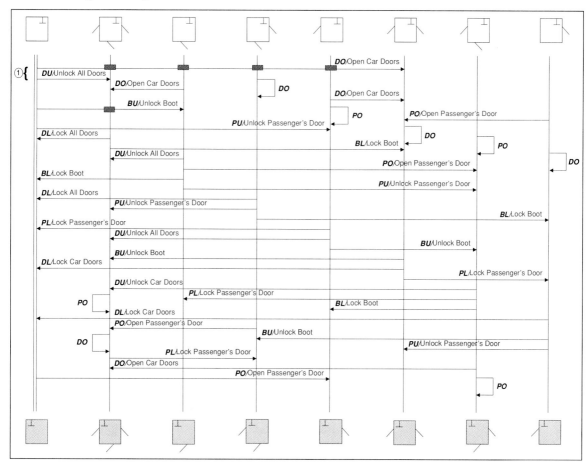

Some points to note are, firstly, the difference in behaviour caused by opening the driver's door compared with unlocking the driver's door (labelled (1) in the diagram above). This may, in fact, be an error in design of the vehicle we modelled (or, alternatively, an undocumented design feature that we could not think of a use for!). Remember the purpose of the state diagram, like all modelling techniques, is to model the system accurately and definitively, whether it is right or wrong, so that it can be used to predict the system's behaviour. To illustrate the prediction capability of the diagram, notice that, if all doors are unlocked and you want to lock all doors except the boot, this cannot be achieved in one step, but must be done by locking all doors (via a DL event) and then unlocking the boot (via a BU event). On the car examined for this exercise, special operations have been provided to allow the boot to be taken off the central locking system (so that operations on the driver's door do not affect the boot) and put back on it again by turning the boot lock a further ninety degrees. The documentation for the vehicle indicates this facility is useful for those times when you trust someone enough to lend them your car, but not enough to let them see what is in the boot! You might like to try adding two new events to this diagram to cater for B- (boot off central locking) and B+ (boot on central locking).

When we designed this state diagram we were amazed at how complex a system it turned out to be, especially as we had not even considered a more standard car with rear passenger doors and child locks. It hardly came as much of a surprise then to find that most colleagues reported problems with their central locking systems, which did not work all the time or did not work as expected under different conditions.

Quality Checking a State Transition Diagram

A number of checks can be applied to state transition diagrams to ensure completeness and consistency. The first is to learn how to read the diagrams to users, in both forward and inverted syntax. A couple of examples were used earlier and full syntax is given later, but to illustrate the point let us look at some syntax that could be used to help check this model, just from the state **only passenger's door locked**.

*The **central locking system** will change from the **only passenger's door locked** state to the **only passenger's door and boot locked** state on the event **boot unlocked (BL)**, causing the **lock boot** process to occur;*

*and to the **all doors unlocked (including boot)** state on the event **passenger's door opened from inside (PO)**, causing the **open passenger's door** process to occur;*

*and will change back to the current state on the event **driver's door opened from inside (DO)**, causing no process to occur (i.e. it has no effect).*

These are the only transitions that occur from this state, is that true?

*The system can only ever enter the **only passenger's door locked** state following a **passenger's door locked with key (PL)** event, after being in the **all doors unlocked (including boot)** state, is that true?*

This level of rigorous questioning will eliminate most errors, but it is best attempted with the help of a CASE tool to construct the questions automatically.

The second of these quality checking techniques, the event/state matrix, is also very simple and effective.

Event/State Matrix

A matrix of state against event is constructed and a tick is entered in a cell for each transition caused by the event when in the state shown. Now you can challenge each state:

"When the system is in this state, are there any events that have any significant effect other than those ticked on the matrix?"

or

"Is it perfectly safe to ignore all unticked events when in this state?"

and also

"Are there any additional (observable or internal) states, other than those listed?"

And then challenge each event:

"The only states in which this event has any effect on the system are those indicated with ticks. Is this true?"

or

"Can this event be safely ignored by the system when it is in all unticked states?"

and also

"Are there any further events that can affect this system?"

Almost inevitably, these cross-checks will identify new states and events and cause you to redraw and evolve the state diagram accordingly.

Unreachable States

Each state on the state transition diagram should be reachable from the start state. That is, there must be some sequence of events which would take the system from its start state to each of the other states: otherwise there is no point in their being on the diagram! These states can be found very simply by taking the diagram, ticking the start state, then ticking all the states that can be reached from the start state (i.e. there is a transition that leaves the start state and goes into the state to be ticked). You then pass through the diagram ticking each of the unticked states that can be reached from an already ticked state. In this way, the ticks will spread out across the diagram with each fresh pass through. Eventually, you will make a pass through the diagram in which you will tick no new states. If any states remain unticked at this stage, then they are unreachable.

Figure 12-11
Unreachable States

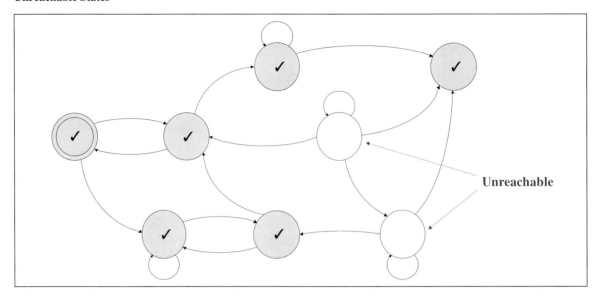

Once these states have been identified, there are a number of questions that arise about each one:

"Is it necessary at all?"

"Is it really the same as one of the other states?"

"Are there one or more missing transitions that should get the system into this state?"

In most cases, the unreachable states are caused by omissions – missing transitions. Sometimes, however, they are important states and there really is no way to reach them. In these cases, a way must be designed; for example, by specifying a process that generates an event to take the system into this state. For example, 'timer' events are added to systems as a fail-safe, so that if nothing happens for a period of time the system can react accordingly. When a modern pocket calculator is left inactive for a period of time it turns itself off to save the battery.

Traps

A trap is a section of the state diagram which the system cannot leave once it has entered it. For instance:

Figure 12-12
Traps

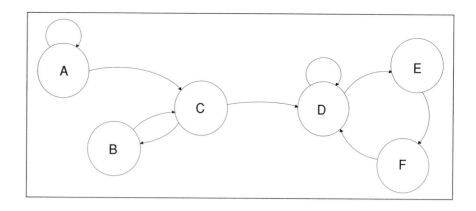

Once the system shown in Figure 12-12 has gone from C to D, states A, B and C become unreachable! This may not be wrong, and in some cases it is very common. It occurs most frequently with electrical and electronic equipment, which uses the power supply to 'remember' its state; if the power is removed, the system 'forgets' its current state and returns to its start state (the state it assumes when it is initially connected to a power supply). Some equipment has battery back-up to enable it to retain its current state should the mains power fail – rather important if you are a patient hooked up to electronic equipment in an intensive care unit in a hospital. A personal computer may have battery back-up, so that it can retain its current state if the main power supply is removed (this battery keeps the internal clock working even when the machine is switched off).

A General Quality Check

It is a good idea to create a matrix of which states can be reached from which other states, as below, using the diagram shown in Figure 12-12.

**Figure 12-13
State/State Matrix –
Completed Cross-check**

To \ From	A	B	C	D	E	F
A	1					
B	2	2	1			
C	1	1	2			
D	2	2	1	1	2	1
E	3	3	2	1	3	2
F	4	4	3	2	1	3

The numbers show how many transitions are required to get from one state to another. So, for example, we can get from state A to state D after two transitions. You will also notice that the trap mentioned above is very clearly shown.

How to construct a quality matrix is covered in detail in the next chapter.

A Familiar Example for Computer Users

Let us quickly have a look at the realtime graphics user interface system that the vast majority of system people will be using every day. Most modern personal computers and workstations have some form of window management system, often supporting a multi-tasking operating environment.

Here we have a very complex system that contains potentially many simultaneous sub-systems under the combined control of at least two pieces of control software. One of these is the underlying operating system, which is a realtime system as it is controlling events such as requests to read a disk, print a line, send a communication package or message. It must also change what it is doing dependent on events that can occur, such as a read failure. Advanced systems will have message passing and event mechanisms to control multiple tasks. For example, one such control mechanism will suspend any process whilst it is waiting for a peripheral transfer to complete, trigger other processes, and restart the original process when the transfer is complete. Further, to ensure that each process on the computer gets a fair (or at least predetermined) allocation of processor power, processes will be suspended after they have run for an elapsed time, a number of instruction cycles or a similar measure so that other processes can be given a chance. Timer events are also common on operating systems, particularly to kill off some process that is quiescent and has been tying up resources beyond some allowed elapsed time limit.

The second and more visible control mechanism is the window manager itself. If you initiate a workstation, open a window and fire off some task, that task will operate completely under the control of the operating system and its own program logic. However, **you** can change what happens. All you have to do is move the pointing device (usually a mouse), click a button, touch a 'touch sensitive' part of the screen, type a character or otherwise stimulate the system. The window management system now has to determine what to do with each event, and there may be thousands of events for even a small mouse movement, as the pointer crosses different pixels on the screen (a pixel is a single dot on the screen). The window manager informs the process that it is running in the window, so that it can decide what to do with the event. As the pointer moves across the window, the underlying process nearly always simply discards the events thereby taking up quite a lot of processor power.

This can be highly visible when you move the pointer across two windows, one active and one passive. When the pointer enters the window that contains an active program, it will typically change to some form of clock to indicate that the program is in an active state. When the pointer enters the inactive window, it will typically become an arrow to indicate that it is waiting for you to type something or otherwise start some process.

Figure 12-14
Screen Pointer in Active and Inactive Windows

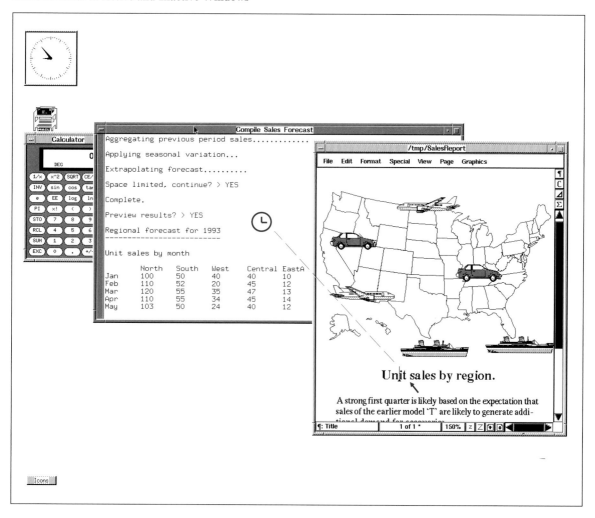

You can see other realtime events very easily if you use scroll bars, move a window on the screen to another position, resize a window, draw a box with a drawing package, and so on. The states are shown by a pointer icon, the transitions are often shown by a shape being drawn or moved. Why not try creating a state transition diagram of just one of those processes using your own workstation as the realtime machine?

Summary

In this chapter we have introduced the concept of realtime modelling using state transition diagramming, which is another useful technique for modelling systems where it is important to know what happens when different events occur, dependent on the state of the system. These tend to be critical control systems, so it is important to be able to check them out with the user in English and using various quality checks. We have also found that realtime sub-systems are an essential component of many computer systems today, and become more important whenever process control and interactive graphics user interfaces are considered.

In the next chapter we will look at some advanced conventions, guidelines for representing states, transitions and events on state transition diagrams, and ways of reading the diagrams using forward and inverted syntax.

13

REALTIME MODELLING
CONVENTIONS & COMPLEX EXAMPLE

In the previous chapter we introduced the concept of realtime modelling with two simple examples of a television set and a central locking system for a car. This chapter covers some more advanced techniques using an extension of the television example, and examines the representation of states, transitions and events on state transition diagrams and ways of reading the diagrams in more detail. This is particularly relevant to the system ⬭ and program/procedure level ▭.

The example at the end of the chapter looks at a rather different aspect of the airline example used in earlier chapters: the fuelling of aircraft on the runway apron by tankers, taking fuel from huge tanks underneath the runway.

Advanced Conventions

We have introduced two alternative representations for a state transition diagram: the 'bubble' notation and the 'fence' notation. Bubbles are more memorable in general because states have a spatial relationship to one another in the diagram. The human mind will happily remember that the 'off' state is roughly at the top-left of a diagram, for example. This helps you to become familiar with a large diagram (and in using it as a communication aid). The fence notation, however, allows you to avoid lots of crossing lines and is much better for defining and checking large diagrams (even if they are not so memorable). In this section, we introduce the concepts of decomposed states and generic transitions as a way of dealing with very large diagrams, using either notation.

Decomposed States

Decomposition should be a familiar notion by now (we have used it on functions to produce a function hierarchy and on processes to produce sub-processes and dataflows). In the case of states, it is possible to decompose them into sub-states and balance transitions to and from them, in a similar way to how we decomposed processes and balanced dataflows on a dataflow diagram (see Chapter 11). Decomposed states are drawn as a circle with points of ellipsis ◯··· (or a line with points of ellipsis |··· in fence notation). For example, we might decompose the 'on' state in the full model of the television to show how the television handles European teletext. (See Figure 13-1.)

The teletext service allows a television set to display pages of text which are transmitted on conventional television broadcasts. The text can be displayed instead of the picture or, alternatively, overlaid on top of the picture, so that both the picture and the text are visible at the same time.

Figure 13-1
Full Model for the Television

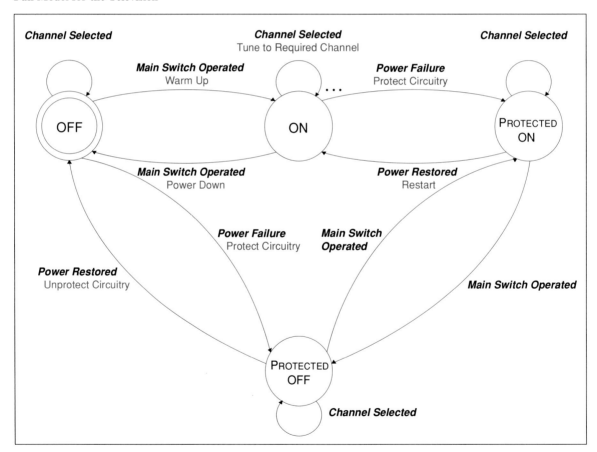

Using this facility, programmes can be subtitled for the hard of hearing, for example, or you can check on the latest news or weather.

There are some rules and conventions governing the use of decomposed states:

1. Transitions **into** the parent state behave as though they have been rerouted into the start state of the decomposition.

The decomposition is itself a state transition diagram (see Figure 13-2), so it must have a nominated start state (in this example, the 'regular picture' state) and it is here that all incoming transitions to the parent state (in this case, the 'on' state) will come. So, the transition from the 'off' state, triggered by the 'main switch operated' event, will go to the 'regular picture' state.

Figure 13-2
Decomposition of the 'On' State

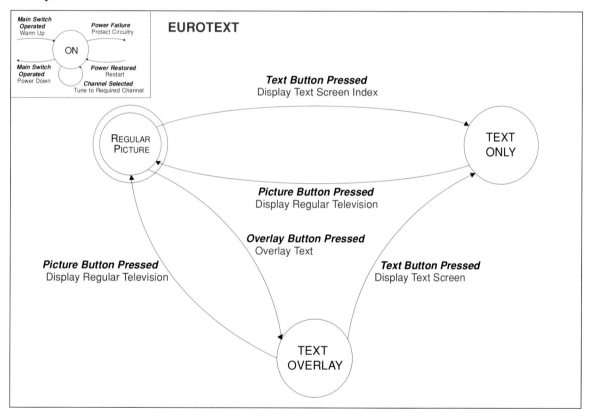

2. Transitions **from** the parent state behave as though each state in the decomposition has a copy of the outgoing transition from it.

In our example, the 'on' state has an outgoing transition triggered by the 'main switch operated' event, which takes the television from the 'on' state to the 'off' state. When the 'on' state is decomposed, it is as though the 'regular picture', 'text only' **and** 'text overlay' states **all** had a transition triggered by the 'main switch operated' event, taking the television back to the 'off' state; and similarly for the 'power failure' event.

3. Cyclic transitions on the parent state behave as though they have been copied **and** rerouted to the start state.

A cyclic transition is both an incoming and outgoing transition and, therefore, the three states in the decomposition will all have a copy of the transition fired by the 'channel selected' event, which returns them to the start state of the decomposition (regular picture). In the case of the 'regular picture' state the transition will still be cyclic, but the other two states will have non-cyclic transitions back to 'regular picture'.

The effect of this third rule in our example is that whenever the 'channel selected' event occurs, the regular picture is displayed, whichever state in the decomposition the television was in. This means that, if the television is showing teletext and the regular picture is overlaid ('text overlay' state) and a new channel is selected, the television will return to the 'regular picture' state, thus losing the overlaid text. This may be the required behaviour or, alternatively, we might have preferred to retain the text overlaid over the new channel.

Figure 13-3
Cyclic Transition on a
Decomposed State

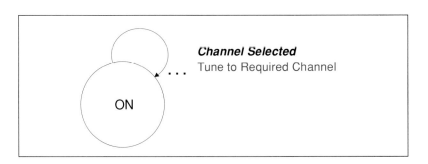

4. A transition in the decomposed diagram is used in preference to a transition from the parent state when both are fired by the same event. The transitions on the lower-level states can be used to override those on the parent state.

For example, an override transition can be added to the 'text overlay' state so that when the television is in this state it responds differently to a 'channel selected' event, retaining the text and overlaying it on the new picture, rather than returning to the 'regular picture' state, which would result from the cyclic transition on the parent state.

Figure 13-4
Override Transition

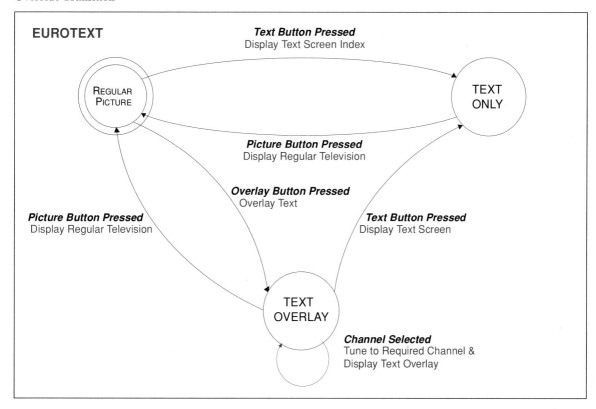

Notice that the diagram above also returns to the regular picture if the television is showing teletext only and a new channel is selected (because of the channel change on the parent state). Again, this may be desirable behaviour; a kind of fast pathway of switching between text and picture by depression of a single button, instead of changing to regular picture and then selecting a new channel. If this is undesirable behaviour, then this transition can be overridden, as we did for the text overlay.

The diagram used to decompose the 'on' state is a completely self-contained unit and can be used more than once (i.e. it can be used as the decomposition of more than one state). In this way a full state transition diagram can be built up with a combination of top-down modelling (based on the externally observable states the system is to exhibit, such as ON, OFF, etc.) and bottom-up modelling with reusable definitions of how the system is to respond to each individual external event.

Generic Transitions

There is a special type of event which the system will always respond to in an identical way, irrespective of the state of the system when this event occurs. This is modelled by a generic transition, which is represented by a hollow arrow. There are two variations. The first leaves the system in a nominated state following the transition. For example:

Figure 13-5
Generic Transition

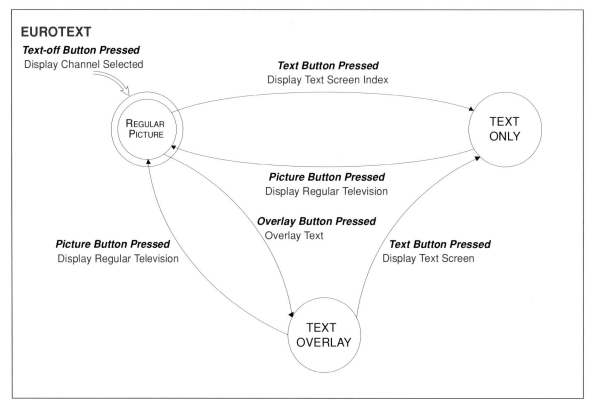

No matter which state the television is in, receipt of a 'text-off button pressed' event will return the system to the regular picture state, having displayed the currently selected channel.

The second variation causes no state change but would cause a specific process to occur. These transitions are listed separately or drawn as looped generic transitions with no state (see Figure 13-6 opposite). This means that no matter which state the system is in when a 'channel selected' event is received, the selected channel is tuned in (but no picture is displayed and no state change occurs). This is equivalent to an identical cyclic transition on every state in the diagram, hence the name generic cyclic transition, and is simply a shorthand to remove clutter from a diagram. By convention it is useful to put these transitions stacked in boxes to the right of the diagram. Note that this has again altered the behaviour of the system: now, if the person using the television is looking at text only and presses a channel change button, the text remains but the channel changes. On some television sets this is the observed behaviour. An indication of the channel being displayed is sometimes available as a digital readout on the set or the remote control unit or by the audio output which is played through the speaker on the television.

Figure 13-6
Generic Cyclic Transition

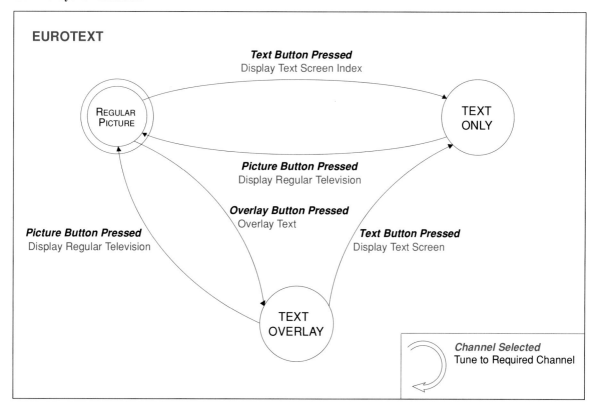

Representation

A summary of the representation of the various objects on state transition diagrams is given below for both bubble and fence layouts.

Figure 13-7
Representations

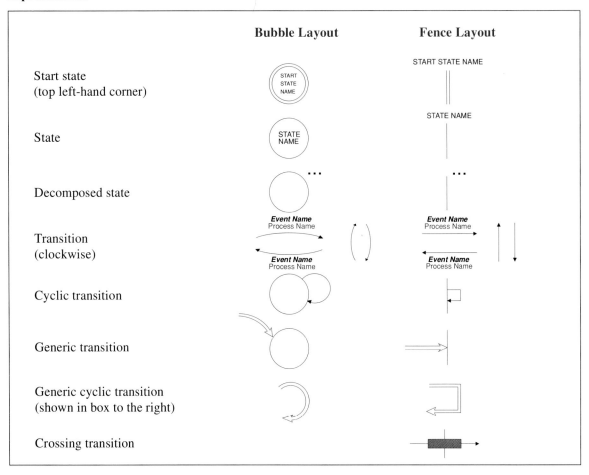

The system or sub-system name is shown as a title to the diagram, along with the date, author and any other useful information.

Having the start event in the top left-hand corner and the transitions going in a clockwise direction helps us to read the diagram easily, checking it as we go. This will tend to be the natural way to discuss the life-cycle of a system.

Syntax

The use of syntax, such as that illustrated below, is to aid communication with users, enabling them to take an active part in the modelling process. As a general guideline, try not to be too pedantic about syntax. You can add in an example part of the way through a sentence, use it to help in telling the story about how the system does or could work, and generally make it interesting whilst checking out the model. You may want to throw in a few questions such as:

"And there is no other way to do it, is there?"

"And there are no exceptions to that, are there?"

"Is that true?"

These are designed to **really** get all the errors out as early as possible.

The System

The [system-name] system starts at rest from the start-name state, is affected by the event-name-1, event-name-2, . . . , event-name-n events, and can exist in the state-name-1, state-name-2, . . . , state-name-n states.

The State

The [system-name] system will change from the current-state-name state

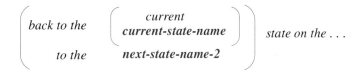

on the event-name-1 event

$$\left[\; , \; causing \; \left(\begin{array}{c} no \\ the \; \textbf{\textit{process-name-1}} \end{array} \right) \; process \; to \; occur \; \right]$$

and will also change from the current-state-name

$$\left(\begin{array}{c} back \; to \; the \\ \\ to \; the \end{array} \left(\begin{array}{c} current \\ \textbf{\textit{current-state-name}} \\ \textbf{\textit{next-state-name-2}} \end{array} \right) \right) \; state \; on \; the \; . . .$$

The Event

The event-name event triggers the [system-name] system to change from the state-name-1 state

$$\left\{ \begin{array}{l} \textit{back to the same} \\ \textit{to the state-name-2} \end{array} \right\} \textit{state,}$$

$$\textit{causing} \left\{ \begin{array}{l} \textit{no} \\ \textit{the process-name-1} \end{array} \right\} \textit{process to occur}$$

or triggers a change from the state-name-n state

$$\left\{ \begin{array}{l} \textit{back to the same} \\ \textit{to the state-name-n+1} \end{array} \right\} \textit{state, causing} \ldots$$

The Process

The process-name process is

$$\left\{ \begin{array}{l} \textit{invoked} \\ \textit{caused} \end{array} \right\} \textit{by the event-name-1 event, that changes}$$

the [system-name] system from the state-name-1 state

$$\left\{ \begin{array}{l} \textit{back to the same} \\ \textit{to the state-name-2} \end{array} \right\} \textit{state,}$$

$$\textit{and is also} \left\{ \begin{array}{l} \textit{invoked} \\ \textit{caused} \end{array} \right\} \textit{by the event-name-n event, that changes} \ldots$$

Generic Transition

Whenever an event-name event occurs [, irrespective of the state of the system,] the [system-name] system will change to the state-name state

$$\left[\textit{, causing} \left\{ \begin{array}{l} \textit{no} \\ \textit{the process-name} \end{array} \right\} \textit{process to occur} \right]$$

Generic Cyclic Transition	*Whenever an **event-name** event occurs [, irrespective of the state of the system,] the system will remain in its current state*

$$\left[\ , having\ caused\ \left(\begin{array}{c} no \\ the\ \textbf{process-name} \end{array}\right)\ process\ to\ occur\ \right]$$

Decomposed State	For any decomposed state you may choose to add to the syntax the phrase:

which is decomposed into more detail.

For lower-level states, you may add the phrase:

*which is part of the **parent-state** state.*

Inverted Syntax

The inverted syntax is used to tease out possible errors or omissions, once more in English, to assure that whenever possible errors are corrected at this early stage. The presenter of a diagram should use this approach when he or she is unsure about some detail, wants absolute confirmation, and as a random cross-check from time to time. The use of this format for EVERYTHING would be excessive. You should, however, be able to use it, starting from any object on the diagram.

The System	*The [system-name] system can only ever be affected by the **event-name-1**, **event-name-2**, . . . , and **event-name-n** events, is that true? There are no other events?*

*The [system-name] system can only ever exist in the **state-name-1**, **state-name-2**, . . . , **state-name-n** states, is that true? There are no other states of this system?*

Note: this is a more useful approach than the normal syntax for the system as a whole. Its use tends to help find missing events and states quickly.

The State

$$\left(\begin{array}{c} The\ [system\text{-}name]\ system\ can\ only \\ It\ is\ only\ possible\ to \end{array}\right)\qquad \left(\begin{array}{c} enter \\ leave \end{array}\right)$$

*the **state-name** state following an **event-name-1** [after being in the **state-name-1** state], **event-name-2**, . . . or **event-name-n** event, is that true?*

[Or are there other events that could directly cause the system to

$$\left(\begin{array}{c} enter \\ leave \end{array}\right)\ this\ state?]$$

Notice that the same general form of inverted syntax shown above can be used to check transitions into and out of a state by reference to their triggering events. Optionally you can add the state(s) that the system could have been in when the event occurred.

The Event

Use the normal syntax, but replace the word 'triggers' with 'can only ever trigger'. You may also add a final question:

There are no other state changes anywhere that are caused by this event, are there?

The Process

Similarly replace the word 'is' in the normal syntax for process with the phrase 'is only ever', and add a final sentence:

There is no other way this process can be invoked, is there?

The Transition

*Did you know that you can only get to the **state-name-1** state from the **state-name-2, state-name-3, . . . , state-name-n** states? And that it is impossible to get to this state from the **state-name-q** state?*

*Did you realise that once you have left the **state-name** state, you cannot get back to it?*

These are useful when you believe that what you have been told is wrong.

Quality Matrix

As was mentioned in the last chapter, constructing a quality matrix is a good general quality check. The following section describes the procedure. A word of warning though: this can be a lengthy process if done by hand, so quality checks of this detail are rarely performed manually. This is one of the areas where automated support for such techniques is invaluable.

**Figure 13-8
State Diagram**

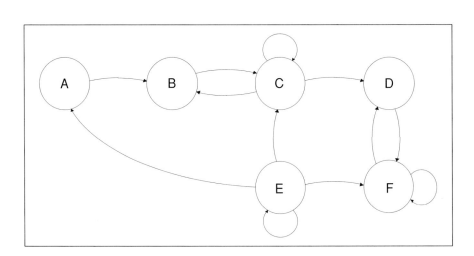

A matrix of state against state is created from the information on the diagram ('from' states along the top, 'to' states down the side). A number one in a cell will mean there is a direct transition from the 'from' state to the 'to' state – you can get there in a single transition. A number two will mean that two transitions are needed to get from the 'from' state to the 'to' state, so there is an intervening state. And so on . . . .

Figure 13-9 is a first-level matrix showing the direct transitions from one state to another. To perform the check we will repeatedly add this matrix to itself (using standard matrix addition). This will tell us the number of transitions needed to get from any one state to any other state, which can be very useful to check if it is indeed possible to get from one state to another indirectly and also to give some guidance on likely performance issues. If it takes a hundred and fifty-three state changes to perform a regular operation, the system designer should suspect a design fault.

Figure 13-9
State/State Matrix Showing only Direct Transitions

To \ From	A	B	C	D	E	F	Total transitions into this state
A					1		1
B	1		1				2
C		1	1		1		3
D			1			1	2
E					1		1
F				1	1	1	3
Total transitions leaving this state	1	1	3	1	4	2	12 in total

Pass 1

Start with column A and go down it until you find a cell with a **one** in it. Row B is the first one we find, which means we can get from state A to state B direct. Now treat state B as the 'from' state and work down column B to find the first cell with **any number** in it – in this case, a one at row C. Add the numbers together and write the total in the relevant row for column A – row C in this case. (Admittedly, our initial matrix only contains ones, but the same procedure applies to any matrix.)

In general terms, for the first pass take each column of the matrix in turn (the 'from' states) and trace down until you find a 'to' state reached by a single transition, shown by a one in the cell. Now treat the state on that row as the 'from' state, go to the appropriate column and trace down looking for any number. Add the number from the first cell to the number you have just found, and write it in the relevant row for the original column being checked. Repeat this for each 'from' state (i.e. a complete pass through the matrix). The example now looks like Figure 13-10.

Figure 13-10
State/State Matrix after First Pass

To \ From	A	B	C	D	E	F
A					1	
B	1	2	1		2	
C	2	1	1		1	
D		2	1	2	2	1
E					1	
F			2	1	1	1

Pass 2

Start a fresh pass using the procedure as before, but look for the number **two** in the initial column search. Continue this procedure, looking for threes, then fours, and so on, in the initial column for all entries in the matrix, until no new numbers result from a pass.

Figure 13-11
State/State Matrix – Completed Cross-check

To \ From	A	B	C	D	E	F
A					1	
B	1	2	1		2	
C	2	1	1		1	
D	3	2	1	2	2	1
E					1	
F	4	3	2	1	1	1

These entries show the **minimum** number of transitions it would take to get from any 'from' state to any 'to' state. Interesting points to note are:

- Blank or sparsely filled rows – a blank row (or one with an entry only in its own column) is an unreachable state, such as E in our case.

- Blank or sparse columns – a blank column (or one with only an entry in its own row) is a state which, once reached, cannot be left.

- Collections of sparse columns – where the only way out is to a state that also has a sparse column. These are traps, for example D and F in our case.

Figure 13-12
Unreachable States

To \ From	A	B	C	D	E	F
A					1	
B	1	2	1		2	
C	2	1	1		1	
D	3	2	1	2	2	1
E					1	
F	4	3	2	1	1	1

Notice that very detailed quality checks are difficult to do (especially finding traps with large numbers of states in) and are often possible only with computer assistance.

More About Events

Timing Details

One strong feature of the state diagramming technique is the opportunity to specify the required timing characteristics of a system. So far, we have concerned ourselves with the simple examples of a television and a central locking system. Now let us consider a third and final example, including all the concepts introduced so far, and use this as a means of specifying the time-dependent constraints on a system.

Timing constraints fall into two categories: how long a system should remain in a state with no activity (i.e. processing when no external events are being received) and how quickly a transition should complete to ensure acceptable behaviour of the system. The first of these categories is normally dealt with by the introduction of a special 'timer event'; an event generated by the system itself to 'remind' it that it has been idle for too long. This has the advantage of being treated like any other event, and it can be adapted or tuned once the system has been built to occur after a suitable period; for example, a fast timeout, in a situation such as controlling a valve on an oil refinery, or a slow timeout, such as turning the display of a calculator off to save battery power. (An example of a timeout event is included in the Fuel Transfer example later in this chapter.) The maximum tolerance on a transition forms a clear goal for the detailed design of a process in terms of how long the process can afford to take.

Event Queues

What happens if an event occurs and our system is already in the process of making a transition? That is, it is not in a recognizable state and therefore cannot deal with the event. In theory, an event is instantaneous; but, in practice, it may last for a finite period of time, or at least the evidence of the event can be detected for a period of time afterwards. There are two ways to view this situation. The first is from a computer-world aspect (mentioned in the last chapter), born in the days when computers were primitive and the entire computing task was carried out by a single processing unit (often called the Central Processing Unit or CPU for this reason). In such circumstances, if an event occurs whilst the CPU is occupied effecting a transition between states and there is no way for the event to be 'remembered', then the event is lost forever. This is undesirable because it leads to behaviour that is dependent on the timing of events rather than the sequencing of events: if you do things faster, something different happens! To deal with this situation, the computer industry first built some fast-switching electronics, so that an event could be detected and the relevant process invoked quickly enough to diminish the likelihood of another event occurring before the first had been dealt with. And secondly, it introduced some purpose-built circuitry to 'catch' events and store them in a queue, passing them on to the processing unit on request. In this way, the limit is on the number of events that can be queued, not the timing of the events. The system limits are then a function of the rate at which events occur and the rate at which they can be dispatched and dealt with (yielding the likely length of the queue, the likelihood of the system being unable to cope, etc.).

In more recent times, however, (and in the 'real world' of realtime and non-computerized systems) more than one processing unit is available to work in parallel. Processing units include machines, people, electronic circuits and computers; anything, in fact, that is capable of implementing a process. This means that events coming into a system can be dispatched more rapidly: while one processor is dealing with one event, another processor can be dealing with a second, providing the opportunity for simultaneous event handling (i.e. true concurrent processing). This gives us a higher capacity and, at the same time, a more complex problem of system design and specification. Because of this more accurate view of the real world having many, concurrent, processing units, we choose to model processes and the dependencies between them using dependency diagrams, which show what **could** happen – each process could be going on in parallel to all the others. We then use this description of what **could** happen (if we had enough processing units) to decide which things **will** happen in parallel, based on the number of processing units we actually do have, or can afford.

State transition diagrams can be used to good effect here by drawing a diagram for each processor that will be used to implement a system, and by defining a protocol through which the processors will co-operate and synchronize. One frequently used way of documenting such synchronization is to introduce a controller sub-system, which is often implemented as the sole means of ensuring proper system behaviour. This acts as a type of watchdog process whose task is to co-ordinate co-operating processes and to clean up those which are unable to cope on their own any more – usually owing to some disaster, such as a design flaw. An analogy might be a controller in a taxi-cab company who receives a continuous stream of requests for journeys and allocates them to a varying number of taxi-cabs, subject to availability and other criteria.

In a state transition diagram representing the design of a system or sub-system that will work in conjunction (and concurrently) with other systems or sub-systems, each of which has its own state transition diagram, some of the processes invoked during a transition will send events to other systems or sub-systems. For example, if we designed an autopilot (one sub-system) and a pressure sensor (another sub-system) to work in an aircraft, then one of the transitions in the autopilot may send a request for a pressure reading to the pressure sensor. This request is an event that triggers a transition in the pressure sensor, which takes a reading and sends the result back to the autopilot. The result is an event that causes a transition in the autopilot, and so on. Note that the autopilot can either wait for the response from the pressure sensor or carry on doing something else in the meantime. In this way, very sophisticated exchanges between systems (communications protocols to give them a technical term) can be documented concisely and accurately.

Figure 13-13
Co-operating Systems

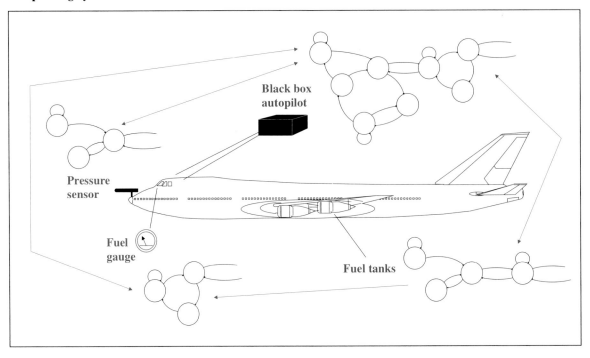

A Complex Example

You might like to think about the problems of modelling a more complex system than a television or a car locking system. Here are a few suggestions:

- weather forecasting
- a bit-mapped user interface
- radar monitoring
- a bar-code reader at a supermarket checkout
- a robot on an assembly line
- signal control on a railway
- a monitor in an intensive care unit
- a photocopier
- a telephone exchange.

One cold and windy autumn day we visited a busy airport to investigate the realtime system for refuelling aeroplanes.

You might have thought that fuelling an aeroplane would be a fairly straightforward activity. In fact, when you look at the rate at which aeroplanes arrive at and depart from busy airports like London Heathrow, you realize that behind the scenes these events have to be handled in quite a sophisticated manner.

The real business problem is how to minimize the number of fuel tankers and personnel involved in catering for a peak number of aeroplanes landing and taking off during both normal and abnormal working days. The solution is a series of systems joined together to provide a complete mechanism for handling any aeroplane as it lands, its refuelling, and making it ready for subsequent take-off. We shall be looking in detail at the fuel transfer system that applies to the refuelling tankers, but before that let us have a look at the overall system.

At some central fuel-control point, information is received on a realtime basis to tell us about the imminent arrival of aeroplanes at the airport. Other information recorded includes changes to the aircraft stand or gate, changes of aircraft for specific flights, unscheduled flights and special requirements for additional fuel or even removing the fuel from an aeroplane.

This information is used to help determine which aircraft should be refuelled and in what sequence. The system, or in many cases the controller, may well then allocate a particular tanker to carry out the refuelling process. In the system being modelled, the process to initiate sending a tanker to refuel an aeroplane is opened by the production of a smart card; this identifies the aeroplane, the flight stand or gate, the departure time, the name of the airline and the fuel supplier, and other necessary details to enable the operator to carry out the fuelling process.

At a later time in the process the tanker may be asked to go and refuel a second or subsequent aircraft, so the smart card is also pre-loaded with similar information for other aircraft, which may subsequently be refuelled by the same tanker. This smart card is then taken by the tanker operator to the tanker and used to help control an onboard system in the tanker cab, which will monitor the amount of fuel dispensed to any aircraft, and subsequently print out a card that will be the basis for invoicing the airline. Details held in the card will also be used afterwards for management information purposes.

We watched a tanker operator during this task. He walked out to the tank and carried out some safety checks. He then logged in to the onboard computer by recording his clock card and inserting the smart card. This smart card is actually a small computer loaded onto a credit-card-sized device; it down loads information about an aircraft to be refuelled onto the onboard computer. It will also down load information about any other aircraft that may be refuelled. The operator immediately checked the details because from any time onwards any instructions may be varied by radio telephone; for example, the aeroplane may have been moved to another stand, or the particular aircraft in question identified by its registration number may be replaced by another aircraft. Once he had confirmed this information and he knew which stand to go to, he drove out to the stand and made a final check. As it was the correct aeroplane he started the fuelling process, which automatically recorded the fuel meter value at the beginning of the pumping process. When refuelling was complete it recorded the final meter value, and in essence all that is required is to print out the details of the aircraft, stand, airline, fuel supplier and the amount of fuel supplied (the basis of the invoice).

Figure 13-14
A Fuel Tanker

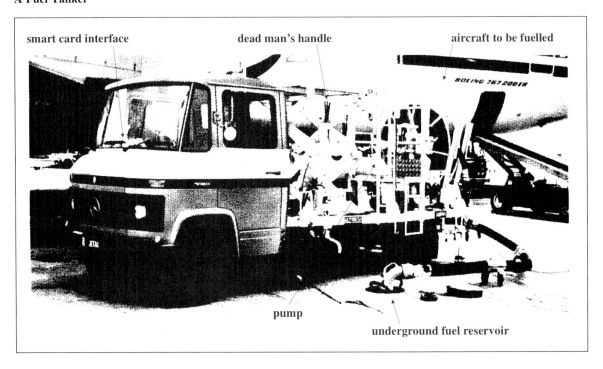

Now in reality this process is actually far more complex than this suggests, as the onboard computer needs to cater for many possible events. These include checking for the release of a 'dead man's handle'. This is similar to the safety device on a locomotive where releasing the handle will automatically cause the locomotive to halt. In the refuelling system releasing the handle will automatically stop the fuel flow. It also needs to cater for exceptional circumstances, such as the aircraft's fuel tanks becoming full before the anticipated volume of fuel has been discharged.

The following diagram shows the onboard system in reasonable detail. Some of the states would need to be decomposed to allow levels of further detail prior to generating this particular system.

Figure 13-15
The Fuel Flow Transfer System

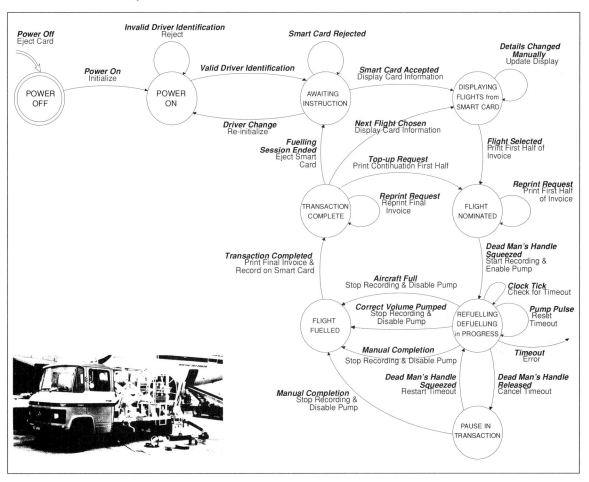

At the conclusion of this process the smart card is updated, and it and the printed card are taken back to the control centre to update the central records, initiate the invoicing process and otherwise complete the transaction.

At any time, prior to returning to the controller, the tanker operator may also be asked to go and refuel another aircraft, which then goes through the same process. The model also caters for other possibilities; for example, after a certain volume of fuel has been loaded into an aeroplane the pilot asks for an additional amount of fuel as a top-up, maybe because the latest weather report indicates a strong head wind.

Notice that in this example we have a generic transition in the top left-hand corner. This is a safety factor that can be checked easily by our users, by letting them read the syntax:

> *Whenever a **power off** event occurs, irrespective of the state of the system, the **fuel flow transfer** system will change to the **power off** state, causing the **eject card** process to occur.*

As you can see, this is quite a sophisticated process, involving the integration of several separate systems. These systems include the air traffic control system, the airline-specific systems (which know about their particular aircraft arrivals and departures), knowledge of the movement of tankers and aircraft around the airport, and manual intervention from many sources. And on board the tanker there is a computerized control system, which is co-ordinating the pumping and metering system on the tanker. Even here the complexities can get even greater to cater for some modern aeroplanes that are refuelled on both wings simultaneously and for different types of tanker, some of which hold their own fuel whilst others receive fuel directly from huge tanks underneath the runway apron.

Have a look at the model and see if you can find any circumstances in an emergency situation which cannot be catered for in a safe manner by this state transition diagram.

Some Further Questions

This model begs a number of questions. See if you can find the relevant part of the model that raised each question.

> *"Is it possible to receive a manual completion whilst actually refuelling? If the dead man's handle is on the end of the hose, can the operator physically reach the manual completion button?"*

> *"Is it possible to end up with the smart card stuck inside the machine?"*

> *"What happens if the operator accidentally selects the wrong flight or refuels the wrong aircraft? What would have to be done to correct it?"*

As a very useful cross-check, for each transition on a state diagram ask yourself:

"How can the system recover gracefully and in an acceptable way if the event that raised the transition was generated incorrectly?"

Complexity

A final word on complexity: when dealing with very large state transition diagrams it is worthwhile reducing complexity by finding commonality and using other generic techniques. The most useful things to identify are those generic transitions which once found will often replace many individual transitions. Look for recursive transitions that trigger the same process – often the events that cause them are the same, but with slightly different names.

In English it is often helpful to use expressions such as:

'the system will also change to the . . .'
'whenever all but . . . occurs . . .'
'whenever *this or that set* of things occurs then . . .' or
'once more causing the . . .'

You might like to collect a list of events into a group or set, give it a name and then use it in such sentences. A good example would be a set of events that fall into the category of 'exceptions', which on the fuel-flow example include 'invalid driver identification', 'dead man's handle released' and 'timeout'.

Your objective is to produce a rigorous, complete and consistent state transition diagram that accurately reflects the need, and is itself as simple and elegant as possible. Good elegant designs are invariably more generic, easier to implement and much simpler to maintain.

Just before we finish with this example let us look at the Fuel Flow Transfer system purely from one of the states to see what the syntax gives us. We will use the 'refuelling/defuelling in progress' state after the event 'dead man's handle squeezed' as this is the essence of the system. In fact we will limit this to the transitions to the 'flight fuelled' state – you will soon see why.

The dead man's handle squeezed event triggers the fuel flow transfer system to change from the flight nominated state to the refuelling/defuelling in progress state, causing the start recording and enable pump process to occur.

(The system would now be pumping fuel.)

*The system will change from the **refuelling/defuelling in progress** state to the **flight fuelled** state on the **aircraft full** event, causing the **stop recording and disable pump** process to occur. The system will also change from the current state to the **flight fuelled** state whenever the **correct volume pumped** event occurs, once more causing the **stop recording and disable pump** process. And finally the system will also change to this state whenever the **manual completion** event occurs, once more causing the **stop recording and disable pump** process.*

*The system will change from the current state to the **pause in transaction** state on the **dead man's handle** event, causing the **cancel timeout** process. And whenever a **power off** event occurs, irrespective of the state of the system, the system will change to the **power off** state, causing the **eject card** process to occur.*

As you can see this is by no means the complete story, even from the viewpoint of this one state, but the diagram contains a wealth of rigorous information. You may have heard the expression 'a picture speaks a thousand words'; this example confirms our notion that 'a diagram can speak ten thousand words – rigorously'.

Summary

As it deals more closely with the complex concurrent activities of the real world, realtime modelling requires a more sophisticated approach to the modelling exercise than has been met previously. State transition diagrams give us the ability to model a system from the viewpoint of the system being in a given state, going through a transition to another state following an event, and possibly carrying out some consequential process. They also allow us to model interrelated realtime sub-sytems and handle queues and concurrent processes, and are particularly appropriate for process control systems and interactive graphical user interfaces.

14

PHYSICAL SYSTEM DESIGN

Introduction

Traditionally this is the part that computer technicians enjoy most, the physical design at the program/procedure level ☐ . Having laboured hard to figure out the requirements, now we can get on with the real job – playing with our adult toys! In reality this attitude is what has caused the rejection of so many systems built in the past and given the information technology industry a bad name. And the design may well encompass manual and other implementation vehicles, not just computers.

So this final step in designing a system is to decide precisely how each process is to be constructed, using the chosen computer language, electronic device, machine or other implementation vehicle. If a specific computer programming language has been chosen, then the structure required to carry out the processing must be designed; if the process is to be implemented manually, then the procedure to be followed must be designed; if an electronic solution has been chosen, then the circuits and hardware devices must be designed; and so on. The level of design applicable before construction can be carried out is dependent on many factors, such as the technology being used, the skill of the people doing the construction and the complexity of the process. In some cases this physical design is not a separate step, but can be done at the same time as the construction of a computer program, manual procedure or hardware circuit. In the computer industry, the very existence of higher levels of abstraction in programming languages is intended to remove this separate step for a progressively larger proportion of processes, hopefully giving higher degrees of productivity and quality. In almost all systems, however, there will be some processes that need a physical design step carried out and reviewed with more care, usually because the cost of error in those cases is high. For instance, in the control software for monitoring an intensive care unit in a hospital the cost of error could be a human life.

In this chapter we look at the qualities desirable in the implementation of a process (e.g. efficiency, flexibility and robustness) and specific techniques for designing usable systems, including presentation design for interactive computer applications and paper forms, and structure charts for computer programs. We also investigate how to use the logical design documentation (dataflow diagrams and state transition diagrams) as the basis for a design.

Choosing the Right Approach

A number of techniques for the physical design of processes in a system are considered in a later section. It is unlikely (although not impossible) that the level of detail we show here is going to be applicable to **every** process; much will depend upon the type of development being undertaken. Usually, only a few processes are subjected to this treatment in any formal way. We strongly recommend that you record your design decisions as you go. However, if you decide not to, we hope that you will use some of the techniques presented here and find them useful.

Factors such as cost and time are often the ones that prevent a formal physical design phase on a whole system – this is a good thing in general, as **whole** systems rarely need such formality. The question then remains, *"Which processes, if any, require this level of formality in their design?"* To help answer this, let us first look at what we are trying to achieve with a physical design and then look at the alternative approaches before examining some techniques in detail.

Aims of Physical System Design

Business Relevance

Physical design is the final activity to be carried out before a system or application system is built and delivered. It is the final point at which we can ensure that the system we are delivering is the best one for the business we are trying to support, given the constraints imposed. Functionally, what the system does must be what the business needs. That is the whole thrust of this book: identifying, improving and now supporting the right functionality for the business. It is also important to retain the terms used in the **business** for menu options, titles, field prompts on screens and paper forms, help and error messages, and so on. That way the users (or operators) of a process are instantly familiar with what is going on and do not have to translate strange terms used by system designers!

Timeliness

Businesses are experiencing such a rate of change that it is becoming essential to develop and deliver systems in increasingly short timescales. Better tools, techniques and attitudes are making this possible, but we must still make an effort to **ensure that it is the right thing that is delivered, in an acceptable timescale.** In more and more cases, it is vital to deliver the system in a given time window, before the business experiences another substantial change in direction, thereby changing the system needs again.

Flexibility

Because it is difficult, or impossible, to produce a system that is one hundred percent right and because things will **always** change in the business and systems that support it, we need to strive for flexibility in what we design. As we shall see later, it is often cheaper and quicker to develop a process with flexibility built in right from the outset.

Flexibility can be considered as having two aspects:

- the ability to carry on providing the same functionality when the environment (such as types of computer hardware or software and external procedures) changes and, also
- the ability of a system to adapt to changing business requirements, and changes in legislation or organization, with minimal redevelopment.

Our ability to deliver a flexible sytem that can cater for a change in the business, a change in technology, or some other factor, can be measured by the investment required to cope with that change. Our aim when designing a system should be to minimize the cost and elapsed time of adapting to such changes. Later in this chapter we look at some tips for designing generic and reusable computer software.

Efficiency

Any system uses resources and the decisions made during the physical design of a process will affect how much (and how well) these resources are used. If the process is a paper implementation, the resources required to use the process will be paper for the forms, ink for the pens to fill them out, and the time of people using them. By changing the layout of a form we might be able to use the same form for more than one process, thus saving on stationery costs. Careful planning of the form might prevent expensive mistakes being made, thus improving the efficiency of the person filling out the forms. When communication experts redesigned a set of forms for an insurance company they were able to reduce the number from fourteen to two and the error rate dropped from one hundred percent (i.e. every form contained at least one error) to fifteen percent. In the computer world, resources such as the disk space and amount of computer processing time required by a process are the resources to be used (and saved) by good physical design.

Usability

An essential quality of any system is that it be usable. The people that interact with and operate the system must find it easy (and preferably motivating) to do so. This is why the relevance to the business is so important; few people use a system simply because it is fun! They use it because it helps them achieve what they are trying to do and are paid for. Assuming the process is doing the right thing, usability is then a measure of how easily the user interacts with it to make it work. Our aim during the physical design of a system is to make sure that each process is usable by the person who operates it (does the operator feel comfortable with it?) and, ideally, is something that is motivating (and fun) to use as well.

This high usability objective can be difficult to achieve as there are differences of approach between different users, alternative user interfaces on different equipment and existing systems to consider. Really high usability systems often cost more to produce initially, although invariably they give a quick payback later.

Other Qualities

Each process you design is an expression of your own individual capability, so the following checklist can be used as a personal challenge. What level of each of the following characteristics do you want in the process you are designing?:

- maintainability (ease of change)
- operability (ease of set-up and use)
- inter-operability (ability to work with other systems)
- integrity (protection against corruption)
- security (protection against unauthorized access)
- resilience and robustness (protection against failure)
- availability (when the process can be used)
- back-up/recovery (the level of resilience if failure does occur).

You may find it useful to examine your design several times, with each of these aspects in mind.

Summary of Objectives

In a system, we are aiming to design processes that are:

- relevant to the business they support
- delivered in a timely fashion
- flexible to changes in technology and the business
- efficient in their use of resources
- usable by the person that operates them
- secure, robust and available to an acceptable level
- based on good practice and relevant standards
- and provide a return on investment and a protection of that investment.

This activity is just part of an iterative design stage that you may be going through. The whole activity is covered in far more detail in the *CASE*Method: Tasks and Deliverables* book in this series, from which the following diagram has been taken to illustrate the iterative and interrelated nature of the design process.

**Figure 14-1
Interdependent
Design Aspects**

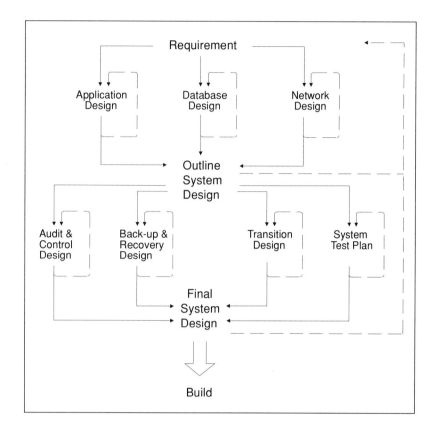

So Where Should We Focus our Efforts?

Our design time will need to be carefully deployed if we are to achieve the best results in terms of these objectives. Every development will be different in how the split of design time is approached. For example, a mission-critical system to control a nuclear reactor might demand very high levels of integrity and robustness and warrant a careful, formal physical design stage (which must also consider a later decommissioning exercise), whereas a paper system to record business expenses for a small consulting company might bypass all formal recording of a physical design in order to deliver something that can be used immediately. Where the system is not at one of these extremes, a choice must be made – which processes should we focus our attention on?

In earlier chapters covering function logic, logical system design and real-time modelling, we referred to critical processes and defined them in a number of ways. We must now consider the efficiency of use of resources that might make a process critical for physical design. Our approach should be to spend eighty percent of our time on the twenty percent of a system that yields the highest value to the business. The remaining eighty percent of the system can be dealt with by an exercise to establish standards and guidelines for certain types of development. The vendors of computer software equipment will usually have standards developed by themselves, or their clients, which are generally available (or for sale) to use as the basis for standards within an organization. For manual systems, literature in the field of ergonomics contains many indicators that can be used to develop a standard or guideline for the development of paper forms, manual procedures, and so on.

Do not lose sight of the real point of any system development. It is to get a job of work done and the system must help in this aim.

Back to Atlantis

To look at how to address the physical design activity using some of the techniques we explored in previous chapters, we will return to Atlantis Island Flights and the example of allocating a seat to a passenger. Let us consider two possible implementations of this – an interactive computer screen and a manual procedure. We will now examine the detailed physical design of the seat allocation process for a computerized process.

Decomposition

Decomposition is probably the most universally applicable technique in the history of design! Almost anything can be broken down into more detail, the components treated individually, and quality checks for completeness and consistency applied.

The Computer Application

Let us look at three different types of language for implementing an interactive computer application to allocate seats. The most important thing this program does is to match an existing seat, which must be free, to a known passenger. (There are many other aspects to making an application of this sort usable; we will consider those later.) Initially, let us just concern ourselves with getting the job done.

With a typical programming language, such`as COBOL, Fortran or 'C', the language imposes some constraints on what can be done. Typically, we write blocks of code that must be executed in sequence, sometimes only when a certain condition applies and sometimes repetitively. These three constructs – sequence, choice and repetition – are the basis of such languages. The code blocks represent the nodes in a decomposition and we might start our design thus:

Figure 14-2
A Structure Chart

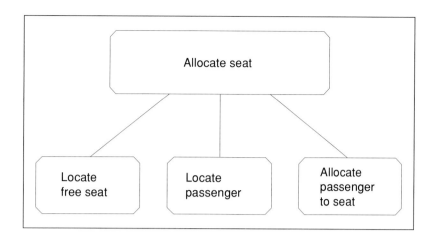

This is sometimes called a structure chart, a decomposition of the code within a computerized process. The decomposition is shown by the lines, which are then read from left to right to give the sequence. The concept of choice (either one thing or another) is shown as a diamond, optionally supplemented by a definition of the relevant condition.

Figure 14-3
A Structure Chart with Choice

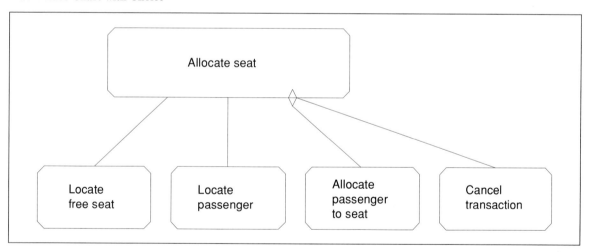

This means that either the seat has to be allocated or the transaction cancelled. Notice that we are starting to address usability here by catering for the fact that something may go wrong and the transaction may need to be cancelled to make the application more tolerant of mistakes. Putting this into a wider context, we need to allow for components that will be repeated.

Figure 14-5
Wider Context of Structure Chart

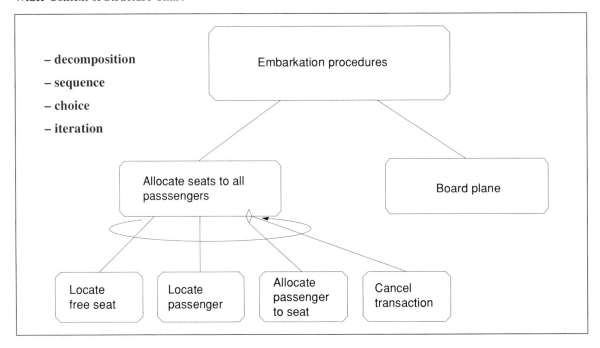

– decomposition

– sequence

– choice

– iteration

Embarkation procedures

Allocate seats to all passsengers

Board plane

Locate free seat

Locate passenger

Allocate passenger to seat

Cancel transaction

The arrow around the decomposition legs indicates that the components at the other end of the legs are to be done repetitively. If this were to be translated now into two different programming languages, we would subsequently end up with:

Figure 14-4
In COBOL

```
    :
    :
EMBARK.

ALLOCATE.
   IF PASSENGERS_BOOKED NOT GREATER THAN SEATS_ALLOCATED
   THEN GOTO BOARD.
   PERFORM FIND_FREE_SEAT.
   PERFORM LOCATE_NEXT_PASSENGER.
   PERFORM ASK_IF_OK.
   IF TRANSACTION_OK
   THEN PERFORM COMPLETE_TRANSACTION
      ADD 1 TO SEATS_ALLOCATED
   ELSE PERFORM CANCEL_TRANSACTION.
   GOTO ALLOCATE.

BOARD.
    :
    :
```

Figure 14-6
In 'C'

```
:
:
while (PassengersBooked > SeatsAllocated)
{
    LocateFreeSeat (Preference, SeatNumber);
    LocateNextPassenger (Surname, Initials, Gender);
    if (CancellationRequired)
    {
        CancelTransaction ();
    }
    else
    {
        Allocate (SeatNumber, Surname, Initials, Gender);
        SeatsAllocated++;
    }
}
BoardPlane ();
:
:
```

Notice how the 'choice' diamond has assumed the syntax of an 'if' statement and the repetition arrow has resulted in one of the language's looping structures (repeat, goto, while, perform . . . until, and so on), which, additionally, have a termination condition on them.

Block Structuring

Some languages support blocks of code that can be invoked separately and to which parameters or arguments can be passed; for example, procedures in Pascal, functions in 'C' and paragraphs in COBOL. These parameters are sometimes shown on the decomposition lines.

Figure 14-7
Block Structuring

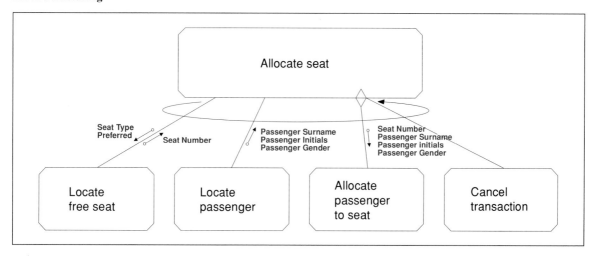

The arrows show whether the data (parameter) is passed into the lower code block (pointing downwards) or returned by the lower code block (pointing upwards). The combinations shown in Figure 14-8 illustrate some of the possible patterns using a structure chart.

Figure 14-8
Some Possible Patterns

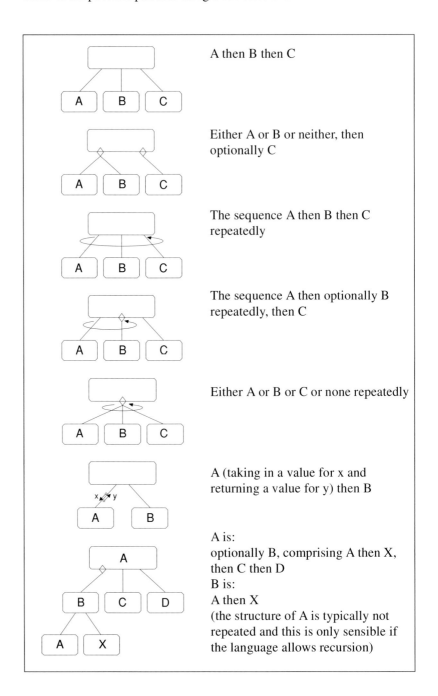

A then B then C

Either A or B or neither, then optionally C

The sequence A then B then C repeatedly

The sequence A then optionally B repeatedly, then C

Either A or B or C or none repeatedly

A (taking in a value for x and returning a value for y) then B

A is:
optionally B, comprising A then X, then C then D
B is:
A then X
(the structure of A is typically not repeated and this is only sensible if the language allows recursion)

Designing User Interfaces

The interaction between the user of a program and the program itself (often called the user interface or the man/machine interface for computer applications) is a key aspect to the physical design of an interactive computer program. The subject is wide and still in its infancy and we can only begin to scratch the surface here. For our example, let us take four principles of good user interface design and show how they might be handled.

The principles are:

- minimize interaction
- offer the ability to cancel an operation
- offer sensible guidance
- handle errors gracefully.

Minimizing Interaction

In some respects, the ideal system would be one that required no interaction whatsoever: it did it all for you. We would then truly be a race of leisure, with systems doing everything for us except enjoying ourselves! (But would we?) Since this is thankfully some way from reality, we will assume that there will be a need for some interaction between our process and its user. However, we would like to reduce the amount of work the operator of the process needs to do in order to carry out the business function.

Let us assume the user (operator of the process) is an airline official, who already has the information required to allocate a seat to a passenger*:

- the identity of the seat
- the identity of the passenger.

How could we tell the system which seat was to be allocated? We could:

a) Type in the identification (e.g. the flight number and departure time plus the seat number).

b) Offer a list of flights, get the user to choose one, and then type in the seat number (since the flight partly identifies a seat).

c) Offer a list of flights, get the user to choose one, and then offer a list of seats and get the user to choose the one to be allocated.

Option a is reasonably effective for a check-in operator who knows the flight details, can type well, and is dealing with different flights all the time. However, if we were to develop a computer screen such as the one in Figure 14-9, it would soon become obvious to an operator at the

---

*   We would know this from dataflow diagrams of the logical system design or possibly from the data dependencies or data usages of the business functions this process is implementing.

departure desk, where most of the allocations are done, that the flight details would be the same for each seat – lots of data entry that is repetitive and identical.

Figure 14-9
A Simple Seat
Allocation Screen

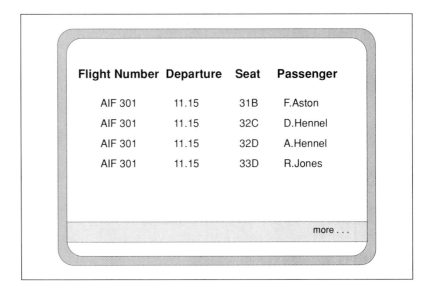

Flight Number	Departure	Seat	Passenger
AIF 301	11.15	31B	F.Aston
AIF 301	11.15	32C	D.Hennel
AIF 301	11.15	32D	A.Hennel
AIF 301	11.15	33D	R.Jones

more . . .

A better design for the operator would provide a place where the flight details could be entered once and then only the seat allocations for that flight would be entered repetitively.

Figure 14-10
Seating Allocation

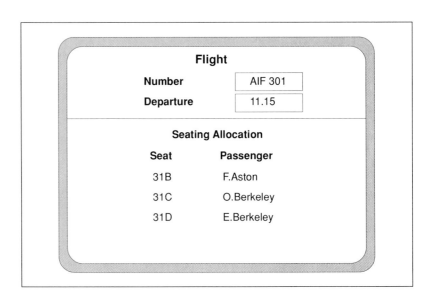

Flight

Number	AIF 301
Departure	11.15

Seating Allocation

Seat	Passenger
31B	F.Aston
31C	O.Berkeley
31D	E.Berkeley

This is a very common technique for reducing the interaction needed (our first principle) for achieving a result by putting repetitive information in a place where it can be entered once and thereafter act as a context for subsequent interaction. Notice again that if each flight is likely to be different for each seat allocation (as might be the case for a reservations clerk) this screen would be a **bad** design because the extra navigation required to move between the flight details area and the seating allocation area would be seen as an overhead; that is, more interaction than **necessary**. For this case, our first screen might be better. This illustrates just how important it actually is to design a process for a role or a user.

We should be able to improve our design further now because we know the seating plan of the aircraft in advance. We could, in fact, provide a list (or even an iconic representation) of the seats and ask the user to choose.

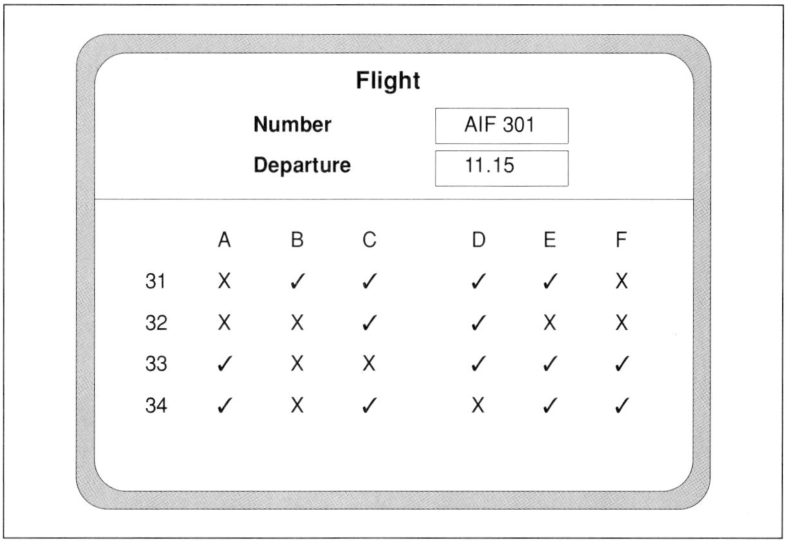

Figure 14-11
List of Seats

This way the user can now 'move' from seat to seat (by pressing some key on the keyboard, for example) until the required seat is found (marked 'x' for free) then type the name of the passenger. Of course, we probably know the passengers that are booked on the flight as well, so a list of the names of passengers on the same row and those in front and behind could be provided too.

As you can see in the next diagram, we have reduced the user interaction from typing the full seat and passenger identification for each seat allocation to simply selecting from lists.

Figure 14-12
Seating Plan

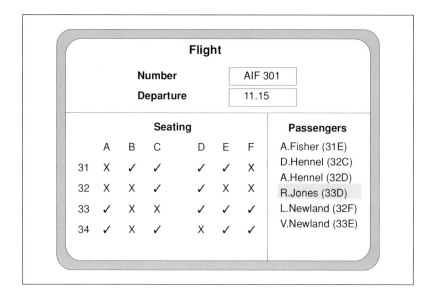

If the technology to be used for the system we are designing is a graphics terminal (quite likely, simply because it offers such a highly usable interface) then the entire operation can be carried out with two clicks of a mouse button or some other pointing device. For example, one possible design is shown in Figure 14-13 opposite.

Offering the Opportunity to Cancel an Operation

Our second principle is to offer the user the opportunity to cancel an operation. Prior to completing an operation, it should be possible to undo any changes made, no matter where a user has reached in the process, and return to a stable point that existed before the attempt to make those changes. We all make mistakes from time to time and, when we do, we need a way out without endangering the business. This is where knowledge of elementary business functions and processes becomes important. For example, assume we have designed either the graphical, or character, screen above and the user selects a seat (either by pointing and double clicking with the mouse or by placing the cursor at the seat and pressing the designated 'allocate' key). If the user discovers that the wrong seat has been selected (or a fickle passenger changes his mind), what will he do? If we provide no way out of this situation, the allocation of the selected seat will have to proceed to completion and then, presumably, be cancelled or revoked somehow before the **correct** allocation can be made. We need a 'cancel' operation – the ability for the user to signal that the allocation is not to proceed and for the screen to deselect the seat and return to where it was before.

Figure 14-13
A Graphical Design

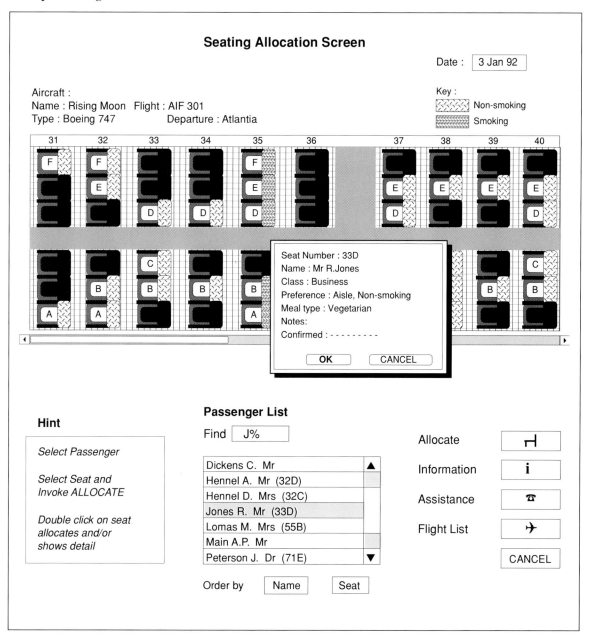

If we are still using a structure chart as our design vehicle, we might develop a new structure to cope with this optional cancellation.

Figure 14-14
Coping with Cancellation

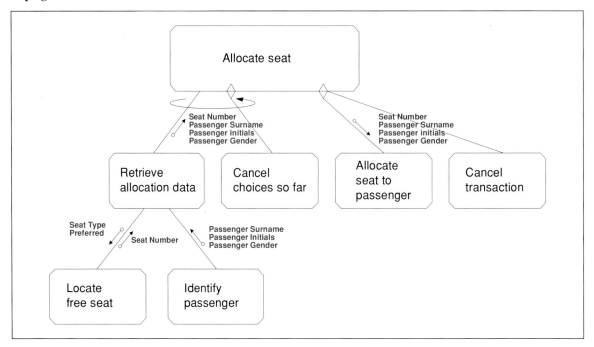

The current design leaves us with a problem: if a seat has been located but the passenger has not yet been identified, and the user wishes to cancel the transaction, cancellation cannot occur until a passenger has been identified. As a general principle, **always** offer the user the ability to cancel **any** operation at **any** point during the operation. It is simple to apply these principles if they are incorporated at the outset, but often murderous to add them in later.

Notice that in offering this possibility (see Figure 14-15) we have given the user more control over the order of the processing, which causes us to ask whether some other sequence of operation would not be better, either instead of or as an alternative to the one chosen so far. What about the user choosing the passenger first and the seat second? This might be a sensible option to allow; it rather depends on your perspective of things whether you feel that seats need passengers (the airline's perspective) or passengers need seats (the passenger's perspective). It would be simple to introduce to our screen design above; we will allow navigation to either the seat or the passenger selection portion of the screen first. But this would cause radical changes to the internal code structure on our structure chart. Now we do not know in advance the sequence of operation, so we must modify our control structure, perhaps to that shown below.

Figure 14-15
Modified Control Structure

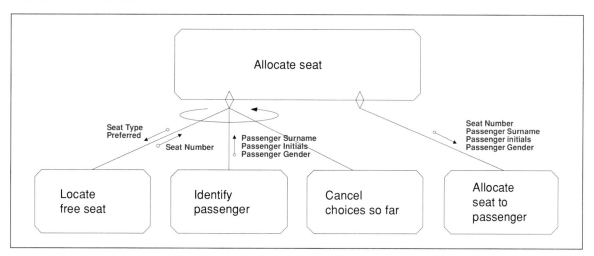

This now gives us the ability to do two things: firstly, the user can now choose seat then passenger, or passenger then seat, as required. This achieves what we set out to do with the exercise but, secondly, the new structure chart allows us to choose a seat, then choose a seat again, by two iterations of the selection block. Presumably we do not want to make the selection actually highlight **two** seats (depending on the definition of the business function), so let us change the selection to 'select a seat **in place of** any that are currently selected'. By doing this, we have an additional piece of usability added to the screen – the ability to change the current selection at any time. Now, if the user selects an incorrect seat in error he can simply select a different one (a kind of implicit cancel), reducing interaction still further.

It is interesting to note that this change in logic has not in fact changed the screen layout in Figure 14-13, but has dramatically changed the way it can be used.

Offering Sensible Guidance

We now have a forgiving screen – the user can choose the order of doing things and can cancel them if they are incorrect with very little inter-action. So we can consider adding more things to help the user.

| Defaults | Perhaps we know the preferred seat for a passenger; one of the stated aims of the airline in Chapter 2 was to: |

improve the service for regular travellers by retaining a record of their preferred seating and special requirements.

We could pre-select the 'most appropriate free seat' for the passenger, if the user chooses to select the passenger first. In this way, the interaction has been reduced to a single operation: that of identifying the passenger to the process! (We are getting close to an ideal system here, but don't panic – the human element still comes in as people often want to change their minds.)

Another illustration of the use of defaults raises an interesting topic – that of the business function that would be difficult, if not impossible, to carry out without technology to help. When a group of people such as a family travels together they usually want to sit together. In this instance, we need to find a block of free seats that are together, one for each passenger in the group. To do so might involve moving passengers with pre-assigned seats, so long as other seats that meet their requirements can be found and ideally they have not yet been allocated boarding cards. Of course, it is possible that a group may also have pre-assigned seats and could be moved to make room for another group and so on. As the plane fills up, the problem of finding acceptable free seats becomes more complex. If a manual implementation is adopted, the cut-off point at which the operator gives up trying to find adequate seats for the passengers and is forced to allocate them less than their ideal seats comes much earlier than with a computerized implementation, which can process thousands of possible options in a very short time.

The introduction of sensible defaults for processing, offering normal options, a list of allowable values for attributes, and so on, can greatly aid the usability of a program. A word of warning, however: poorly chosen defaults have precisely the opposite effect because users are continually correcting them, causing frustration and loss of time. Our structure chart now looks like Figure 14-16.

Use of Terms in Help, Hints, Titles and Prompts

Be sure to consider the user (and, more specifically, the terms that each type of user is familiar with) when designing titles, prompts, error messages, help and other visible text in a program. We have discussed the use of familiar terms in various contexts; in particular, the benefit to be gained by using clearly understood and simple language when naming functions. This is never more relevant than in the design of screens, reports, forms and other mechanisms available to users. We have probably all experienced the frustration of trying to operate a machine (e.g. a vending machine, a ticket dispenser, a video recorder) and finding that the guidance offered does not help us achieve what we are trying to do.

Figure 14-16
Structure Chart with Defaults

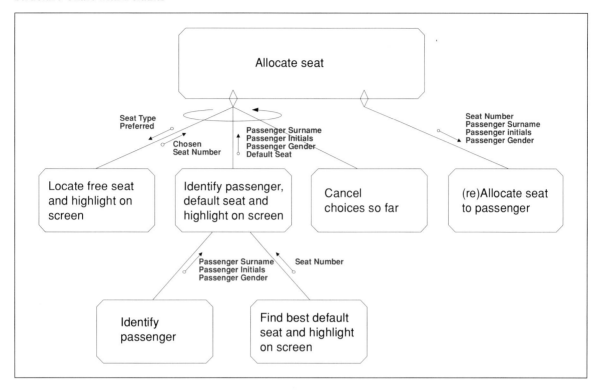

Somewhere in every mechanism there is, or should be, a route that can be taken to achieve a function; that is, it can be made to do something that is useful. The aim of clear language in help, hint, titles and prompts is to show this route and guide the user effortlessly through it. Let us take each of these areas in turn and give a few examples to illustrate the point.

Titles and Prompts

Make sure each screen, report, menu and form has a sensible title by which the user can refer to it, and make the title indicative of what the mechanism is for. For instance, our screen for allocating a seat to a passenger, or group of passengers, might be called:

Seat Allocation
Passenger (group) Allocation
Passenger Location or
Passenger Placement.

Avoid technical jargon; and use business jargon cautiously, because it does change from time to time and is frequently different, depending on the user. Where business jargon is used, make sure the appropriate term for the particular user appears. The ideal would be that a new user could tell what the mechanism is for at the first glance at the title. Much the same applies to prompts, field names, report headings, and so on (i.e. the names of areas that hold specific items of information for the user). On our seat allocation screen, we might find that the flight is expected to depart at a known date and time, so we might label an area:

Figure 14-17
Seat Allocation Screen

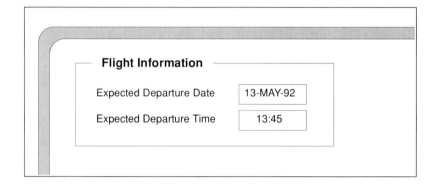

Avoid ambiguous labels such as:

Figure 14-18
Ambiguous Labels

This will just raise questions in the user's mind and give him more to remember: which date? – departure date, arrival date, today's date?

Where the same context is used for more than one item of information, these items can be grouped under a common heading to avoid repeating the common part of the prompt. For example:

Figure 14-19
Common Heading

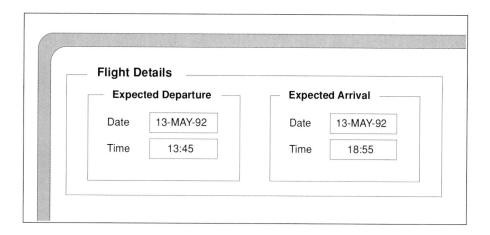

Help and Hint Guidance

Novice users, or trainees, are often in need of **help** to resolve questions they have about a mechanism or, in fact, the business function it is trying to support. For these times, a means of answering questions is an essential part of the detailed physical design of a system. The help information itself might be held in one of several forms; for example, on a computer and available online, on paper as a procedures manual, on a video or audio tape. To be of use, these will all need a sensible index and means of navigation around the information.

A hint is a short description of what the user should do next and, typically, changes every time a user does something, such as fills in a field or makes a choice from a list. When the hint changes according to what the user is doing, it is known as 'context sensitive'. Context sensitivity is about the best form of index there is: the user does not have to do anything specific to use it.

Help information is a more detailed description of what is required from the user, what the effect of an action will be and, perhaps most important, why the user is being asked to do this. Help information should form a strong link between the physical system and its purpose; that is, supporting specific business functions.

Error Handling

Error handling is an art form of its own. You may have come across a system like the apocryphal program that gave the following message:

Error 0000   Software or hardware error

We must, therefore, consider very carefully what should happen to our program if an error occurs. There are numerous things that could go wrong; we have already discussed the possibility of user-invoked errors, but there is always the possibility of a power failure or failure of the computer hardware, failure within the process itself (either a design or construction error) and, probably most common, an attempt to carry out an invalid operation. With any error, there are two key things to remember:

- do not compromise the integrity of the business
- help the user to repair the error or somehow continue, if at all possible.

The first returns us to the concept of an elementary function or process. If a seat has been selected but no passenger has yet been selected, when the computer fails we must make sure that the seat is still free to be allocated when the computer is again available. Modern database management systems take care of much of this for you – as a designer, all you have to do is to be sure to group the right database activities into what is called a 'transaction', 'commit unit' or 'success unit' and the integrity of the transaction is guaranteed. If the software being used does not offer these facilities, then caution must be taken to ensure that partial transactions are not applied to the data being stored, unless they are automatically reversed out following a power failure or other serious hardware failure.

For the majority of business systems in which information is being shared amongst a number of separate users, it is common to introduce a scheme for preventing more than one individual from modifying shared information at the same time. This is similar to the scheme that would be found in a paper-based or manual system, such as our example in Chapter 2 where seat allocation was done using coloured sticky paper. In this scheme, when one booking clerk removes a sticky paper, everyone else can see that the seat is no longer available – the clerk has reserved that seat for 'sole use' by picking up the sticky paper. In computer systems this is known as a 'locking scheme'. It exists to ensure that in a situation where two or more users could potentially conflict in their use of shared information (e.g. both trying to allocate the same seat) an initial attempt is made to lock the information (a seat in our example), but if this fails an error message is displayed, such as that shown in Figure 14-20.

For critical processes, alternative back-up systems may be needed so that a secondary system allows the process to continue if the primary system is unavailable for some reason. In our example, we would not want to prevent the departure of the flight if the flight departure computer broke down, so we would design a back-up manual procedure for seat allocation to be used in the event of such a failure.

Generally, errors are somewhat less serious than this. An error might not render a whole system unusable, but might prevent a transaction from being completed; for example, if there were two seat allocation screens operating, one at the check-in desk and one at the departure desk, the seat selection might coincide for the same seat at the same time. We cannot allow both screens to allocate the seat so one must 'fail', and it is at this point we should design some error handling to deal with the situation. Firstly, we should inform the user of what has happened and give a suggested course of action to recover from the error, using business terms wherever possible, as illustrated by the error-reporting screen below. Notice that a good error message may also remind the operator about what he was doing – in this case, trying to reserve the specific seat 32B.

Figure 14-20
Reporting an Error

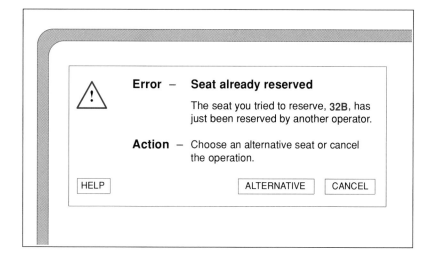

This shows the error that has occurred in both terse and lengthy forms (the expert user will typically only need the former, whereas novice users will need both) and an action that will resolve the error. Notice the keys are labelled to allow the user direct invocation of the action they choose.

Designing Paper Forms

Some of the section on interactive computer-screen design can be applied to designing manual forms, particularly the section on minimizing interaction with the user and providing sensible defaults. But when using paper as a medium, the objective now is to minimize writing and have prefilled forms when the information can only take some known value. For example, in our organization we log our work on a time-recording sheet each month and the heading information is filled in with the month and department number once and then photocopied for the whole department, thus saving each individual having to fill in those particular boxes each time.

Figure 14-21
Example Form

Atlantis Immigration Form – for use on aircraft by visitors only

Welcome to Atlantis. Please fill in each box on this form carefully and legibly. Ask your flight attendant for help if you have any difficulty. In some cases there is a prefilled answer in red, which you should check. In others you may select from some options by ticking them. For example, if your title is 'Mrs' please tick the box like this ☑ Mrs or enter your title in the box below e.g. *Doctor*

1	Your name	Title	Mr	Mrs	tick one or fill in the box below
		Gender	Male	Female	
		Forenames			
		Surname			

2	Normal country of residence		

3	About this visit	Date of arrival	**29-April-1992**	
		Approximate length of stay		
		Purpose of visit	Business	Pleasure	tick one or fill in the box below

4	Passport details	Number			
			Day	Month	Year
		Date of expiry			
		Place of issue			

5	Visa details	Number			
			Day	Month	Year
		Date of expiry			
		Place of issue			

	Flight details	Number	**AIF216**
		From	**Heathrow (LHR), London, England**
		To	**Atlantia (AA), Atlantis**

Thank you for filling in this form. We hope you enjoy your visit.
A copy of sections 1-5 will be attached to your passport and act as your exit permit from Atlantis.

Ideas to consider when designing paper forms include:

- using colour for emphasis and clarity
- providing sufficient space for long fields
- multiple choice check boxes when there is a limited number of alternative answers
- putting simple instructions on the form beside the appropriate fields, or on the back of the previous form
- multiple usage forms with carbonless paper copies
- avoiding asking for information that you already have readily available or is implied by other answers (e.g. having to give your age if you have already given your date of birth)
- sequencing and grouping of fields in recognizable ways.

It is a good idea to look at your most hated forms and remember what their designers did wrong whenever you have to design a new one. Some of our pet hates include forms with all the fields to fill in on one side of a sheet of paper and detailed instructions all on the other side; forms that ask for your full address in a field with four lines, when you actually need seven lines (these can be fun when the system at the other end makes an apparently random selection, permutating any four from seven, but our Post Office does a brilliant job coping with these!); and probably our number-one hate form hides the advice that you only need to fill in certain sections at the very end of the form, after you have wasted hours completing **all** of the sections.

Report Layout

The design of reports that come from a computer or are produced by other means also needs attention – more than can be given in this book. Most of the same principles apply but extra emphasis should be placed on certain areas. Good questions to ask include:

- who needs it?
- what is it for?
- how would the **users** need to use it?
- in what sequence and format will the information be most usable?

Some of the things we typically get wrong when designing computer reports are now classics:

- printing five blank pages before and after every report
- headings that only make sense to the programmers
- vast amounts of data printed out just because it was easy to produce
- insufficient space for big numbers, which then magically turn into XXXXXXX.

Remember, there is nobody stopping you adding text to a computer report to help people understand it. And of course there is always the acid test:

"Will it make any difference to the business if we stop sending out this report?"

Keep it Simple

The main guiding principle for good paper form or report design should be 'keep it simple': obvious, clear naming to indicate what is required in each field of the form (using business terms only, of course) with the minimum number of fields needed to perform the business function.

Summary So Far

We have looked briefly at how to design a user interface for an interactive computer application and introduced the principles of minimizing interaction and the ability to cancel an operation, and how to provide sensible defaults and handle errors as guidelines to the task. Structure charting as a stylized form of decomposition was used as a way of describing a structure for a process in a typical computer programming language with sequence, choice and repetition constructs. Finally, we looked at designing paper forms and reports for presenting information in a usable form. Let us now move on to look in more detail at how state diagrams, function/process dependencies, dataflow diagrams and function/process logic can be used as the basis for physical design.

Aside – Ideal Usability

Let's imagine a finance director who rarely uses a computer. He blows the dust off his terminal and turns it on. Immediately it lights up and gives him three choices. He selects one and a beautifully designed screen appears: no jargon, nice layout, plenty of open space, good use of colour, fields arranged in the expected order and labelled in familiar terms.

He skips from field to field and a friendly hint message tells him what to do. A context-sensitive, multi-level help system is available – this has hypertext capabilities, fast navigation, full glossary of terms and pictorial examples in case he needs them. He still cannot remember how to use it, so hits the tutorial button and works through the in-context tutorial – the same one he used when he was on his short training course. But still he cannot get the hang of it. No problem; he spots the sound icon and presses it. It says:

"Well Peter, you had trouble last time you used this screen. Let's go through it again slowly . . . "

Finally, in desperation, he presses the video button and watches a full-motion video window that shows him how somebody else could use the screen. All becomes clear, he completes his task, and sends a note to his colleagues telling them about this wonderful system he has.

Moral: high usability can be attained with modern technology and some imagination. However, if you find some people are so incompetent that they still cannot succeed you might want to consider a *final* screen, which offers a prefilled termination pro forma with the reason for termination given as 'gross incompetence in the face of a real user-friendly system'.

Physical Design from State Diagrams

In the next sections we look at designing physical implementations for a computerized process from a logical design expressed as a state diagram. This is relatively technical as it is targeted at readers who are involved in the lower levels of design. We consider computerized implementations, concentrating on programming languages, such as COBOL, 'C', Ada and Pascal (third-generation languages) and proprietary interactive application tools (often called fourth-generation tools). Finally, we look at manual, electronic and mechanical implementations. We shall also visit this physical design at two levels of computer processor concurrency. The first is currently more prominent in the computer world and assumes the existence of a single processor in a single computer – the most common environment for implementing processes in commercial data processing systems. The second is more prevalent in realtime systems and massively parallel computers, where multiple processors (often many hundreds or even thousands) are all available and executing processes in parallel.

A State Machine Driven Program

To start with, let us look at a simple case of designing a third-generation language program to implement a process for which we have a realtime model or state diagram on a single processor computer (such as a personal computer) or a computer with a multi-tasking operating system (such as UNIX, VMS or MVS). The general structure of an event-driven program designed from a state diagram has two parts.

**Figure 14-22
Program Structure**

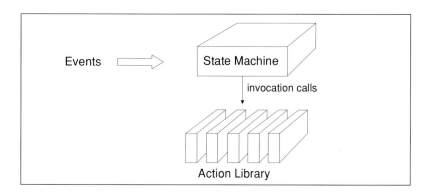

The state machine directly translates the state diagram, handles incoming events and decides which action to invoke. The action library is a collection of routines that do the work of the program (the computations, data manipulation, input and output to other devices, and so on). In fact, what we have done is very simple; we have separated out some of the control structure (usually expressed as 'if', 'perform . . . until', 'repeat . . . until' and other looping and conditional statements) and put them in a separate part of the program called the state machine. Let us look at the detail of the state machine first; this must perform a number of activities.

- 'catch' events (and possibly queue them)
- maintain the current state of the program
- decide which action to invoke for each event and invoke it.

A structure chart of this part of the program might look like Figure 14-23.

Figure 14-23
Structure Chart

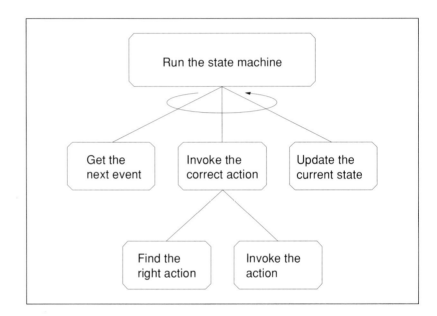

There are a number of common ways of implementing each of the parts of the state machine, each with advantages and disadvantages. The methods covered are the state array, dynamic memory state driver and hard coded.

The State Array

The state diagram is recorded in a two-dimensional array, indexed on its axes by state and event. In modern systems such an array is often dynamically loaded from a table or file at start up; older systems tend to have the array hard coded in read-only memory. Each array entry is a simple transition and holds an indication of which action to perform and the state that becomes current after the action. For example, the transition from state S2 to S4 in Figure 14-24 is triggered by the event E2. This is achieved by indexing the array with the current state (S2) and the event that has just occurred (E2) to find the entry in the array which indicates the action (A1) and the next state (S4).

Figure 14-24
The Array-driven State Machine

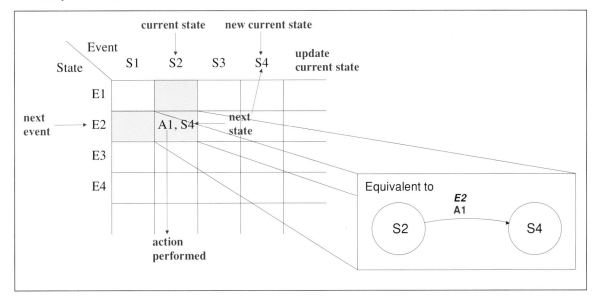

The driver code then retrieves the next event, uses it plus the current state (simply a program variable) to index the array, retrieves the array entry, decodes the action and invokes it, and then uses the next state to update the current state and repeats the cycle.

The details of how each of these can be implemented are highly dependent on the language. For example, in 'C' the action in the array entry could be a pointer to a 'C' function, which can be invoked directly, whereas in COBOL the actions must be paragraphs and, since a pointer to a paragraph is not supported in the language, a variable in the array must be decoded (with 'if' statements or a 'perform depending' statement) to perform the right paragraph.

Dynamic Memory State Driver

Variations on the array data structure which work just as well include dynamically allocating memory for (only) those entries in the array that are filled in (i.e. those state/event pairs that fire a transition) with pointers to the next state. For example, see Figure 14-25. This is much more economical on memory for very large state diagrams, especially if there is a large number of possible events, but only a small number of transitions (i.e. only a small number of events fire a transition in any one state), at the expense of the state machine having to scan down the list of events from the current state each time, which **may** be slower than accessing the array by index.

Figure 14-25
Memory Structures for a Dynamic Memory State Driver

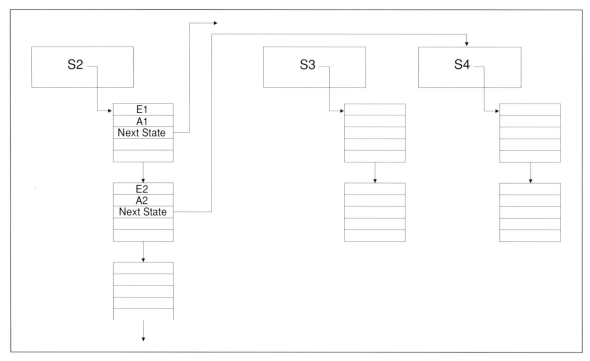

There are many other possible implementations of the state table; the key point being that the state table is a direct translation from the state diagram. It is possible, for example, simply to generate code that tests each event (see Figure 14-26 opposite). In general, the array is more easily understood and hence more easily maintained, in that it is easy to change the table and often this will require no coding changes. This is a very powerful technique for producing flexible software because the separation and formalizing of the control structures makes it simpler to modify the behaviour required from complex sequences of events.

Event Handling

In our structure chart, we had a repetitive 'get next event' box performed at the beginning of each cycle. This will work if the hardware and software in the environment catch and store events without any interaction from the process, so further refinement is unnecessary. This is the case with most operating system software when the events are such things as key depressions, which get buffered automatically by the

Figure 14-26
A Hard-coded
State Machine

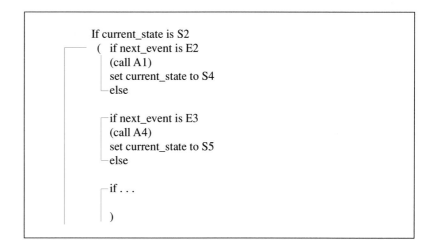

```
If current_state is S2
  (  if next_event is E2
     (call A1)
     set current_state to S4
   else

   if next_event is E3
   (call A4)
   set current_state to S5
   else

   if . . .

   )
```

operating system. In some cases, however, events may need to be trapped as they occur; that is, the operating system will not guarantee to keep the information about the event unless your program reacts to it immediately. This happens frequently when software is being designed for control of hardware or machinery, where there may not be an operating system at all. In these circumstances, it is common to build a queuing mechanism, which is populated by a piece of asynchronous code. A typical event handler is shown below. This code might be part of the same program or a different program with shared memory, or some other implementation, depending on the operating system.

Figure 14-27
Event Handling

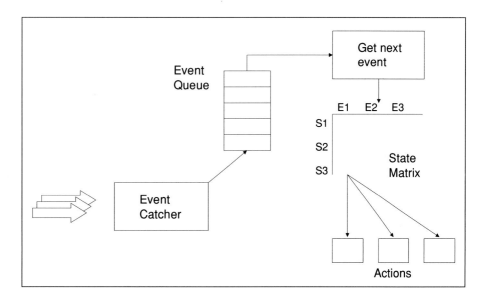

Designing Actions

The remainder of the process is implemented as a set of program components arranged as an 'action library'. This could be a collection of COBOL paragraphs, 'C' functions or Pascal procedures that can be called by the state machine. These do the real work of the program and may be further designed in detail with structure charts or other physical design techniques depending on the degree of complexity and the level of detail needed before the program can be built.

Physical Design from Dataflow Diagrams

Designing from dataflow diagrams centres around the conversion of each dataflow into the design of the physical medium to be used for it. Some possible implementations of a dataflow might be:

- electronic or normal mail
- a telephone link
- a satellite communications link
- facsimile
- computer communication (physical wire or inter-process communication)
- one block of code invoking another within a computer program
- microwave transmission
- voice
- semaphore
- or any combination of the above.

For those 'manual' communications techniques, such as voice, the process on either end of the dataflow is likely to be manual – that is, carried out by a person – although voice recognition and voice-controlled computing systems are starting to become available. A dataflow implemented as 'voice' flowing into a datastore might mean dictating orders into a hand-held recording device. For manual communications of this sort little design is required, simply an indication of what information needs to be communicated (the dataflow definition).

In many parts of the world, dealers buying and selling company stocks and shares on the floor of a stock exchange still use a kind of frantic semaphore to communicate the type and price of the items to be bought and sold. For other forms of communication, the main part of physical design is the design of a protocol, that is, a format that the information to be moved will adhere to. An example might be an electronic mail template for an order.

Electronic mail is a computerized means of composing and delivering letters, memoranda, notes, and so on, by communicating across a computer network, by wires, satellite or other means. In the example below, a template (like a preprinted form) has been provided; the fields in

Figure 14-28
Electronic Mail Example

To	: Sales
From	: RSADEGHI (Regional Sales Representative – North)
Copy to	: Finance, Shipping
Subject	: Sales Order – URGENT

| Customer | : R.R.Inc. | Date of Order | : 12 June |
| | | Date Delivery Promised | : 12 July |

Product Description	Quantity	Price Agreed
Sheet Titanium (6mm)	500	10,000
Sheet Steel (3mm)	1,000	5,000

Kind regards
Roger

A company dedicated to customer service

red are filled in by the electronic mail service and the sales representative fills in the blanks. Electronic mail can be a cheap implementation and provides a fast mechanism for communicating information widely and an optional audit trail, saving the mail after dealing with it. This would work especially well if the communication is across a large geographical distance or where the processes at either end have to be on separate computers in separate companies.

**Dataflows by Computer
Programming Languages**

When considering implementation by computer program, dataflows fall into two categories; those which are wholly contained within a single execution unit (such as an operating system process) and those between execution units. For example, in the dataflow diagram in Figure 14-29 dataflow 'b' is between execution units X and Y, whereas dataflow 'a' is contained internally within execution unit X.

An execution unit is a concurrent thread of control, either true or simulated concurrency. Good examples of true concurrency are found in a multi-processing computer or where people are the processors – you may be reading this book whilst drinking your favourite beverage, crossing your legs, and of course breathing. (Alternatively you may be falling asleep!) Examples of simulated concurrency include those offered by a multi-tasking operating system, such as UNIX, VMS or MVS. Within a single execution unit (dataflow 'a' above) the information can be passed between blocks of code using parameters (arguments) or global variables. This can be shown on a structure chart as in Figure 14-30.

Figure 14-29
Execution Units

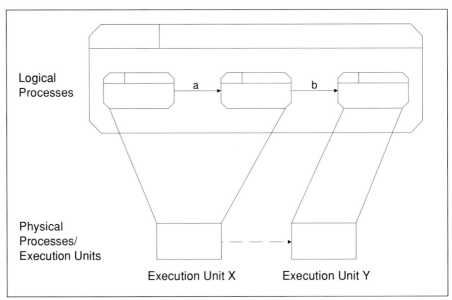

Logical
Processes

Physical
Processes/
Execution Units

Execution Unit X   Execution Unit Y

Figure 14-30
Structure Chart

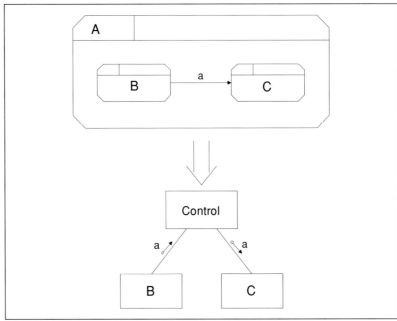

In the next structure chart the dataflow has been implemented by a call to B (to produce the information) and a call to C (to process it). The box marked Control is introduced to dictate the sequence in which things are done, so that there are two alternative sequences. This is possible because (from the rules of dependency and dataflow diagramming) the order in which C and D are done does not matter.

Figure 14-31
Structure Chart with Control

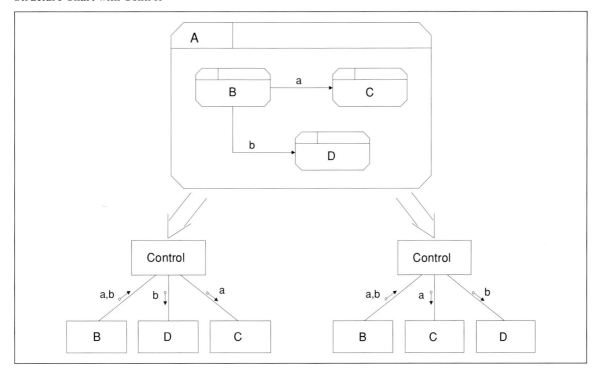

There is also the third possibility of splitting the code that generates 'a' and 'b'. Whether or not this is possible will depend on how 'a' and 'b' are produced. If, for example, they are the result of a single calculation, to do them separately would be poor design because the calculation would have to be done twice – B1 and B2 . But if 'a' is completely independent of 'b', the split may be a good design, especially if C is optional, since 'a' need only be produced if absolutely necessary.

Figure 14-32
Splitting the Code

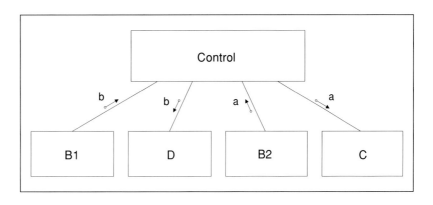

The structure of the code developed to implement a dataflow will depend on many factors, such as:

- the capability of the computer programming language (e.g. whether or not it can be modular and pass parameters)

- code development standards (e.g. never use global variables)

- individual style (e.g. *"I prefer to separate the control flow from the data processing in my structure"*).

Dataflows between Execution Units

Where a dataflow is between two execution units, a protocol must be designed to effect the data transfer between them. Many operating systems offer facilities to do this directly (such as 'pipes' and 'sockets' on UNIX systems, 'mailboxes' on VMS) or provide low-level facilities, such as shared memory management. If not, there is always the option of writing the information to a file or database from one process and then reading it back in from the other. The actual implementation will vary enormously, depending on which mechanism is chosen and which operating system is being used. As a result, it is a good design practice to isolate these highly environment-specific parts of the code from the generally applicable parts, so that the environment-specific ones can be changed if the implementation is changed. For our dataflow diagram, we might choose to have B and C in one execution unit and D in another. The dataflow 'b' is then between execution units.

Figure 14-33
Dataflows between Execution Units

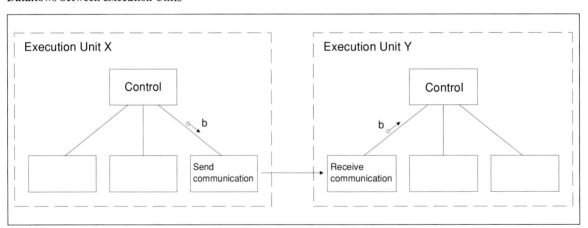

Typically, the sending and receiving of information between execution units takes some setting up and control and this tends to be very specific to the type of communication method and operating system. The error handling in these situations also requires particular attention as there may be complex exception situations to handle and we must remember that the poor user does not want to learn that a pipe or socket has been lost.

Within the 'Send communication' and 'Receive communication' boxes, we can design for this specific environment, knowing that, if we need to change the method later, there is only one place in which this needs to be done. An example of the structure with the 'Send communication' box might be:

Figure 14-34
Example of 'Send communication' Box

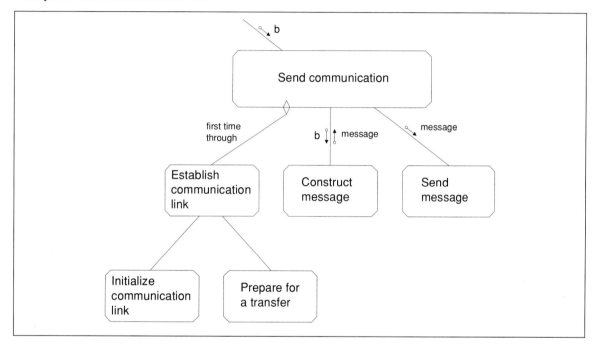

Summary

Designing a system to a level of detail necessary for it to be built successfully demands design work to be done with knowledge of the physical implementation language, machinery or other implementation vehicle. In this chapter, we have looked at aspects of the functional design activity with a particular bias towards designing computerized systems that are:

- relevant
- usable, and
- flexible.

We looked at how techniques such as decomposition, dependency and dataflow diagrams provide a good starting point for a physical design, and we saw how decomposition, in the form of a structure chart, can be used to record the results of a physical design for a procedural computer programming language.

A Final Analogy

As a final reminder about the importance of proper analysis and preparation throughout all the stages of creating information systems, let us consider the analogy of decorating a room in your home.

It is spring and you get the urge to redecorate, so you rush out to the hardware shop and buy lots of lovely paint, wallpaper, new paint brushes, and so on. Then you come home and at least you have the sense to move the furniture out of the room or at least cover it up while you are working. A quick cup of tea (after all that rushing about) and you set to with the paint brush (it really is such fun painting you can't wait to get to work). Result: you run out of paint, or you have loads left over, it is badly done, the cracks and the holes and the old flaking paint still show through, your children hate the colour!

The 'fun' bit at the end will only be successful if you get the requirements and the design right – what colour, what type of paint, how much, will you still like the pattern in three years' time? Then you must construct the sytem properly. Decide on the order of the preparation work: sanding the paintwork, preparing the walls, washing them, filling the cracks, and so on. Work out the order for the actual physical design: which bit will be painted first, how many coats of paint, how long between coats, and so on.

Now you can actually start coding (painting).

Chapter

15

WHEN TO USE WHAT

Introduction

During this book we have introduced several techniques for modelling functional activity and shown how these techniques can be used to model business functions and processes and the physical structures used by some computer, manual and electronic implementation mechanisms. But what techniques should we choose? When are they appropriate?

Some of these techniques, such as hierarchy modelling, enable a large scope to be covered quickly, but provide insufficient detail to aid full comprehension or implementation. Others, such as realtime modelling, are highly rigorous and definitive, but cause people to lose sight of the broader picture. These more detailed techniques are often very good for modelling certain aspects but have to be contorted in their use to cover other situations (e.g. using dataflow diagrams to model real-world events). Further, some techniques are excellent for modelling the existing situation or a newly envisaged concept, or for that highly creative intermediate step of developing a new concept.

The environment in which systems are to be designed will often decide which techniques are chosen and how they are applied. For a Health Service organization building large, complex, life-critical systems, all of these techniques may apply at some stage for modelling some broad or detailed aspect. As a consequence, the development may need to be thoroughly checked and reviewed, particularly for consistency. This contrasts with a low-risk development of a simple, low-cost personnel system for a start-up company in which a quick business analysis exercise may be followed by a couple of rounds of prototyped applications before final construction of the system.

This chapter explores the various ways in which these techniques may be deployed and the conditions that best suit each technique to guide you in selecting the techniques that are applicable to your organization, project and specific goals. We will also look in outline at the subjects of business process (re-)engineering, fastpath system development, reverse engineering, package evaluation and large-scale, mission-critical, system development.

Technique Relevance

We start off by looking at each of the techniques presented in this book and how each relates to the different levels of abstraction that we may need to use to model our business and systems. There is then a discussion of each of the major techniques, followed by a table of strengths and weaknesses.

Instant Index

The diagram below enables you to find the relevant chapters quickly for each of the techniques, at the appropriate level of abstraction, indicating whether a primary or optional technique at this level. Chapters containing definitions of terms for the particular technique are shown in bold. To find key sections for other concepts, such as *event*, please use the index.

Figure 15-1
Index to Using the Techniques

Modelling Technique	Business Level	System Level	Program/ Procedure Level	
Hierarchy	Ch. 2, **3**, 5	Ch. 5, **10**	Ch. 5	Acts as scope for all functions
Dependency	Ch. 6, **7**	Ch. 6, **7**	Ch. **7**	Interdependent functions
Dataflow	Ch. **11**	Ch. **11**	Ch. 11	Flow orientation
Realtime	–	Ch. **12**, 13	Ch. **12**, 13	Event driven
Logic	Ch. **9**	Ch. **9**	Ch. 9	Detail for any of the above requiring explicit logic definition
Structure chart	–	–	Ch. **14**	
General Ch. 1, 15, App. C	Function Ch. 2, **3**	Process Ch. **10**	Program Ch. **14**	Key ▢ – primary technique ▢ – optional technique

Concept to Level

The three abstraction levels at which we model use different subsets of the concepts covered in the book. This is shown in the table below.

Concept	Business Level	System Level	Program/ Procedure Level
Function/common/sub	✓	–	–
Process/common/sub	–	✓	–
Program/common/sub	–	–	✓
Event	✓	✓	✓
Dependency	✓	✓	✓
Dataflow	✓	✓	✓
Datastore	✓	✓	✓
Detailed logic	✓	✓	✓
Objective/aim	✓	✓	✓
Constraint	✓	✓	✓
Entity/attribute	✓	✓	–
Relationship	✓	✓	–
Table/column/join/view	–	–	✓
Business view	✓	✓	–
State/transition	–	✓	✓

Hierarchy Modelling

This simple technique has broad applicability at all three levels of modelling: business, system and procedure. It can be used for quick creation of a top-down view of a new concept. The approach would be to define the whole, and then repeatedly break it down into its constituent parts, adding detail as you go. However, hierarchy modelling can also be used to create a bottom-up view of some business process or system that already exists. In this case, a list of functions or processes can be grouped together and the groups further aggregated until you get to the top.

Both of these methods involve arbitrary grouping and different people may get different results. This is actually a useful aspect: it is often highly effective to get two or even three people to work separately and quickly to produce a top-down model of some area, whilst another person produces a bottom-up model, and then compare and consolidate the various models. This makes use of the human ability to spot inconsistencies, role play, add new ideas, think laterally and otherwise extend thinking during this simple modelling process. Getting more than one person to model using the other techniques is rarely, if ever, cost effective, except perhaps with a life-critical system where accuracy and completeness is the overriding concern.

Dependency Modelling

Dependency modelling may also be used at all three levels, but it has a more focused applicability and is generally used for detailed definition. It is particularly useful for modelling existing or new situations where simple, event-driven, interdependent functions or processes exist. This technique is not rigorous enough to handle complex realtime situations. Where processes are initiated by the arrival of data or change in data value, dataflow modelling is normally better.

The key to the use of dependency modelling is, therefore, when the analyst or designer continually finds functions or processes that:

– are triggered when another finishes
– are caused by some real-world or system event
– happen periodically or at some predetermined time
– or where knowledge of interdependence is the critical aspect.

This approach is a flat modelling technique in that it is rarely easy or useful to use the decomposition or group (aggregation) approach to dependency modelling. You simply use a single model of a particular need and include all its interdependent functions on it. Thus the functions (or processes) may appear all over the place on the hierarchy diagram. Only about twenty to forty percent of elementary functions or processes in a hierarchy would tend to be shown on a function dependency diagram.

We find that it takes some time to produce an accurate model when using this technique, so it is rarely used for scoping. It can, however, be an excellent technique for drawing a (non-rigorous) diagram of a complete sub-system and is particularly useful when trying to convey the concept to engineers. Dependency modelling will also appear at the more detailed breakdown of such a sub-system, where it is most applicable.

Dataflow Modelling

Dataflow modelling is a popular and well-tried technique; it has been used for decades in the system area, and for much longer in various guises in general commerce. It is excellent for modelling exactly what currently happens, particularly in a flow-oriented situation. In most cases where new systems are envisaged, the existing systems are manual in nature, and document flow (letters, forms, reports, requests, etc.) is often the main driving force. Computerization in the office has often mimicked the original, replacing the flow of real mail with electronic mail as opposed to re-engineering the process. By all means use dataflow modelling to gain an understanding of an existing system, but beware of thinking that this is what you need next time! (One company we know had tens of filing cabinets of dataflow diagrams of their existing business processes. These had been laboriously drawn over a two-year period and they did not know what to do with them: but we did! – they were none too pleased with the idea of junking so much stuff.) The trap is that you will simply create a more streamlined, computer-assisted version of what you already have. Order of magnitude improvements can often be made by re-examining what is **really needed** and then synthesizing a model of that.

In general, we find this technique too cumbersome and restricting for use in a highly creative, problem-solving situation. Ideas can be flying around rapidly and it simply takes too long to get them down using this approach (or for that matter using dependency or realtime modelling), although it may still be useful here for checking some specific detail. However, we do find it very useful to model the outcome of such a creative session rigorously, when dataflow modelling is the appropriate technique.*

Dataflow modelling lends itself to top-down and bottom-up modelling techniques. It is not as quick as hierarchy modelling, and to do it properly you have to keep ensuring that all the flows are connected in at the 'right' level and that the whole model is balanced and consistent. Our advice is to use it primarily at the bottom of a hierarchy, not for the structure of the hierarchy itself – it is time consuming and the intermediate levels are rarely, if ever, needed later. It is also excellent at the very top level for giving a non-rigorous but useful overview of the whole.

At a more system level of detail, dataflow diagrams have always been useful for batch computer systems and for transaction processing or dialogue-style procedures. They are also useful when there are lots of separate files, data sources and intermediate results, which you tend to find in offices or older computer systems. These diagrams are still one of the best and most accepted ways of defining many manual processes. With the newer integrated databases, which can hold structured data, documents, text, image, sound, diagrams, pictures and full motion video, the concept of separate datastores is less useful. In addition, with the advent of fourth-generation languages and other design techniques, we often have the situation that within the scope of a transaction we can create, retrieve, update, delete, archive and perform sophisticated concept navigation around all sorts of interrelated data in whatever manner we choose. Being constrained to a predefined dialogue flow can be most inappropriate – even if it is easier for the designer to understand.

---

* This is, of course, our subjective opinion. There are excellent modellers who prefer the discipline and slightly slower pace of this to other techniques when in a creative mood.

So in summary, use dataflows to help understand existing situations and model new ones where flow and prescribed processes must be adhered to.

Realtime Modelling

Realtime modelling is really only applicable at the system and program/procedure level. The approach assumes that we not only know **what** has to be done but that **we are asserting precisely how it must be done** (or we are modelling how it is currently done). This convention is useful for many shop-floor situations and interruptable, event-driven human situations and, of course, for a myriad of multi-processor, event-driven, computerized applications. It is not useful for most simple functions and processes: in fact, in these cases it may be a complete waste of time.

Often, a set of dependency diagrams may need to be converted into realtime models as sophistication is added. A key trigger for this change of convention is when an event occurs and, irrespective of the process in hand, the system must stop and change what is done. The convention is also important when the concept of 'states' is frequently mentioned.

Realtime modelling is perhaps the most rigorous and time-consuming technique described and, as such, should be used with care on only those processes where the realtime aspect is clear. In many commercial and government general applications you may never need to use this technique at all. It is still worth learning, however, as it is invaluable when it does apply (a little like that special spanner in your tool box that you use only once a year, but when you do it is 'just the job'.)

Realtime modelling has proved an excellent way of finding out how an existing computer system or machine probably or actually works. Quite complex realtime systems have often been built without the benefit of this modelling technique and then problems cannot be easily resolved or even diagnosed. Yet more frequent is the situation where the existing system is required to be used in some new circumstance or with greatly extended capability – it suddenly becomes vitally important to know how it works currently. Given that understanding, the model will help in identifying logic errors in the current design and it is also useful when synthesizing a model of the envisaged extensions.

For totally new situations it obviously makes a lot of sense to spend a small amount of time modelling a new, complex, event-driven machine or computer system before going to the expense (often vast) of building it and correcting errors afterwards. This modelling approach benefits greatly from the exercise of checking it out, in detail, with a representative set of expected scenarios. In particular, it pays to concentrate on exception handling. We often build prototypes or simulations to be really sure that it is correct before the real system is built. These do not need to be complete

– they simply focus on those aspects that are most critical, complex or where there is doubt.

We have deliberately used conventions that apply to by far the majority of realtime situations, rather than complicating and confusing the issue with some concepts that occur only rarely in general commerce. These techniques do not embrace the situation where two or more sophisticated realtime systems interact extensively with one another. Simple interaction can be catered for by producing a single model that covers the whole. More sophisticated interaction involves concepts of queue theory, tokens, message passing, and so on. We envisage that some new modelling conventions will become available over the next few years to cater for massively parallel computer processes, when multiple server processors coexist and interact. Such processors will be able to spawn clones of themselves wherever there are performance bottlenecks to give a co-operative server concept. These initiatives will be associated with distributed processing, dynamically self-adjusting networks, distributed database, dynamically relocating data records, and so on.

Simple Description

Obviously, every function, process or program will have a clear simple description, in natural language, to describe what it does, how it does it and what its purpose is. **This is often all you need to describe a function or process in sufficient detail for full comprehension** or to act as guidance for someone to build what is needed. We find that at the business level a simple description is perfectly adequate for up to half of the elementary functions. As we get closer to the implementation level the number falls to only five or ten percent.

When writing descriptions, take the opportunity to put in examples, illustrations, analogies and references to people or other sources to aid the reader in complex situations or identify sources that already give adequate detail. This can save a lot of time, effort and error-prone duplication.

Logic

Function, process, program and procedure logic is only used when absolute rigour and detail are needed. At the business level it is necessary for perhaps ten or fifteen percent of elementary functions. At the process level it is used a lot, and at the program or procedure level there is a wide choice of procedural and non-procedural languages that may be relevant.

As a word of warning, there was one large account where a project team identified around two thousand elementary business functions: they defined detailed function logic for them all. This activity took somewhere between five and ten man years and was of dubious value as it all had to be coded again later in another implementation language. The useful bits were where the business rules, algorithms and constraints were critical, complex or just had to be right for legal and other business reasons.

When it is needed, it is useful to write simple pieces of logic, each of which is to define the detail of some sub-process or sub-program for which the structure or architecture is already defined on a realtime model or structure chart. This enables you to imply a large amount of the logic from the rules covered by the other conventions, such as sequence, choice, iteration, event handling, state transition, and so on.

Structure Charts

These detailed diagrams are extremely useful for defining most sophisticated single processor styles of solution. They do not cater very well for interactive processor scenarios or for realtime situations.

Traditionally, they have been used for manual and computerized batch situations, and for defining complex bits of functionality within large computer processes. They are particularly effective when the process logic maps on to the structure of some data structure cleanly.

Strengths and Weaknesses

The tables below indicates the relative strengths and weaknesses of these various techniques plus a few other related techniques.

Modelling Technique	Strengths	Weaknesses
Hierarchy	–quick and easy to do and learn –gets 80% very fast –good presentation medium at high level of hierarchy and can be used to focus attention on individual functions with careful layout styles	–hard (and subjective) to check for quality –cannot handle complex interactions between functions or complex algorithmic definitions –not very good presentation medium for detailed or large hierarchies
Dependency	–good at identifying key sequences of business functions –good for medium complexity function definitions –good presentation tool	–time consuming to do without computer –difficult if diagrams are very large
Dataflow	–shows system structure as a whole –good for developing top-down systems without losing detail –good for presentation of systems to management	–poor at handling complexity –poor at maintaining balanced hierarchy when requirements are changing rapidly

Modelling Technique	Strengths	Weaknesses
Realtime	−good at handling complex event-driven situations −good at controlling quality in multi-process systems −can be quality checked by some algorithms (especially useful with computerized tools)	−large diagrams are difficult to manage and evolve if designs change
Volumes & frequencies	−good for spotting trends, peaks, troughs and other anomalies −good at focusing on important aspects of model −good for spotting inaccuracies and conflicting information	−only useful in conjunction with other techniques −large and complex sets of volumes are difficult to manage
Description	−easy and quick to do −often sufficient on its own	−not rigorous −requires human interpretation (which can be a benefit or an issue, depending on the person)
Logic	−good for modelling complex algorithms and procedural logic −good for determining complex function interaction via elementary functions	−time consuming −error prone (in analysis) −hostile to non-technically-oriented business people and users −hard to learn
Structure chart	−helps to spot and capitalize on reusable components −easy to evolve and change −natural for procedural programmers (easy to learn, good discipline)	−cannot easily model some situations (e.g. recursion) −only applies to procedural specifications (no good for declarative languages)
Flowcharting	see structure chart	
Decision tables	−simple model for complex decision paths −can be optimized for efficient implementation (e.g. take most qualifying decisions first)	−applicable to a limited niche
Matrices	−general applicability −easy to learn and simple to deploy −good completeness check	−hard without computer support: most good CASE tools have a facility (use a spreadsheet package if necessary)
Formulae	−excellent for complex process logic and precise engineering/scientific functions	−applicable to a limited niche

Overlapping Techniques

There is often overlap between different techniques: after all, they only produce models as opposed to the real thing. Use the guidance above to help you select the 'right tool' for the job. Sometimes there is no clear single choice and a number of techniques have equal validity; use the one that **you** like best or that is most acceptable to your users or colleagues. Remember, these techniques are only being used to act as communication tools and a means to an end.

In some circumstances you may only need to introduce a sophisticated technique, say realtime modelling, for just a couple of situations. It can be useful to continue using a less rigorous but more familiar technique as the primary communication vehicle to avoid confusing people and slowing them down. You will often have to add some extra text to describe **some** of the detailed considerations: **then** provide the more sophisticated model, as an appendix perhaps, to those few people who really do need the full rigour.

How the Techniques Relate to System Activities

We have looked at the techniques in their own right. Now let us have a look at some of the types of activity that progressive organizations are conducting as part of their way of running their businesses and creating new or revised systems. We will look at:

- Business process (re-)engineering
- Fastpath system development
- Reverse engineering
- Package or solution evaluation
- Large-scale system development life-cycle.

Business Process Re-engineering
– Synthesizing a New Way to Run the Company

In many organizations, an executive-led activity is underway to re-examine how they run their businesses. This is something that enlightened companies have always done intuitively, but now it is being carried out consciously.

The general concept is to readdress the basic objectives of a company and its interfaces with suppliers and clients, and to use a 'clean sheet of paper' approach to thinking about how the business could be run, given changes in business practice, market influences, advances in technology, and pressures on productivity and margins.

Obviously, many of the techniques of business function and process modelling are highly relevant to this task. As the key players include executives, it may be necessary to ensure that the models you use look slightly simpler and somewhat different from those traditionally used for defining new systems. It is perfectly acceptable to use differently shaped boxes and connectors, and to add or eliminate detail as required, to aid communication and understanding. The most useful techniques to help in this activity are hierarchy, dependency and/or dataflow (probably simplified), matrix and simplified entity relationship modelling. These must be associated with structured lists of newly defined business objectives, assertions of approach, constraints, and other categories of executive direction.

Appendix A on quality and completeness checking also covers some considerations that are essential when carrying out this task or designing a new system.

Fastpath System Development
Rapid Application Development

Sometimes, speedy development of a business system is necessary or desirable. Perhaps a window of opportunity such as the end of a financial year is close; or an existing system is about to exceed capacity; or simply whim on the part of the company's management is the compelling reason to 'get something delivered quickly'. Fastpath or 'rapid development' is an approach to system development which cuts corners in order to reduce the time required from the initial idea to final delivery and operation of a system. Many of the techniques in this book still apply, although a different attitude towards their use is needed to make a fastpath development successful.

A fastpath approach is rarely appropriate for complex overlapping systems, realtime applications or with large-team or other complex situations which would benefit from a more rigorous approach.

Building the Team

Building a team with the right mix of skills is key to the success of a fastpath development. The ideal would be a small number of people, practised in the use of all the system development techniques in this and other CASE*Method books, with a keen sense of when things may be omitted without incurring an unacceptable risk. Such a rich variety of techniques now exists that it is rare, if not impossible, to find a single person well versed in all of them, so assembling a team with an adequate mix of skills is in itself a skill.

The approach often relies on the skills and abilities of the people in the team to work together really effectively to minimize how much has to be written down or explained about new ways of working. Business awareness is probably the most difficult skill to acquire in a system development team, and for this reason business people, usually managers, are an essential part of the team.

The skills necessary for success are:

- Business awareness:
  - of general business practices
  - specific knowledge of the organization
- System development skills:
  - problem analysis and solving
  - specific skills for computer, manual and other systems
  - generic modelling
  - clarity of thought and concept
- Team and project management skills
- Communication skills:
  - within a small team
  - between the team and other parties.

As speed is of the essence in a fastpath exercise, the team must remain focused on deliverables and goals. A strong team or project manager is needed to keep up the pressure and maintain the continued involvement of the business community, ensuring a high level of effective communication betweeen team members and between the team and other parties.

Guess and Check

One approach to speeding up the development process is to guess what is required – an 'educated' guess based on existing knowledge of this or other organizations – and then check that the guess is reasonable. This approach invests heavily in the abilities of the people doing the guessing: the risks are obvious. If these people are highly skilled in the right areas, the guesses are more likely to be correct, and rapid focus on key aspects of a system can be achieved at a low level of risk of getting it wrong. The initial interview and analysis stages can be shortened, with fewer interviews needed to establish a business model very quickly.

By forcing decisions on what (and how) to implement from the business model (again, partly based on guesswork) but reducing the risk by designing for change (we will get some things wrong so we need room to manoeuvre), we can deliver prototype or operational systems very quickly. In a development of this type, this initial implementation should be followed by a phase in which substantial modifications or even planned replacement of a system can take place.

Fastpath Techniques

The most useful techniques on a fastpath development are entity relationship and hierarchy modelling, which can set the scope very quickly. Critical core components would be modelled using dependency diagrams and then much reliance is put on the skills of the team to 'fill in the gaps'; in other words, the things that should be obvious to this carefully selected group of people.

The fastpath approach also lends itself well to the use of good CASE tools, fourth-generation languages, prototyping and other high-level computer languages. Adoption of sensible, not necessarily ideal, standards can streamline the activity and cut out those endless debates on esoteric differences in style.

The more detailed techniques shown in this and other books should only be used if absolutely necessary. Concept diagrams are, however, vital, as so much reliance is put on each team member sharing the same vision.

Reverse Engineering

Reverse engineering is the act of reclaiming knowledge from existing systems, so that these systems can be:

– maintained
– rebuilt (to take advantage of new technology, for example)
– replaced
– enhanced or modified.

Some aspect of reverse engineering is, in fact, essential in virtually all systems development where a new or replacement system must coexist with existing systems. In practice, what is required is the ability to access (or derive) technical documentation describing the physical implementation of a system so that, during the development of other systems that will coexist with or replace it, the necessary links feeds and other intersystem communications can be designed.

In theory, there should be no need for reverse engineering, because existing systems should be fully and correctly documented – but how often are they? So, reverse engineering is about analyzing the physical structure of an existing system, using techniques such as creating structure charts and dataflow diagramming to show what is actually in existence. This can then be modified to provide a development path for the existing system to enable it to integrate (communicate and share information) with any new systems.

Figure 15-2
Integrating with
Existing Systems

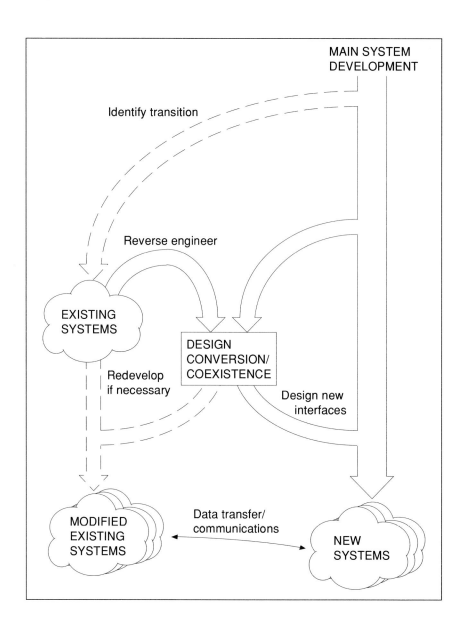

The diagrams opposite show a modification to the existing billing system for customers of an electricity supply company. The new part of the structure chart is shown in red on Figure 15-3. Now, each time a customer's bill is printed, information is to be passed to a new system.

Figure 15-3
Modifying a Structure Chart

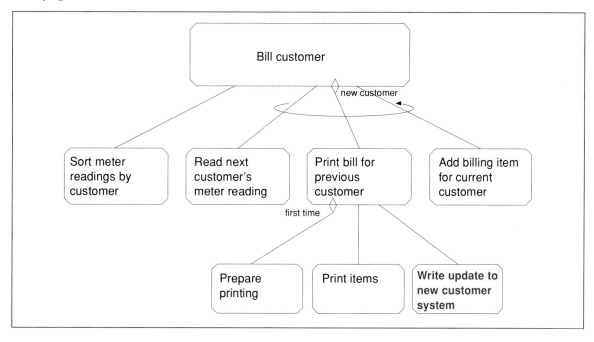

This might appear in our new system documentation as a dataflow on a dataflow diagram.

Figure 15-4
New System Dataflow

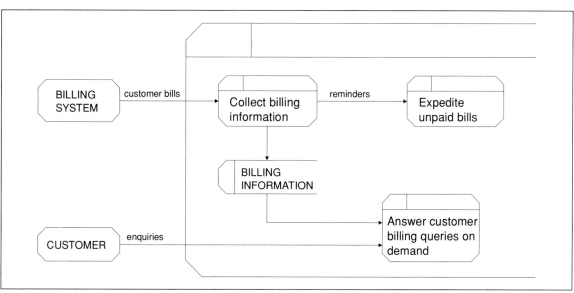

Package or Solution Evaluation

When evaluating alternative forms of solution, in particular, packages and the reuse of existing systems, it is vital to have a clear understanding of the requirement **prior** to looking at the possible solution. (The solution may give you additional facilities that you may choose to use, but always be guided first by the need.) So all the scoping, architectural, concept and completeness techniques apply well.

Given a function hierarchy, an entity diagram and lists of important concepts, you can evaluate a possible solution against your predetermined need. Many companies weight each of the evaluation aspects as critical, mandatory, optional and 'nice to have'. However, it is perfectly acceptable to select a package that has some missing 'mandatory' feature if, on balance, it is the best and most cost-effective way of meeting the business requirement. Such a decision is often strongly influenced by the urgency of the need and the relative availability of different solutions.

In many cases, a system is so critical that the buyer may want to check that the package or other possible solution was built sensibly and exactly meets some important processing or data need. You may, therefore, deploy these and other techniques to reverse engineer key parts of it into diagrammatic form to check the design and other aspects. Many vendors are pre-empting this issue by supplying at least some of the diagrams and details needed in the documentation of the package. In rare cases, packages may be delivered with complete repository and CASE diagrams.

The main modelling techniques from this book used for evaluation are lists of functions, dependencies, volumes and frequencies, logic for key areas, matrices and formulae. There are also other important aspects like usability, standards, ease of use, ease of learning, vendor viability, support, and so on, that one always needs to consider when buying anything. It is just like buying a new car or a cooker. If you are anything like we are you produce lists and criteria, read up on it carefully, get all the independent reviews: then buy the one you like best in your price bracket.

A Story with a Moral

One of us once bought a cooker (an excellent cooker, in fact) because it fulfilled all the criteria and it looked beautiful. The only problem was it was just a tiny bit too large for the space in the kitchen (a volume error?), so two of us then redesigned a new kitchen around the beautiful cooker. And it was a **really** beautiful kitchen, but what an expensive way to buy a cooker!

**Large-scale System
Development Life-cycle**

This and other books in the series are really focused on large-scale system development and thus all these techniques will apply at some point or other. And each of the concepts of business process (re-)engineering, fastpath development, reverse engineering and package evaluation will be part of any enterprise-wide system endeavour. So in many senses we could simply say to use it all. To give some guidance, however, on this large-scale topic, we have included yet another of those useful matrices on the next two pages to help you focus on when to use what.

In addition, it is worth while remembering a few pieces of general advice to help you handle such a complex endeavour. Firstly, ensure that you have people who can work at this scale: if you cannot find them inside your organization, hire top consultants. These people need to be experts in concept diagrams, generic modelling, clarity of thought, and articulation in visual and written form. Once again, business acumen and strong communication skills are essential.

Managing the scale is difficult. It requires the ability to break the work into movable chunks, control overlaps, set and meet expectations, deliver useful subsets regularly to a high level of quality, and to balance many factors such as urgency, accuracy, ease of change and cost.

In many cases, this scale of work is being done by multinational corporations, using dispersed development units. The target may be a system for users working in different languages, complying with different legislation, and acceptable in different cultures.

Those companies that attempt to produce integrated modern systems that can react to changing business practice and technology without using powerful modelling techniques and computer-aided tools are very unlikely to succeed.

Key to tables:
- ✪ key technique and very good
- ✓✓ very good and important
- ✓ of some use
- T useful for top level
- R rarely useful

Technique	Business Process (Re-)Engineering	Fastpath System Development	Reverse Engineering	Package or Solution Evaluation
Function/Process				
Hierarchy	✪	✪	✓	✓✓
Dependency	✪, T	✓	✓✓	✓
Dataflow	✓✓, T	✓	✪	✓
Realtime	–	✓	–	–
Description	✓	✓✓	✓	✓✓
Logic	–	✓	–	–
Structure chart	–	✓	✓	–
Prototyping & simulations	–	✪	–	✓
Volumes & frequencies	–	✓	✓✓	✓
Flowcharting	–	–	✓	✓
Decision tables	–	–	–	–
Matrices	✓✓	✓	✓	✓
Lists	✓✓	✪	✓	✓✓
Concept diagrams	✪, T	✪✪	✓	✪
Business views	✓	✓✓	✓	✓
Entity/data model	✪, T	✪	✪	✪
Use of CASE tools	✓✓	✪✪	✓✓	✓
Common sense	✪✪	✪✪	✓✓	✪

Technique	Strategy	Analysis	Design	Build	Transition	Production/maintenance	Complex	Algorithmic	Varies over time	Mission critical	Performance critical
Large-scale System Development							**Other Categories**				
Function/Process											
Hierarchy	✪, T	✪	✓✓	–	–	✓	–	–	–	✓	–
Dependency	T	✪	✪	–	✓	✓	✓	–	✓	✓	✓
Dataflow	T	✓	✪	✓	✓	✓	✓	–	✓	✓	✓
Realtime	–	R	✪	✓	–	–	✓✓	–	✓✓	✓	✓✓
Description	✪, T	✪	✓	✓	✓✓	✓✓	✓✓	–	✓	✓	–
Logic	–	–	✪	✪	–	✓	✪	✪	✓	✓✓	✓✓
Structure chart	–	–	✓✓	✪	–	✓	✪	✪	✓	✓	✓✓
Prototyping & simulations	T	✓	✓✓	✓	–	✓	✪	✓✓	✓	✓	✪
Volumes & frequencies	✓	✓✓	✪	✓	✓	✓	✓✓	–	✪	✓✓	✪✪
Flowcharting	–	–	✓	✓	✓	✓	✓	–	–	✓	–
Decision tables	T	✓	✓	✓	✓	✓	✓	✓✓	–	✓✓	✓
Matrices	✪	✪	✓✓	✓	✓	✓✓	✓✓	–	✪	✪	✓
Lists	✪	✓	✓	✓	✓✓	✓	✓	–	✓	✓✓	✓
Concept diagrams	✪, T	✓	✪	✓	✓✓	✓	✪	–	–	✪	✓
Business views	–	✪	✪	✓	–	–	✓✓	–	–	–	–
Entity/data model	✪, T	✪	✪	✪	–	✓	✓✓	–	✓	✪	✓
Use of CASE tools	✓	✪	✪	✪	✓	✓	✪	–	✓	✓	✓
Common sense	✪✪	✪	✪✪	✪	✪	✪	✪	–	✪	✪✪	✪

Column group headers (staircase): Large-scale System Development — Strategy, Analysis, Design, Build, Transition; Production/maintenance. Other Categories — Complex, Algorithmic, Varies over time, Mission critical, Performance critical.

REFERENCES AND SUGGESTED READING

References

1. Barker, R. et al (1990). *CASE*Method Tasks and Deliverables*. Addison-Wesley, Wokingham, England.

2. Barker, R. (1990). *CASE*Method Entity Relationship Modelling*. Addison-Wesley, Wokingham, England.

3. Fowler, H.W. and F.G. (1987). *The King's English*. Oxford University Press, Oxford.

4. Bjorner, D., Jones, C.B. (1978). The Vienna Development Method: the Meta Language, *Lecture Notes in Computer Science*, **Vol. 61**. Springer-Verlag, Berlin, Heidelberg.

5. Spivey, J.M. (1992). *The Z Notation: A Reference Manual*. Prentice Hall, Hemel Hempstead.

6. Barker, R. (1990). *CASE*Method Entity Relationship Modelling*, Appendix G. Addison-Wesley, Wokingham, England.

7. Adams, D. (1991). *The Hitchhiker's Guide to the Galaxy: A Trilogy in Four Parts*. Heinemann, London.

Suggested Reading

What makes the difference between a competent technician and a skilled modeller? The former can follow a method rigorously and with any luck produce an adequate result, just. The latter is a creative thinker, able to see things from fresh perspectives, to find patterns, to use analogies, to innovate, to imagine, to draw on all sorts of intellectual resources. Many of the things that stimulate fresh thinking are personal – a particular story, a poem, something a friend says. How often do we say, "I never thought of it like that before" and then dismiss this alternative viewpoint? We have given a very short list of books, books that we personally enjoyed reading, to encourage you to take a fresh look at 'life, the universe and everything'.[7]

On the power of using analogies:
> Goldratt, E.M. and Cox, J. (1991). *The Goal*. Gower, Aldershot.

On designing for usability:
> Norman, D.A. (1990). *The Design of Everyday Things*. Doubleday, New York.

On thinking techniques:
> de Bono, E.(1990). *Lateral Thinking*. Penguin Books, London.

On many techniques for designing nearly anything:
> Jones, J.C. (1980). *Design Methods: Seeds of Human Futures*. Wiley, New York, Chichester.

On changing business concepts into action ('getting things done'):
> Harvey-Jones, J. (1989). *Making It Happen*. Fontana, London.

A

QUALITY AND COMPLETENESS CHECKS

FOR SYSTEMS AND RE-ENGINEERED BUSINESS FUNCTIONS OR PROCESSES

Throughout the book, as we have covered the different techniques we have examined ways of checking the quality of the models and diagrams produced. The overriding question here is: *"Is it complete and accurate?"* Then we need to consider the way in which these models will be translated in a system. Now the first question should be: *"Does it do what I want it to do or, more importantly, what the business needs it to do?"* Of course, all those other important aspects have to be considered: cost and timescales (for both writing and using a system), flexibility and reusability (can it cope with changes in the requirements, in the business, in the hardware, etc.), robustness, ease of use, and so on.

We have frequently referred to asking questions to test out your model (*"what if . . . ?", "does it . . . ?", etc.*), presenting your ideas for feedback to the users, cross-checking the model developed by one technique against that from another or comparing the results of applying the same technique from different starting points (top down versus bottom up), and we have used matrices, more matrices and yet more matrices. Sections dealing with quality and completeness checking will be found on the following pages:

This appendix contains some additional guidance and checklists. The lists should not be considered comprehensive since every project is different, so you will want to construct project-specific lists. Bear in mind that technology is continually changing and such lists can rapidly become out of date. Other books in this series contain more checklists, some specific to the techniques and others of particular relevance to the stage-by-stage process of developing information systems (the Business System Life Cycle).

Remember, if your system passes all the following checklists, it merely proves that it has passed the checklists.

Completed checklists should not be taken as the sole evidence that you have a good system. They are rather like intelligence tests – these tend to show how good you are at passing intelligence tests, not how intelligent you really are! At the end of the day your users will perform the ultimate quality check and tell you if the system is any good.

The System as a Whole

System Overview

- Are the **business** reasons for developing the system clear? And how will you measure whether the system helps the relevant business objectives?

- Is the purpose of the system clearly described?

- Are the system's objectives, aims and critical success factors clear?

- Is the boundary of the system clearly defined?

- Are interfaces to other systems defined?

- Are the different user groups clearly identified?

- Is there a complete list of functions to be implemented?

- Is there a description of the system architecture?

- Are the client's acceptance criteria for the system as a whole known and documented?

- Do we know the cost, benefit, timescale and scope?

- Have the executives, users and system people all bought into the concepts?

**Business Model
(functional components)**

Function Definitions:

- Is there a function hierarchy in which the functions to be implemented are broken down to elementary business functions?

- Is there adequate, accurate and unambiguous documentation of all the elementary business functions to be implemented?
    - what triggers each function?
    - how often does each function occur? By location if necessary?
    - what does the function consist of in terms of detailed function logic?
    - what entities and attributes are accessed, and how?
    - what functions are triggered?
    - do dataflow, function dependency, state transition or other diagrams exist where relevant?

- Has the correctness of the model been confirmed by user representatives?

- Have automated consistency checks been run against the business model?

- What changes are expected when considered over a period of time?

Business Direction

- Is it clear what the business is that the system is going to support?

- Are there clearly-defined business objectives, aims, priorities, constraints, critical success factors, problems and issues that may be wholly or partially addressed by the system?

- Is it clear which business functions correspond to these business directions? Similarly, does the entity relationship model cover the data required to predict and monitor against any quantifiable business indicators?

We will come back to the system checklist again at the end of this appendix, in particular to look at design issues as they apply to systems or to re-engineering a business process/function.

Strategy Study Checklist

Terms of Reference

Check that:

- objectives are brief (with well-chosen words), measurable, achievable, apt
- scope is as explicit as possible
- acceptance criteria clearly express how the system will be judged.

Functions

- Does each function have a concise and meaningful description that starts with a verb?

- Is the sum of the functionality of the child functions equal to the functionality of the parent node?

- Are there any parent nodes with excessive numbers of children (say ten or more) that could be further split?

- Do any functions refer to objects that are not entities, synonyms of entities, attributes or business views?

- Do the functions reflect what the executives think the business should do in the future?

Diagrams

- Are crossing lines reduced to the minimum possible? Is it cluttered?

- Does the diagram have a label indicating the name of the drawing, version number and author?

- Is the diagram clear and unambiguous?

- Are the conventions on how to interpret the diagram clear?

System Boundary

- Is the boundary of any proposed system clear?

- Are any cross-system interfaces clear?

- Are key transition, conversion and coexistence issues clearly identified and at least some form of viable solution envisaged?

Analysis Checklist

Functions

Each function should:

- have a concise meaningful description, that starts with a verb
- have a unique function reference within the context
- have a set of children whose functions perform all the functions of the parent, apart from bottom-level functions
- have frequencies specified, if the function is a bottom-level function
- as far as possible appear only once, or common functions should be defined
- not refer to a mechanism unless the mechanism is recognized as unchanging and compulsory within the business
- refer only to entities that are in the scope
- refer to entity names in the description
- have leaf functions that are elementary business functions

- have function logic specified, if it is a complex elementary business function
- have entity, attribute and relationship usage, and mode of usage specified
- have triggering events defined
- have dependent functions and dependencies defined
- have user-required response and deadlines defined.

Consider some or all of the following:

- the number of steps to perform a function:
  complexity, effort
- the number of different roles involved for a function:
  communication responsibilities
- functions that do one thing versus functions that do the same things many times (batch):
  flexibility versus economy of scale
- an acceptable/unacceptable error rate:
  the cost of quality
- decision points:
  optimization for key factors and impact of errors
- interaction across internal or external boundaries:
  simplification of processes
  removal of redundant processes
  streamlining of the business.

Do some of the functions cover the following?

- audit requirements
- back-up
- recovery
- security and access control
- privacy enforcement
- monitoring
- manual procedures
- set-up, transition or coexistence.

System Transition

- If data is to be derived from existing systems then specify:

  - the sources of data
  - the procedure for export from the old system
  - data conversion procedures
  - procedures for import of data into the new system
  - timescales and resources needed.

- If not, have default values, derivation rules or sources of value been defined?

- Has all old data either been catered for or has it been agreed that it is no longer required?

- If existing systems overlap the new system then specify:

  - replacement functionality
  - changes to procedures
  - the removal of redundant processes in the existing system.

- Are acceptable periods for transition defined?

- Are transition plans viable and agreed?

- Has user education and training been planned?

- Are expectation levels being set sensibly?

- Are the peak demands of transition catered for?

- Has a sensible time in business terms been allowed for transition?

Dataflows

Each dataflow must be:

- named
- between two functions or
- between a function and a datastore or
- between a function and an external entity or function
- made up of known attributes of entities or data items whose destination or source is clear.

Also see page 213.

Datastores

Each datastore must be:

- named
- made up of known attributes of entities or data items whose destination or source is clear
- capable of construction from its input dataflows
- capable of acting as a source for any output dataflows.

Also see page 213.

State Transition Diagrams
(realtime modelling)

Each state must be:

– named
– separately identifiable, ideally in real-world terms
– able to be entered (input transition)
– able to be exited (output transition).

Each transition:

– must be caused by one and only one event
– may trigger one or zero processes
   (the process may itself be decomposed).

Each event must be:

– named
– clearly defined.

Each process must:

– be triggered by one or more events
– comply with the normal checklist for a process.

Check for:

– duplication/redundancy
– excessive complexity
– infinite loops
– areas that can never be accessed
– appropriate notation for complexity of diagram
      if simple use bubble notation
      if complex use gate notation
– sensible use of generic transitions to simplify design
– interrelated diagrams.

Users

Each user role should be defined along with:

– the acceptable or relevant style of working
– the type of working environment and potential working constraints (e.g. no desk for a terminal)
– cross-reference to functions carried out
– ownership of data
– access rights and levels of working.

Design Checklist

This section is targeted at a relational database implementation only, but reflects the sort of list that would be needed for any aspect of design.

System Architecture

- Is it clear what databases, processing and communications nodes will exist and their geographic location?
- Are the major components of the system defined, along with their interrelationships?
- Is the intended application of vendor and in-house technologies clear?
- Is it clear how different technologies will fit together?

**Program Module/
Procedure Design**

- Is each module cross-referenced to the function(s) it supports?
- Does the module definition or specification have the following?
  - a header
  - a user overview
  - a technical overview
  - process logic and insertion/change/deletion rules
  - tables (and columns used), and mode of usage
  - the vehicle for implementation
  - the degree of complexity
  - assumptions
  - limit and exception handling
  - interface definitions, if necessary, between clerical, computer, mechanical and other mechanisms.
- Are the weighting factors for programming specified?
- Are the weighting factors for procedure or other definitions specified?
- Are they realistic, given the experience of development staff?
- Does the user interface match the user working style?

Paper and Computer Forms

Each form should be:

- clear in purpose
- legible
- arranged in a sensible sequence
- laid out logically and in an aesthetically pleasing manner
- and it should contain necessary instruction on how to use it.

Check that forms:

- encourage accuracy
- avoid clutter
- do not overlap with other forms
- cross-reference other relevant forms
- utilize the chosen medium well (colour, fonts, etc.)
- do not cause real annoyance when used. If they do then determine why
- and where a form is to replace some other one, check that the old one is actually withdrawn!

System and Business Process Design Checklist

Many different things may cause a system to 'fail' at the design stage, for instance:

- the design is too complex to be understood
- the system or business process would take too long to develop to be of value
- the people responsible for building the system do not have the necessary skills or experience
- the cost of building the system would be too high.

These factors should be seen as very real constraints on the design options available and we recommend identifying them explicitly by making a list under relevant headings. The following may be used as a checklist of things to consider as constraints or issues worth considering:

- time
- money
- people:
    numbers, skills, experience, technical capability, existing teams, morale
- physical location and resources:
    space/buildings, machinery, . . .
- communications
- degree of reliability needed
- throughput
- bottlenecks, queuing
- responsiveness
- availability
- ease of change
- maintainability

- acceptability:
  - to key people
  - to the culture of the organization
- impact, attitude and acceptability from different points of view:
  - customers
  - suppliers
  - government
  - auditors
  - other third-party organizations
- national language, culture and regional legislation
- impending technology changes
- computer software, hardware, . . .
- organizational structure
- legislation
- expectations
- dependencies on external resources
- rate of change of all the above!

In many senses this checklist is being used to identify success factors and those factors that will cause total or partial failure if ignored. It is important to build your own checklist for **each** project – then and only then use it as a guideline to whatever else may be important.

Appendix

B

VALID CONSTRUCTS

Each modelling technique lays down simple rules for construction. In this appendix we will identify some useful valid constructs, some special cases and, perhaps most important, some invalid constructs. Most of the more obvious cases covered earlier have been omitted.

Hierarchies

Valid Constructs

Figure B-1
Multiple Hierarchies

These are illustrated at the system level, but apply at all three levels.

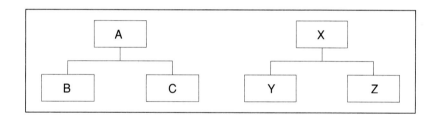

Multiple hierarchies are allowed, as an intermediate step in thinking.

Invalid Constructs

Figure B-2
Recursion in a Hierarchy

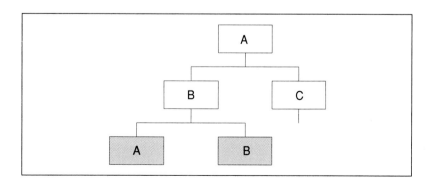

A node in a function or process hierarchy cannot be a parent of itself, nor any form of ancestor. However, at the implementation level, recursive structures can be valid, so long as there is a means to terminate a possible infinite loop of recursion in all situations.

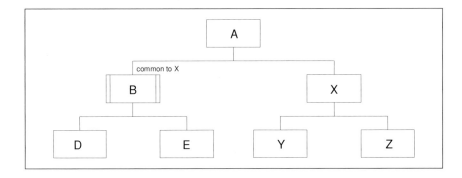

B is common to X, but fails two rules for common functions:

– it is obviously not the same function
– only the master function should be decomposed.

Dependencies

These are illustrated at the business level, but apply at all three levels. In addition to Figures B4-B7, see Figures 7-8 and 7-9.

Valid Constructs

Figure B-4
Simple Constructs and Their Meanings

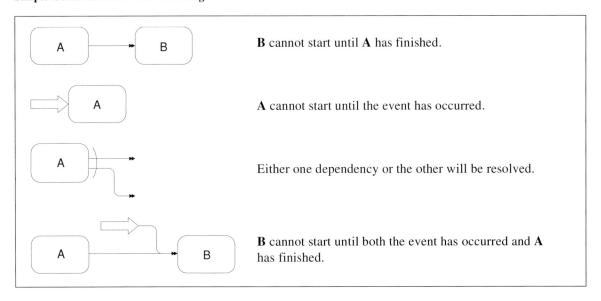

Figure B-5
More Complex Constructs and Their Meanings

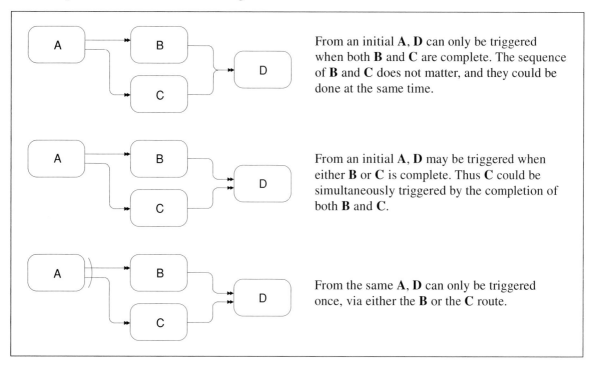

From an initial **A**, **D** can only be triggered when both **B** and **C** are complete. The sequence of **B** and **C** does not matter, and they could be done at the same time.

From an initial **A**, **D** may be triggered when either **B** or **C** is complete. Thus **C** could be simultaneously triggered by the completion of both **B** and **C**.

From the same **A**, **D** can only be triggered once, via either the **B** or the **C** route.

Figure B-6
Dependencies with Recursion

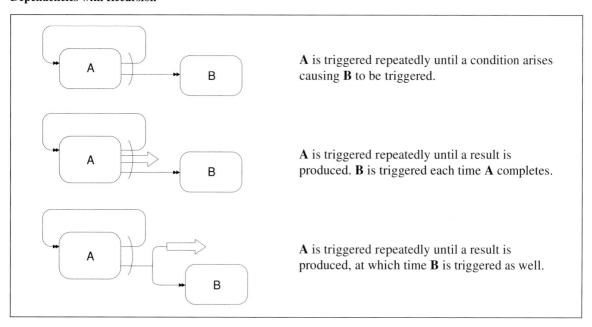

A is triggered repeatedly until a condition arises causing **B** to be triggered.

A is triggered repeatedly until a result is produced. **B** is triggered each time **A** completes.

A is triggered repeatedly until a result is produced, at which time **B** is triggered as well.

Invalid Constructs

Figure B-7
Invalid Constructs and Infinite Loops

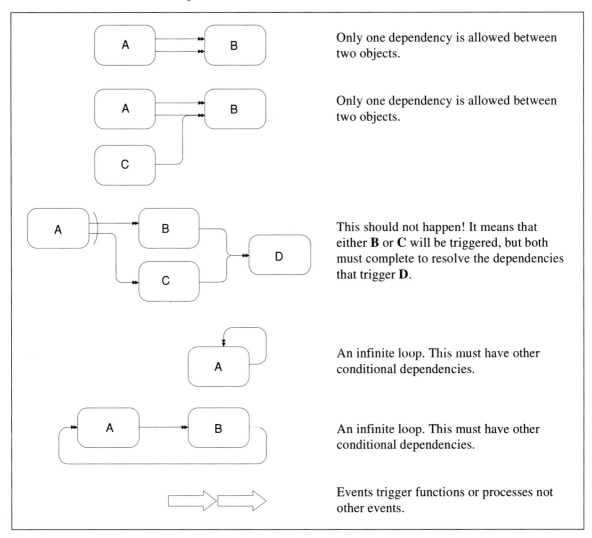

Only one dependency is allowed between two objects.

Only one dependency is allowed between two objects.

This should not happen! It means that either **B** or **C** will be triggered, but both must complete to resolve the dependencies that trigger **D**.

An infinite loop. This must have other conditional dependencies.

An infinite loop. This must have other conditional dependencies.

Events trigger functions or processes not other events.

Dataflows

These are illustrated at the system level, but apply at all three levels. By convention, objects on a diagram at the system level are shown with subdivisions for labels and names. In addition, see Figures 11-21 and 11-22.

Figure B-8
Valid Constructs

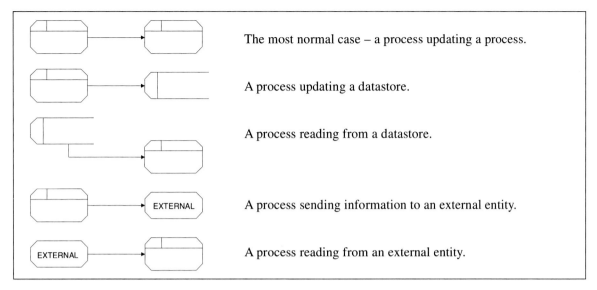

The most normal case – a process updating a process.

A process updating a datastore.

A process reading from a datastore.

A process sending information to an external entity.

A process reading from an external entity.

Figure B-9
Invalid or Incomplete Constructs

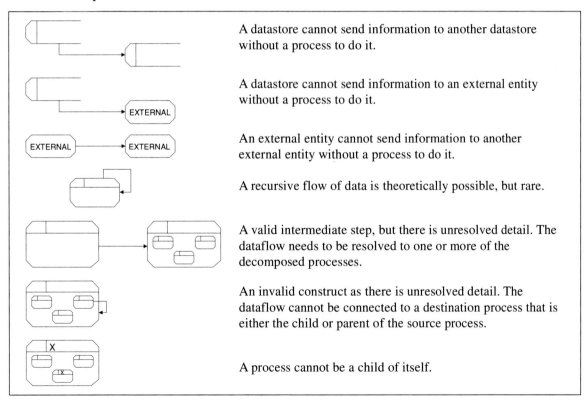

A datastore cannot send information to another datastore without a process to do it.

A datastore cannot send information to an external entity without a process to do it.

An external entity cannot send information to another external entity without a process to do it.

A recursive flow of data is theoretically possible, but rare.

A valid intermediate step, but there is unresolved detail. The dataflow needs to be resolved to one or more of the decomposed processes.

An invalid construct as there is unresolved detail. The dataflow cannot be connected to a destination process that is either the child or parent of the source process.

A process cannot be a child of itself.

Realtime Models

Also called state transition diagrams, these are not used at the business level.

Figure B-10
Valid Constructs

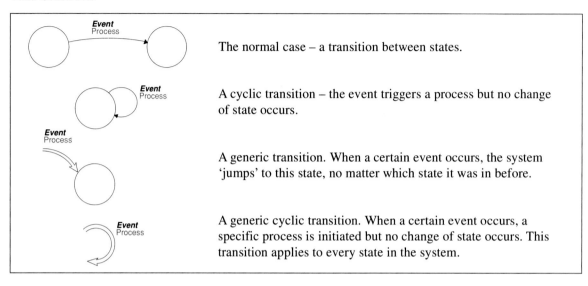

The normal case – a transition between states.

A cyclic transition – the event triggers a process but no change of state occurs.

A generic transition. When a certain event occurs, the system 'jumps' to this state, no matter which state it was in before.

A generic cyclic transition. When a certain event occurs, a specific process is initiated but no change of state occurs. This transition applies to every state in the system.

Figure B-11
Invalid Constructs

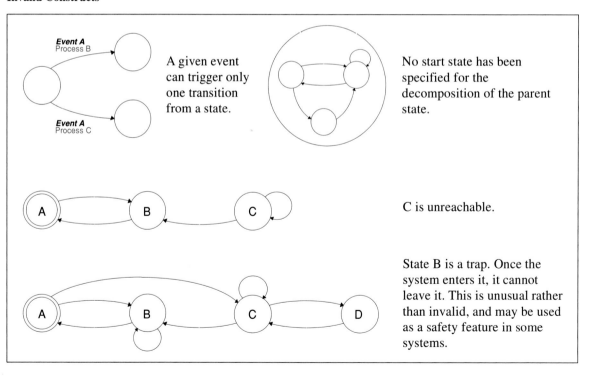

A given event can trigger only one transition from a state.

No start state has been specified for the decomposition of the parent state.

C is unreachable.

State B is a trap. Once the system enters it, it cannot leave it. This is unusual rather than invalid, and may be used as a safety feature in some systems.

Appendix

C DETAILED DEFINITIONS

This appendix covers the detailed definitions for the concepts in this book. Standard paper forms are shown mainly for the business level, but you may plagiarize them for the other levels. It is preferable to use a CASE system to record this information. The forms included are:

C2   Application (system)
C4   Geographic Location
C5   Business Unit
C10 Business Function Hierarchy
C11 Elementary Business Function Definition
C12 Business Function Frequency (general frequencies)
C13 Business Function Frequency (distributed requirement)
C14 Input Dataflow   C15   Output Dataflow
C16 Function Logic
C17 Datastore Definition
C29 Matrix (general form)
C30 State Definition
C31 Generic Transition   C32   Generic Cyclic Transition

You will find you need lists and matrices of many things, in particular:

Business Function (or Process):	Entity; Attribute/Data Item; Business Unit; User Role; Process; Event; Objective; Aim; Critical Success Factor
Program/ Procedure:	Table/File/Record Type; Field; User Role; Event; Node; Other Program/Procedure
State:	Event; Process; State

Not all the fields on a form may be needed each time; they are there as reminders. You may also find extra fields useful. Add these yourself direct to the paper form or via the user extensibility feature in your CASE tool.

ORACLE® ——————— APPLICATION (BUSINESS)

THE RELATIONAL DATABASE
MANAGEMENT SYSTEM

Name . . . .   Parent application . . . .

Business description

Business objectives/aims/priorities/constraints/performance indicators

Notes

Form	Team	Project	Analyst	Date	Sheet .... of ....
C2	User	Activity	Checked by	Date	

ORACLE®

_THE RELATIONAL DATABASE
MANAGEMENT SYSTEM_

GEOGRAPHIC
LOCATION

Geographic Location Name . . . .

Reference . . . .

Type . . . . e.g. Site

Spatial Reference . . . . e.g. Grid reference

Within Location Name . . . .

Reference . . . .

Type . . . . e.g. Town

Description/constraints

Distances to other geographic locations

Other Location Reference	Name	Absolute Distance	Unit e.g. km	Notes

This form should be used to identify any site, town, city, region, country, etc. at which business
location(s) may be found. They would later be refined to sites for nodes on a network.

Form	Team	Project	Analyst	Date	Sheet .... of ....
C4	User	Activity	Checked by	Date	

ORACLE®

THE RELATIONAL DATABASE
MANAGEMENT SYSTEM

BUSINESS UNIT

(Company/Department/Organization unit)

Business Unit Name . . . .

    Reference . . . .

        Type . . . .   e.g. Department

Subordinate to . . . .

    Reference . . . .

        Type . . . .   e.g. Company

	Purpose of Unit
Address	
. . . .	
Post Town/City	
Postal Code	
Country	
Location Ref	

User Group

Name	Description	Named Users (optional)		

Form	Team	Project	Analyst	Date	Sheet .... of ....
C5	User	Activity	Checked by	Date	

ORACLE ® ——— BUSINESS FUNCTION HIERARCHY
THE RELATIONAL DATABASE
MANAGEMENT SYSTEM
(Process/Operation Hierarchy)

Reference ....

Form	Team	Project	Analyst	Date	Sheet .... of ....
C10	User	Activity	Checked by	Date	

Detailed Definitions   337

ORACLE®

THE RELATIONAL DATABASE MANAGEMENT SYSTEM

ELEMENTARY BUSINESS FUNCTION DEFINITION
(Process/Operation)

Reference ....

Function Ref .... Name ....

Inferior to Function Ref .... Name ....

Available to .... Authority Level ....

....

Frequency	per	Urgency/Response needed
		see continuation for more detail

Triggered by	Trigger for

Description

Usage of entity (attribute)	Method/action

Notes/remarks

Form C11	Team User	Project Activity	Analyst Checked by	Date Date	Sheet .... of ....

338 Function and Process Modelling

ORACLE®

THE RELATIONAL DATABASE MANAGEMENT SYSTEM

BUSINESS FUNCTION FREQUENCY

(General Frequencies)

Function Ref . . . .   Name . . . .

Detailed Frequency (for some functions)

	Frequency or	% growth	Per e.g. day	Urgency	Notes
Current frequencies					
Projected: Period 1					
Period 2					
Period 3					
Period 4					
Period 5					

Available to User Group Name	Authority Level	Named Users (optional)		

ORACLE ®

THE RELATIONAL DATABASE
MANAGEMENT SYSTEM

BUSINESS FUNCTION FREQUENCY

(Distributed Requirement)

Reference ....

Function Ref . . . .   Name . . . .

BUSINESS UNIT

Reference . . . .

Name . . . .

Initial Freq . . . . per . . . .

Average Freq . . . . per . . . .

Growth Rate . . . . % per year

Detailed Frequency (for some functions)

	Frequency or	% growth	Per e.g. day	Urgency	Notes
Current frequencies					
Projected: Period 1					
Period 2					
Period 3					
Period 4					
Period 5					

Available to User Group Name	Authority Level	Named Users (optional)			

ORACLE ®

THE RELATIONAL DATABASE
MANAGEMENT SYSTEM

ELEMENTARY BUSINESS
FUNCTION DEFINITION
INPUT DATAFLOW

Reference ....

Function Ref . . . .   Name . . . .

Dataflow Source Type . . . .   Source Name . . . .

 Source Description . . . .

   Dataflow Name . . . .   Dataflow Type . . . . .

	Entity	Attribute	Usage
Data Item			

Dataflow Source Type . . . .   Source Name . . . .

 Source Description . . . .

   Dataflow Name . . . .   Dataflow Type . . . . .

	Entity	Attribute	Usage
Data Item			

Where: Dataflow Type = Input / Retrieval / Interprocess
       Dataflow Source Type = Datastore / External entity / Function or Process
       Description entered only if function/process or datastore

| Form | Team | Project | Analyst | Date | Sheet .... of .... |
| C14 | User | Activity | Checked by | Date | |

ORACLE®

THE RELATIONAL DATABASE
MANAGEMENT SYSTEM

ELEMENTARY BUSINESS
FUNCTION DEFINITION
OUTPUT DATAFLOW

Reference ....

Function Ref . . . .   Name . . . .

Dataflow Destination Type . . . .   Destination Name . . . .

Destination Description . . . .

Dataflow Name . . . .   Dataflow Type . . . . .

Entity	Attribute	Usage
Data Item		

Dataflow Destination Type . . . .   Destination Name . . . .

Destination Description . . . .

Dataflow Name . . . .   Dataflow Type . . . . .

Entity	Attribute	Usage
Data Item		

Where: Dataflow Type = Input / Retrieval / Interprocess
       Dataflow Destination Type = Datastore / External entity / Function or Process
       Description entered only if function/process or datastore

Form C15	Team User	Project Activity	Analyst Checked by	Date Date	Sheet .... of ....

ORACLE® ———— FUNCTION LOGIC ————

THE RELATIONAL DATABASE
MANAGEMENT SYSTEM

Function Ref . . . .   Name . . . .

On ┬ date attribute . . . . . . of entity . . . .
   ├ completion of action . . . . . of function . . . .
   ├ date / time . . . .
   └ external trigger / whim . . . .

Step	Action	Action Freq	Attribute changes and other notes

Form C16	Team User	Project Activity	Analyst Checked by	Date Date	Sheet .... of ....

Detailed Definitions   343

ORACLE®

— THE RELATIONAL DATABASE
MANAGEMENT SYSTEM

DATASTORE
DEFINITION

Datastore name . . . . Reference . . . .

Description . . . .

	Entity	Attributes
Data items		

Input dataflow		from	

Output dataflow		to	

Form	Team	Project	Analyst	Date	Sheet .... of ....
C17	User	Activity	Checked by	Date	

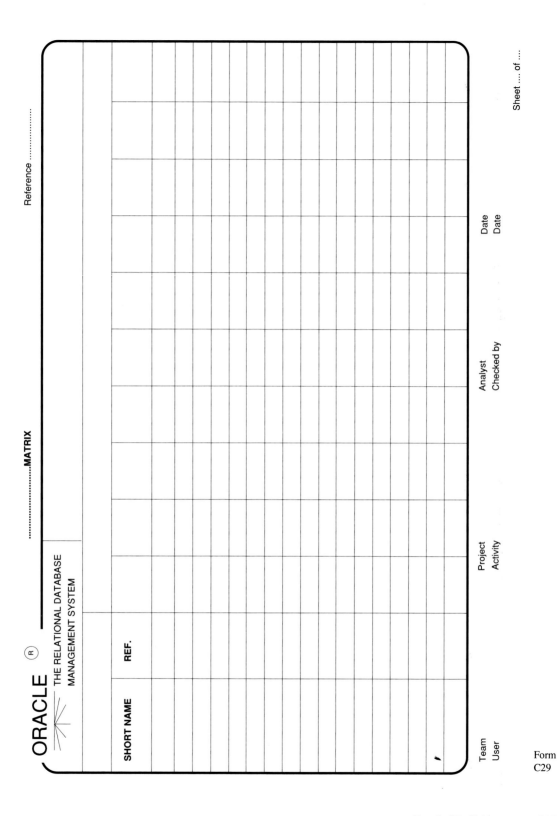

ORACLE ®

THE RELATIONAL DATABASE
MANAGEMENT SYSTEM

................................MATRIX

Reference ....

SHORT NAME	REF.															

Team   Project   Analyst   Date
User   Activity   Checked by   Date

Sheet .... of ....

Form
C29

ORACLE® ———— STATE DEFINITION ———— Reference ....

THE RELATIONAL DATABASE
MANAGEMENT SYSTEM

Name .... Sub-state of ....

Decomposed?   Yes/no

Description ....

....

....

....

Externally recognizable by ....

....

....

Transitions from this state

Triggering event	Process invoked	Resulting state
....	....	....
....	....	....
....	....	....
....	....	....

Form	Team	Project	Analyst	Date	Sheet .... of ....
C30	User	Activity	Checked by	Date	

ORACLE®

THE RELATIONAL DATABASE
MANAGEMENT SYSTEM

GENERIC TRANSITIONS

For (Sub) System ....

Each of these transitions will cause a change from ANY state.

Triggering event	Process invoked	Resulting state

Note: Direct transition will cause a new state to be entered irrespective of the initial state
when the event occurred. A process may or may not be triggered as a result.
The event name uniquely identifies the transition. Also see generic cyclic transitions.

Form	Team	Project	Analyst	Date	Sheet .... of ....
C31	User	Activity	Checked by	Date	

ORACLE® ———————— GENERIC
THE RELATIONAL DATABASE   CYCLIC
MANAGEMENT SYSTEM   TRANSITIONS

Reference ....

For (Sub) System   ....

Each generic cyclic transition will leave the system in the same state it was in when the event occurred.

Triggering event   Process invoked

....

....

....

....

....

....

....

....

....

....

....

....

Note: Cyclic transitions do not cause a change of state and may or may not invoke a process.

The event name uniquely identifies the transition. Also see generic transitions.

Appendix

D

USE OF ORACLE CASE TOOLS

The Oracle CASE tools comprise a family of products, all based upon the portable distributed repository CASE*Dictionary. The products support CASE*Method and many of the techniques used by other methods.

CASE*Dictionary

CASE*Dictionary is a multi-user database that acts as a repository for all information relating to an application system under development, and also acts as a database for each of the products described below. It supports all the stages of the Business System Life Cycle using interactive form-fill screens for maintaining and querying information, thus replacing the need for the paper forms shown in Appendix C. The data is fully cross-referenced and can be examined, checked and communicated to others by a wide range of reports, and completeness and consistency checks. In particular, CASE*Dictionary maintains a complete definition of the requirement and the detailed design. It also provides utilities to help application and database design, sizing, and interaction with database management systems and with application generator programs. It is available through a menu-driven forms interface on personal, mini and mainframe computers.

CASE*Designer

CASE*Designer provides a mouse-driven, multi-tasking, window-based, high-resolution graphics interface to the dictionary. This workstation interface allows interactive update to the dictionary database via diagrams and pop-up windows.

Alternative diagrams, providing different views, may be used for update or presentation purposes. Subsequently, these can be plotted or laser printed. Diagram types include Entity Relationship Diagrams, Function Hierarchies, Dataflow Diagrams and sophisticated matrix handlers. CASE*Designer provides a versatile workbench environment on workstations such as SUN, HP, VAX and powerful PCs, which can be networked into a multi-user, distributed dictionary database.

CASE*Generator

CASE*Generator is a family of products, each of which takes the definition of the requirement held in the dictionary along with a definition of the target environment and installation preferences, and generates appropriate computer programs. The types of program that may be generated include menus, interactive forms and reports.

CASE*Project

CASE*Project is a multi-user project management system to support CASE*Method. It may be used to estimate and control the tasks and deliverables in an overlapping multi-project environment where key resources may be working on several projects. The system integrates, where appropriate, with elements held in the dictionary, including such objects as diagrams.

CASE*Bridge

CASE*Bridge is a family of products that enable users of the Oracle CASE tools to coexist with tools from other CASE vendors. Information from one repository may be extracted to a standard repository protocol and then loaded or merged into the CASE*Dictionary or vice versa.

Overviews

To use the Oracle CASE*Dictionary and CASE*Designer products fully you should refer to the appropriate tutorial, reference information or training course. The following diagrams illustrate in overview how these and other CASE products might be used during the Business System Life Cycle, and the rough sequence of events.

CASE SUPPORT
for the
BUSINESS SYSTEM LIFE CYCLE

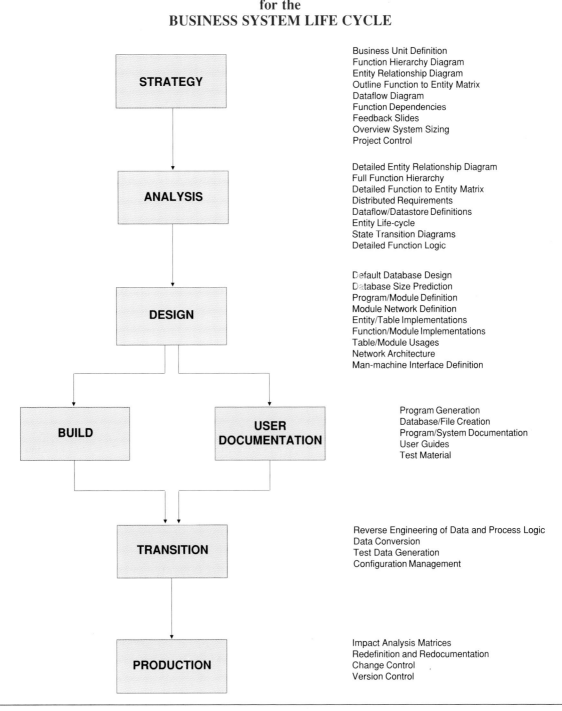

STRATEGY

Business Unit Definition
Function Hierarchy Diagram
Entity Relationship Diagram
Outline Function to Entity Matrix
Dataflow Diagram
Function Dependencies
Feedback Slides
Overview System Sizing
Project Control

ANALYSIS

Detailed Entity Relationship Diagram
Full Function Hierarchy
Detailed Function to Entity Matrix
Distributed Requirements
Dataflow/Datastore Definitions
Entity Life-cycle
State Transition Diagrams
Detailed Function Logic

DESIGN

Default Database Design
Database Size Prediction
Program/Module Definition
Module Network Definition
Entity/Table Implementations
Function/Module Implementations
Table/Module Usages
Network Architecture
Man-machine Interface Definition

BUILD

USER DOCUMENTATION

Program Generation
Database/File Creation
Program/System Documentation
User Guides
Test Material

TRANSITION

Reverse Engineering of Data and Process Logic
Data Conversion
Test Data Generation
Configuration Management

PRODUCTION

Impact Analysis Matrices
Redefinition and Redocumentation
Change Control
Version Control

Screenshots of Diagrammers

The following screenshots from the Oracle CASE*Designer product illustrate some of the advantages of using computer-aided tools rather than paper-based systems for system development. The pictures show the use of a function hierarchy, entity relationship, dataflow and matrix diagrammer. These represent the primary diagrammatic techniques used in the strategy and analysis stages to encompass the information and functional needs of a business, in this case a hypothetical airline.

Each of the windows has a set of buttons and devices to carry out actions such as:

- make a window fill the entire screen
- resize the window to a chosen size and aspect ratio
- where several overlapping windows are being used, 'stack' the windows so those required are to the front or back as appropriate
- iconize the window so that it may be temporarily represented by a small icon or symbol until needed again.

Diagrams can be any practical size required. A subset of a diagram can be seen and manipulated using further devices, which include:

- scroll bars to pan the visible window (or diagram drawing surface) horizontally or vertically across the diagram
- buttons to zoom in or out by degrees or to preset magnification levels
- buttons to select objects on the diagram and then both menu options and further buttons to manipulate the object in some way; for example, delete, edit or run a report.

Further menu options and buttons are used to redefine preferences on how to use the facility, request tutorial hints or help messages, run utilities, load/save diagrams, invoke other tools, system windows, output options and so on.

All these facilities are available in a similar manner under different workstation configurations, using different window management systems; however, the appearance or precise manner of use will vary with the different environments.

Function Hierarchy Diagrammer

This diagrammer is used to define what functions occur in a business and to group the functions into sensible sets for consistency and completeness checking. Facilities exist to add and delete functions and to reconfigure the structure of the hierarchy in various ways; for example, give a function a new parent function.

The analyst in this case has chosen preferences to lay out the diagram in a classic organization structure format and has deliberately used a medium-sized box for each function, which doubles the number of functions that can be viewed and manipulated on the drawing surface. Note that this box size truncates the function descriptions, but these can be accessed in full by scrolling or resizing the box.

Any changes to this or any other diagram interactively update the contents of the CASE*Dictionary and are automatically subject to management facilities such as back-up, recovery, version control and multi-user access to the diagram and underlying objects.

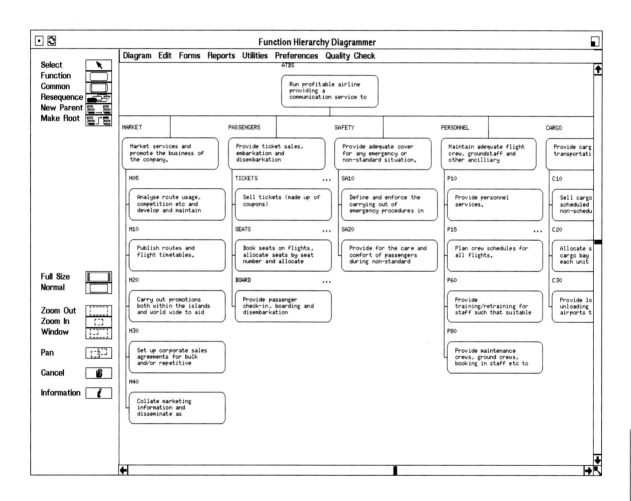

Dataflow Diagrammer

The dataflow diagrammer is used to show the flow of information between different functions. The functions are shown by the larger boxes, and are a subset of the same functions shown on the function hierarchy diagram. A two-level function decomposition is shown by the large function box encompassing four of its child functions. Dataflows are shown by the arrows and a datastore by the open-ended box in the centre. Boxes around the outside can represent source or destination external functions or entities.

This form of diagram covers the complex interrelationships between the business functionality and the corresponding information needs. Notice that useful quality checks are provided to ensure completeness and consistency.

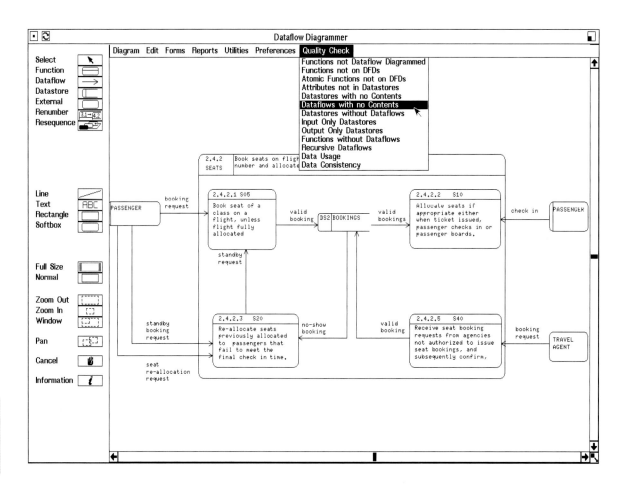

Matrix Diagrammer

The matrix diagrammer is a general-purpose tool that may be used to show the interrelationship between different objects held in the dictionary. In this case the business functions are arranged across the columns and their associated entities (with their average volumes) are shown down the rows. Where the rows and columns intersect, data can be displayed to indicate more detail about any association.

Here the analyst is checking a function for which the description starts 'Hold details of normal aircraft' against the entity AIRCRAFT. This association was initially created by a lexical analysis utility, which scans the function description for the names (or synonyms) of entities already known to the dictionary – a useful, time-saving utility. Now the analyst has qualified the information by recording the fact that the function may retrieve and update information about AIRCRAFT.

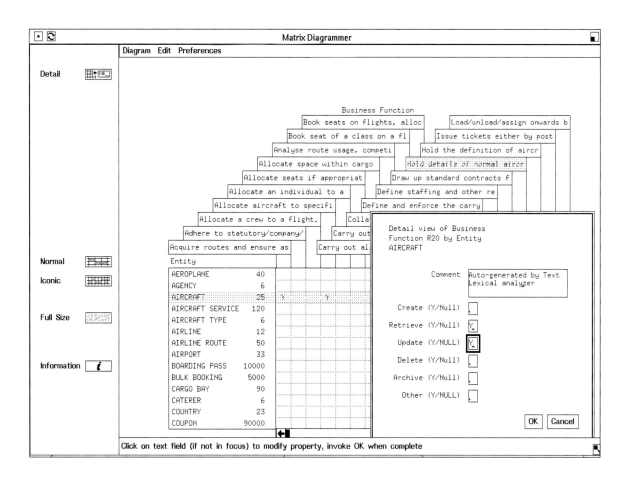

This diagrammer is a very flexible input/output device, and is particularly useful for fast input, quality and completeness checking. The data may be sorted in many ways for either or both axes, enabling the user to view and check the information from many alternative perspectives.

The same diagram can be used for many other purposes, such as manipulating:

- critical success factors to business functions
- program modules to tables
- business units/location to entities
- processing nodes to program modules.

Workstation Use

The workstation interfaces enable the system engineers to gain access to each of the CASE tools, along with other tools or facilities available on their computer network. Multi-tasking capability aids productivity, along with the ability to switch between different and complementary views of related information. Productivity gains of fifteen to twenty percent are often claimed by workstation users, even without such software productivity tools.

Team Orientation

This type of CASE tool has caused some interesting changes in the way that development teams are set up and conduct their day-to-day work.

The central dictionary or repository enables all the members of a team to work on their application system at the same time, thus speeding up communications and minimizing duplication of effort. Multiple teams can share overlapping definitions, under the control of the dictionary management system, and version control enables a controlled evolution of the systems being engineered.

In the past, analysts and designers have used template-drawn diagrams and whiteboards. Now their efforts are focused on the shared database, CASE*Dictionary, and the user interfaces enable them to share their work with their colleagues in real time.

Footnote

Not all the techniques mentioned in the CASE*Method books are fully supported by this or any other CASE tool, yet. This is because new techniques evolve far more quickly than it is possible to provide computer support for them. The tools tend to lag behind the techniques by about twelve to eighteen months.

Appendix

E COMMONLY OCCURRING & FORGOTTEN FUNCTIONS

Introduction

Businesses are, by their very nature, similar in many respects. They all need staff, funds, facilities, and all the other trappings of running some form of enterprise. This similarity across apparently diverse businesses is probably one of the reasons that analysis and synthesis by analogy is such an effective technique.

When analyzing a business, however, it is all too easy to concentrate on the new, the complex, the critical and the problematic. We sometimes forget the apparently more mundane functional areas that may well provide golden opportunities for improvement. Most businesses will have personnel functions covering recruitment, training, hiring, firing, and so on. And obviously many accounting functions will be common to all businesses. It is also interesting how many functions from less obvious areas, perhaps from manufacturing, provision of services, sales or marketing, will frequently be done in similar ways, despite the businesses they support being radically different.

In this appendix we have identified some of the areas that are often overlooked. The best way of using this set of ideas is to ignore them completely until you believe you have finished your initial analysis; then have a look at them before the presentation to your sponsors and users. In this way, you can use these lists as a checklist for things that may have been forgotten, but which are, nonetheless, very important. Do not fall into the trap of including them all. If you do, the likelihood is that your executives will lose focus on those aspects of the business that really need their attention.

In general terms, identifying functions can often be likened to examining the business from the perspective of different aspects – looking at their life-cycles. Let us have a look at a classic business life-cycle, defined as functions, for a business producing and selling products. A similar set would be appropriate for a service-oriented business, but for a retail organization the functions would be subtly different.

A Classic Business Cycle

- Plan the nature of the business, define objectives, approach and timescales it will operate in:
    - set objectives and critical success factors
    - analyze the industry in which the business will operate:
        e.g. for competitors, markets, competitive products
    - formulate and state a business strategy in financial, product and other terms
    - decide the tactics to be deployed.

- Acquire funding, physical, human and other resources:
    - raise capital to fund the business
    - recruit, train and motivate staff
    - purchase (or otherwise acquire) building, machinery, furniture, vehicles, etc.
    - takeover or merge with other businesses
    - ensure availability of resources provided by third parties.

- Market and sell goods, services and products:
    - educate marketplace(s) and make aware of product
    - identify and qualify prospects
    - match product to prospect needs and complete sales
    - manage accounts.

- Develop and produce products and deliver to consumer:
    - research new product opportunities
    - design and develop product
    - produce product
    - deliver product to customer.

- Support and maintain products:
    - resolve faults, complaints and product enhancement requests
    - identify and diagnose root causes of faults in product
    - expedite correction through product development or delivery, as applicable.

- Monitor and control business operations:
    - assess performance against plan

- identify and take action to correct dangerous anomalies and trends, and so on
- instigate replanning if deviation is large enough.

Government

Many central and local government organizations have a life-cycle that is geared to a budget and the provision of relevant services. The functions that apply often fall into the simple pattern shown below:

- Derive and agree budgets for operating period
- Define levels of service provision within budget
- Staff department to level adequate for provision of planned services
- Allocate budget by service for operating period
- Carry out service and log operating costs
- Monitor spend against budget.

Generic Human Resource Functions

The list below applies in whole or part to virtually all businesses, as it relates to recruiting and maintaining employees:

- Define corporate culture and employment policies, particularly for:
    - health, safety, hiring and retention, dismissal, benefits, training, career progression, expenses, relocation, employment conditions, disabled staff and visitors, unions and other employee groups, . . .
- Define job, role, position or other vacancy
- Market the corporation or business
- Advertise job or position
- Liaise with third-party sources of applicants
- Screen applicant
- Interview and test applicant
- Offer job to or reject applicant
- Hire employee
- Take on contractor
- Train and educate
- Pay employee
- Review employee or contractor
- Promote employee
- Warn, reprimand, downgrade and/or fire employee or contractor

- Conduct redundancy procedure

- Reorganize the business and redeploy people.

For other potential key functions, scan through books on human research, management and other related topics. It is interesting to look at how few of these would typically need complex system support. On the other hand, to 'pay an employee' implies a vast amount of additional functionality, possibly encompassing cross-country legislation, bonuses, time recording, shifts, part-time work, and so on.

Forgotten Topics

It would take many months to collate the numbers of generic functions that recur across different businesses, and the result would be pretty boring. So instead, to conclude this appendix, we have identified some of the topics that are often forgotten. It is relatively easy to determine a simple set of functions to support any of these topics as each tends to have its own, reasonably obvious life-cycle. Remember that guessing is a perfectably acceptable modelling technique and feel free to add topics that we have forgotten to this list.

We have arranged the list in alphabetical order as there is no intent to show special groupings; the list is provided purely to help trigger ideas.

Administration	Health	Research
Audits	Insurance	Resilience
Building acquisition/	Integrity	Safety
relocation/disposal	Legal/legislative needs	Sales
Catering	Maintenance	Security
Communications	Management	Social activities
Community relations	Manufacturing	Special projects
Computer services/	Marketing	Sponsorship of
internal systems	Personnel	charities
Controls	Physical resource	Standards
Credit	Policy on . . .	Stores
Development	Printing	Supplier policy
Disabled visitors	Projects	Support/maintenance
Disaster recovery	Publications	Third-party alliances
Ecology/conservation	Public relations	Training
Energy use	Quality management	Transportation
Entertainment/rewards	Recreation	Visitors/reception
Finance	Recycling	Waste management
Forecasting	Refurbishment	
Good practice	Repairs	

F   Meta Model

What is a Meta Model?

A meta model, put simply, is a model of a model.

We have been modelling actual functions, states, events, and so on, using various functional modelling techniques. The concepts we have used on these diagrams can be represented as entities; so for the entity FUNCTION, an instance of that entity would be an actual function such as *'check availability of seats on identified flights'*. The connections between these various concepts can be represented as relationships, and anything that describes them (name, description, etc.) will be an attribute.

The meta model shown overleaf is an entity relationship model of the main concepts of the techniques covered in this book. You may want to read the earlier section on information modelling (pages 34-36) or the *Entity Relationship Modelling* book in this series to understand how to read the diagram. We have given two examples to illustrate the understanding you can gain from being able to read an entity diagram (meta model) of complex events.

The term **data unit** has been used on this diagram as a unifying concept to cover the terms dataflow and datastore, because these are very similar ways of aggregating the information needed by groups of functions.

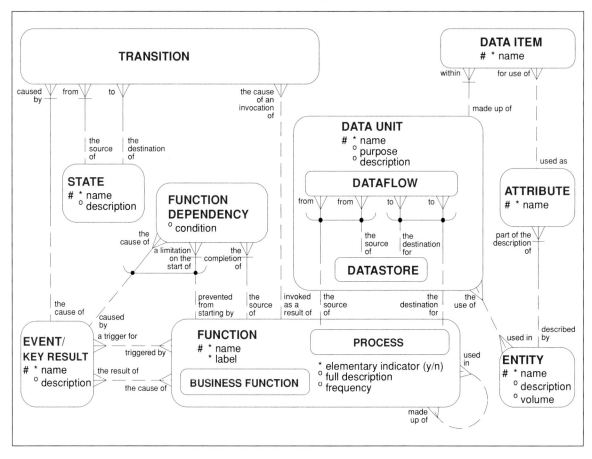

A BUSINESS FUNCTION, described by a name, label, description and frequency, may be the source of one or more FUNCTION DEPENDENCY(s), each of which must be either a limitation on the start of another BUSINESS FUNCTION or the cause of an EVENT or KEY RESULT (which itself may be a trigger for one or more BUSINESS FUNCTIONs).

Each DATAFLOW, described by a name, purpose and description, may be made up of named DATA ITEMs, which may be for use of known ATTRIBUTEs, which are part of the description of an ENTITY. Each DATAFLOW must be from either a FUNCTION or a DATASTORE and must be to either another FUNCTION or DATASTORE (additionally DATAFLOWs between two DATASTOREs are not allowed).

GLOSSARY OF TERMS

This glossary contains a useful subset of the terms used in the CASE*Method references and associated documents. Some of the words may not appear in this particular document, but they are included here for completeness and understanding. You will also find that a few dictionary definitions have been added to illustrate the definitive meaning of a word in **current** English usage. These have been taken from *The Concise Oxford Dictionary of Current English 8th edition*, © 1990 Oxford University Press.

Action Diagram   A partly diagrammatic language for defining the detailed processing carried out by a business function. See also **Function Logic Language** and **Process Logic Language**.

Activity   Anything that needs to be done to complete a task. See **Task**.

Aim   See **Business Aim**.

Application   A forms-based program, report, utility or other self-contained unit that may be used to access database tables.

Application System   A name given to a collection of business functions, entities, programs and tables, which can be further described by system documentation of various forms. It will typically be used to describe a unit of related work as in a project, sub-system or data subject area. An application system may change status (e.g. frozen) and new versions can be created. It is also a unit of access control to the collection of elements contained therein. Elements may be shared between application systems.

Arc   A means of identifying two or more mutually exclusive relationships. See **Exclusive Arc**.

Association   A significant relationship between elements of the same or different type within a CASE environment. See also **Element**.

Atomic Function   A business function that is not further decomposed into consistent business functions once analysis of the function is complete. See **Leaf Function**.

Atomic Process   A process that is not further decomposed into consistent processes once definition of the process is complete. See **Leaf Process**.

Attribute   Any detail that serves to qualify, identify, classify, quantify or express the state of an entity.
or
Any description of 'a thing of significance'.

Note that each entity occurrence may only have one value of any attribute at one time.

attribute *n.* **1 a** a quality ascribed to a person or thing. **b** a characteristic quality. **2** a material object recognized as appropriate to person, office, or status (*a large car is an attribute of seniority*) ...

Business   An enterprise, commercial house or firm in either the private or public sector, concerned with providing products and/or services to satisfy customer requirements; for example, a car manufacturer, a refuse collection company, a legal advice provider, an organization providing health care.

Business Aim   A statement of business intent that may be measured subjectively; for example, to move up market or to develop a sustainable level of growth. See also **Business Objective**.

Business Constraint   Any external, management or other factor that restricts a business or system development in terms of resource availability, dependencies, timescales or some other factor.

Business Function   What a business or enterprise does or needs to do, irrespective of how it does it. See **Elementary Business Function**.

Business Location   A uniquely identifiable geographic location, site or place from which one or more business units may be wholly or partly operating.

Business Model   A collection of models representing a definition of a business. Components include models of objectives, functions and information. See **Entity Relationship Diagram** and **Function Hierarchy**.

Business Objective   A statement of business intent that may be measured quantifiably. A quantifiable goal or target. Aims and objectives are similar concepts but the achievement of an objective is measurable in some specific manner; for example, to increase profit by 1% during the next financial year.

Business Priority   A statement of important business need or requirement within an ordered list.

Business Process (Re-)Engineering   The activity by which an enterprise re-examines its goals and how it achieves them, followed by the disciplined approach of redesigning how the business is carried out. Typically, this can also result in radically improved

systems, which remove redundant activities, streamline and optimize resource utilization. In CASE*Method, new function and/or process definitions may result from this activity, depending on the scope.

Business System Life Cycle   The structured approach for the task of developing a business system. The seven major stages are strategy, analysis, design, build, documentation, transition and production. (Also called the development life-cycle.)

Business Unit   Part of an organization which is treated for any purpose as a separate unit within the parent organization; for example, a department.

Business View   A frequently used subset of information, readily intelligible to users and defined in business terms, derived from definitions held in an entity model. It is based on one entity and can encompass (renamed) attributes from this base entity and any other entity that is associated with it unambiguously.

CASE   Computer-Aided Systems Engineering is the combination of graphical, dictionary, generator, project management and other software tools to assist computer development staff engineer and maintain high-quality systems for their end users, within the framework of a structured method. It is also sometimes referred to as Computer-Aided Software Engineering.

CASE*Designer   CASE*Designer is a workstation-based development environment, designed for use by system engineers such as analysts and designers. It provides a multi-windowed, multi-user, networked access to many development tools. It also provides a set of interactive diagrammers and plotting facilities to enable concepts, such as entity relationship models, to be manipulated and output graphically.

CASE*Dictionary   A multi-user repository for system development staff to record all significant results from the strategy, analysis, design and implementation stages of the system development.

CASE*Exchange   A software tool that enables information to be transferred from a third-party CASE tool to the Oracle CASE tools, or vice versa.

CASE*Generator   A family of software products that use information held within the repository to generate application programs in various languages to produce interactive forms, reports, queries, menus, etc.

CASE*Method   CASE*Method is a structured approach to engineering systems in a data processing environment. It consists of a set of stages, tasks, deliverables and techniques, which lead you through all steps in the life-cycle of a system. It is delivered via training courses, books and consultancy support, and can be automated by a combination of CASE tools.

CDIF   CASE Data Interchange Format, a standard for exchanging data between CASE tools.

Change Event   See **Event**.

Character   A single location on a computer system capable of holding one alphabetic character or numeric digit. One or more characters are held in a field. One or more fields make up a record, and one or more records may be held in a file or database table.
or
The format of an attribute, which may contain alphabetic characters or numeric digits.

Cluster   A means of storing data from multiple tables together, when the data in those tables contains common information and is likely to be accessed concurrently.

Column   A means of implementing an item of data within a table. It can be in character, date, number or other format, and be optional or mandatory.
or
An implementation of an attribute or (part of) a relationship.

Common Business Function   A business function that appears in more than one place in a hierarchy. During analysis, the objective is to eliminate identical functions wherever possible by overlapping, making them more generic or recognizing that they were not identical in the first place. When this is not practicable, one or more common functions may be created, each of which is a copy of a master function. Only the master function may then be further described, whilst the copy functions can appear in different parts of the function hierarchy, as required.

Company   A commercial business.

Constraint   See **Business Constraint**.

Copy Function   An alternative word for a common function. See **Common Business Function**.

Corporation   A group of businesses acting as part of a single legal entity.

Critical Success Factor   Any business event, dependency, deliverable or other factor which, if not attained, would seriously impair the likelihood of achieving a business objective.

Database   An arbitrary collection of tables or files under the control of a database management system.

Data Definition Language (DDL)   A subset of SQL which is used to create, alter, drop and otherwise change definitions of tables, views and other database objects.

Data Dictionary   A database for holding definitions of tables, columns and views, and so on. See also **CASE*Dictionary.**

Dataflow   A named collection of entities, attributes, relationships and as yet unformalized information (data items) passing from one place to another, either between two processes or between a process and a datastore or external entity. Dataflows may also be used with business functions. See **Business Function**, **Process**, **Datastore** and **External Entity**.

Dataflow Diagram   A diagram representing the use of data by business functions or processes. See **Dataflow**, **Dataflow Diagrammer**, **Datastore**, **External Entity** and **Process**.

Dataflow Diagrammer   A software facility that enables you to interactively draw and change Dataflow Diagrams within the context of a version of an application system. The diagrams are dynamically stored within a repository. Functions/processes, datastores and dataflows may appear on more than one diagram.

Data Item   In CASE*Method, the term data item is used on a dataflow or in a datastore to define an item of data that is not an attribute of a known entity. This will be converted to an attribute when the analysis is more complete.

In some other methodologies the definition of a logical data item is equivalent to an attribute at the business level. When used with non-ORACLE database management systems, a data item is a means of implementing an item of data within a file.

The term data item is sometimes used as an equivalent to column. See **Attribute** and **Column.**

Datastore   A named collection of entities, attributes, relationships and as yet unformalized information (data items), as used by specified business functions/ processes, which needs to be retained over a period of time. Storage may be temporary or permanent. During the early stage of analysis a datastore may contain data items, which are subsequently converted to attributes.

DBMS   A database management system, normally encompassing computerized management facilities that are used to structure and manipulate data, and to ensure privacy, recovery and integrity in a multi-user environment. Modern databases can handle different data modelling paradigms, such as relational, and manipulate numbers, text, dates, sound, images, drawings, documents, video, and so on.

DB2   The SQL-based database management system that is available from IBM.

Delivery Vehicle   A term that describes the mechanism for producing or implementing something; for example, 'C' and SQL*Forms are both means by which a computer program may be produced.

Denormalization   Initial database designs are often normalized such that information is recorded once, and once only, and cross-related to all related data. This gives a very flexible design, which can sometimes give poor performance. Denormalization is the design process by which means there is controlled replication of information, the introduction of derived columns and, in rare cases, repeating data to enable the system to meet some performance goal.

Dependency   See **Function Dependency** and **Process Dependency**.

Derived Attribute   A value that is derived by some algorithm from the values of other attributes; for example, profit, which is the difference between income and costs. See also **Derived Column** and **Derived Field.**

Derived Column   A value that is derived by some algorithm from the values of other columns, and is automatically updated in the database wherever the value of any of its source columns changes. The value

of a derived column should not be separately updated. See also **Derived Attribute** and **Derived Field**.

Derived Field   A value that is derived by some algorithm from the values of other columns or fields, and is only available within the scope of some program, such as a screen or report. The value is not stored in the database, for which see **Derived Column**. See also **Derived Attribute**.

Descriptor Column   A relational table has a primary key that is often inappropriate for use with end users. It is useful to define a column that uniquely describes rows in a table; this is known as a descriptor column. In some cases a combination of more than one column may be needed. This is particularly useful to show the user intelligible descriptor columns, whilst using the primary key to perform relational join operations. Descriptor columns are sometimes used to support business views. See **Column** and **Primary Key**.

Development Life-cycle   See **Business System Life Cycle**.

Distributed Database   A database that is physically located on more than one computer processor, connected via some form of communications network. An essential feature of a true distributed database is that the user and/or program work as if they had access to the whole database locally. All processing to give this impression is carried out by the database management system.

Distributed Processing   The ability to have several computers working together in a distributed network, where each processor can be used to run different activities for a user, as required.

Domain   A set of business validation rules, format constraints and other properties that apply to a group of attributes.

For example:

- a list of values
- a range
- a qualified list or range
- any combination of these.

Note that attributes and columns in the same domain are subject to a common set of validation checks.

Element　An element, in CASE, is a thing of significance about which system engineers need to record information in order to define a system requirement and implementation. Elements are further described by properties and associations to other elements. For example, you may need to record information about three tables (each of which is an occurrence of an element) and two program modules (two occurrences of a different element). The association between them would be which program uses which table and how. A company may often need to extend a repository by adding new elements, properties and associations.

Element Type　Any element held in the repository is classified as being of a particular type. Examples of element type are entity, attribute, program module, process, table, diagram, text, softbox. Occurrences or instances of these are called elements.

Elementary Business Function　A business function which, if started, must be completed successfully or, if for some reason it cannot be completed successfully, any changes it makes up to the point of failure must be undone, as though they had never happened. See **Function Hierarchy**.

Elementary Process　A process which, if started, must be completed successfully or, if for some reason it cannot be completed successfully, any changes it makes up to the point of failure must be undone, as though they had never happened. See **Process Hierarchy**.

End User　The person for whom a system is being developed; for example, an airline reservations clerk is an end user of an airline reservations system.

Enterprise　An undertaking or business, especially a bold or difficult one.

Entity　A thing of significance, whether real or imagined, about which information needs to be known or held. See **Attribute**.

entity *n.*　**1** a thing with distinct existence, as opposed to a quality or relation ...

Entity Relationship Diagram　A part of the business model produced in the strategy stage of the Business System Life Cycle. The diagram pictorially represents entities, the vital business relationships between them and the attributes used to describe them. See **Entity, Attribute**, **Relationship** and **Entity Relationship Diagrammer**.

The process of creating this diagram is called entity modelling. The terms entity model, entity relationship model and entity/relationship model are all synonyms for Entity Relationship Diagram.

Entity Relationship Diagrammer　A software facility that enables you to interactively draw and change complete (or subset) Entity Relationship Diagrams within the context of a version of an application system. The diagrams are dynamically stored within the repository. Entities and relationships may appear on more than one diagram.

Event　A thing that happens or takes place, or an outcome or result: the arrival of a significant point in time, a change in status of something, or the occurrence of something external that causes the business to react. There are four types of event, all of which may act as triggers to one or more business functions.

> **Change Event** – the status of something changes, and data is created or changed in such a manner as to act as a trigger for some business function(s); for example, when an entity is created or deleted, the value of an attribute is changed, or a relationship is connected or disconnected.

> **External Event** – something happens outside the control of the business but is significant to the business in some way.

> **Time or Realtime Event** – under specified conditions, real time reaches a predetermined date and time.

> **System Event** – something significant within the control of the business occurs, such as completion of a particular function; and this acts as a trigger to initiate further functions.

Exclusive Arc　Two or more relationships (or dependencies) are diagrammatically shown to be mutually exclusive by means of an exclusive arc. See **Arc**.

Extensibility　It is often useful to add new elements, properties and associations into the Dictionary. This is achieved by a facility known as (user) extensibility.

External Business Function   A business function, outside the scope of the application system, that may act as a source or recipient of dataflows.

External Entity   A thing of significance, outside the scope of the application system, that acts as a source or recipient of dataflows. An external entity might be a person, a business unit, another application system, or any other thing that might provide or receive information from a function within the application system.

External Event   See **Event**.

Field   A means of implementing an item of data within a file. It can be in character, date, number or other format, and be optional or mandatory.

File   A method of implementing part or all of a database.

Foreign Key   One or more columns in a table that implement a many-to-one or a one-to-one relationship that the table in question has with another table or itself. This concept allows the two tables to be joined together.

Form   In computer terms, normally used to mean a rectangular area of the screen, which has the appearance of a paper form, through which you can view and change details in a database or repository. It has fields to fill in with prompts and descriptive help information. Validation may be applied at field level or across several components of the form. A form may often be used to query, insert, update or delete information.

Format   The type of data that an attribute or column may represent; for example, character, date, number, sound, image.

Function   See **Business Function** and **Elementary Business Function**.

Function Decomposition   Any business function may be decomposed into lower levels of detail that are business functions themselves, and so on, until reaching the business functions that are atomic. This function decomposition gives rise to functions arranged in groups/hierarchies known as a business function hierarchy.

Function Dependency   Often a function cannot commence until some condition has been fulfilled. Where this condition is the completion of another function there is a dependency between the two functions. Functions may also be dependent on events.

Function Dependency Diagram   A visual means of recording interdependencies between business functions, and showing events that cause functions to be triggered.

Function Hierarchy   A simple grouping of functions in a strict hierarchy, representing all the functions in an area of a business. This forms part of the business model produced in the strategy stage of the Business System Life Cycle. See **Business Function** and **Function Hierarchy Diagrammer**.

Function Hierarchy Diagrammer   A software facility that enables you to create and change complete (or subset) function hierarchies interactively in the repository, within the context of a version of an application system. The layout of the diagram is dynamically produced in one of several user-chosen layout styles.

Function Label   A unique reference, within an application system, for a business function.

Function Logic   The detailed definition of precisely what a function does, including the way it manipulates information, business policies and algorithms (e.g. an algorithm to work out staged payments for a building contract), is defined as part of the function's logic.

Function Logic Language   An English-like pseudo-code for defining in detail the actions that make up an elementary business function. The actions may be structured within a syntactic or diagrammatic framework that represents sequence, choice or iteration. Sometimes the term action diagram is used.

Function Name   A short, succinct sentence, starting with a verb, describing what a business does or needs to do. See **Function Label**.

Fuzzy Model   An important modelling concept that conveys understanding without being rigorous or definitive. Especially useful as a communication aid with senior executives. Commonly known as a 'bullshit diagram'.

Glossary   A compilation of terms with their meanings; it shows a tendency to grow exponentially.

Homonym   A word with more than one meaning; for example, the word **form** has many meanings, including a shape, a hare's home, a criminal record, a document with spaces for information to be filled in, and the way something manifests itself.

Incremental Development   A technique for producing all or part of a production system from an outline definition of the need. The technique involves iterations of a cycle of build/refine/review so that the correct solution gradually emerges. This technique can be difficult to control, but nonetheless is very useful when properly used. Also called quick build and iterative development.

Index   An access mechanism to documents or data. A means of accessing one or more rows in a table with particular performance characteristics, implemented by a B-tree structure on ORACLE. An index may quote one or more columns and be a means of enforcing uniqueness on their values.

Information Model   See **Entity Relationship Diagram**.

Information Systems   That part of an organization responsible for the development, operation and maintenance of computer-based systems. Also known as Information Technology, Information Systems Technology or Data Processing.

Instance   See **Type and Instance**.

Iterative Development   See **Incremental Development**.

Key   A way of accessing something. Any set of columns that is frequently used for retrieval of rows from a table. See also **Unique Identifier** and **Column**.

Key Performance Indicator   A significant measure used on its own, or in combination with other key performance indicators, to monitor how well a business is achieving its quantifiable objectives.

Key Result   The outcome a business is trying to achieve upon receipt of an event. A key result is, in fact, simply an important event.

Leaf Function   A function at the bottom of a function hierarchy; that is, a function that has not been decomposed. It may be a leaf function because definition is incomplete. See **Atomic Function**.

Leaf Process   A process at the bottom of a process hierarchy; that is, a process that has not been decomposed. It may be a leaf process because analysis is incomplete. See **Atomic Process**.

Location   See **Business Location**.

Logical System Design   The task of designing a system to support business needs without making final decisions regarding the physical implementation. The same logical design should be appropriate for many physical implementations using, say, different versions of a database management system.

Master Function   When the same function appears in more than one place in a function hierarchy, one of these will be designated the master function. The other copies will be designated common functions to that master. Only the master can have the full detailed definition recorded against it, including the ability to have further function decomposition. See **Common Business Function**.

Matrix Diagrammer   A software facility that enables you to create and change matrices interactively. Matrices are between two or more associated element types and include:

- Function: Entity
- Function: Business Unit
- Function: Process
- State: Event
- Module: Table
- Module: Module
- Node: Module
- Process: Business Unit: Period.

Any new element type added to the repository by a user extensibility facility may also be matrixed to its associated element types.

Mechanism   A particular technique or technology for implementing a function. Examples might be a telephone, a computer, an electronic mail service.

Meta Model CASE tools provide various alternative modelling techniques at both the business and implementation levels, such as entity relationship modelling. When designing a CASE tool we have to model these models – this is known as meta modelling. A simple example would be to add new properties into the CASE tool. See **Extensibility**.

Module A procedure that implements one or more business functions, or parts of business functions, within a computer system. Subsequently, a module will often be implemented by a computer program.

Module Network Modules (or program modules) may be arranged in a network in the sense that:

- A module may be broken down into sub-modules.
- A module may be used as a sub-module of several others (e.g. a common subroutine).

By this means a network of modules may be created.

Network This may be used to mean:

- a module network (see definition)
- an interconnected network of computers as referred to in distributed processing.

Node A computer network typically has a series of nodes. Each node would normally represent a single computer or group of computers or a mechanism for handling some communication traffic through a particular point on the network.
or
The word node is occasionally used to represent a particular instance of a function on a Function Hierarchy Diagram.

Normalization A step-by-step process that produces either entity or table definitions that have:

- no repeating groups
- the same kind of values assigned to attributes or columns
- a distinct name
- distinct and uniquely identifiable rows.

Null In some implementations of database management systems a column, field or data item may be required to reserve a value that means 'there is no current value' – this is known as a null value. Other implementations, such as paper, implement this concept by having 'no value' to signify there is no current value.

Objective See **Business Objective**.

Operation In other methodologies the term operation has the same meaning as business function or elementary business function when used in a business context. See **Business Function** and **Elementary Business Function**.

ORACLE RDBMS The relational database management system from Oracle Corporation, available on most hardware environments worldwide.

Performance Indicator See the entry for **Key Performance Indicator**.

Phase In the context of CASE*Method, phase refers to a part of the business that is being taken through the stages of analysis to production.

Primary Index An index used to improve performance on the combination of columns most frequently used to access rows in a table.

Primary Key The set of mandatory columns within a table which is used to enforce uniqueness of rows, and which is normally the most frequent means by which rows are accessed.

Priority See **Business Priority**.

Process A definition of how one or more business functions are to be carried out by a system. A business function is what a business needs to do; a process is what a system needs to do; a mechanism is how the system does it. See **Elementary Process**.

Process Decomposition Any process may be decomposed into lower levels of detail that are processes themselves, and so on, until reaching the processes that are atomic. This process decomposition gives rise to processes arranged in groups/hierarchies know as a process hierarchy.

Process Dependency Often a process cannot commence until some condition has been fulfilled. Where this condition is the completion of another process there is a dependency between the two processes. Processes may also be dependent on events.

Process Dependency Diagram   A visual means of recording interdependencies between processes, and showing events that cause processes to be triggered.

Process Hierarchy   A simple grouping of processes in a strict hierarchy, representing all the processes in an area of a system. See **Process** and **Process Hierarchy Diagrammer**.

Process Hierarchy Diagrammer   A software facility that enables you to create and change complete (or subset) process hierarchies interactively in the repository, within the context of a version of a system. The layout of the diagram is dynamically produced in one of several user-chosen layout styles.

Process Label   A unique reference, within a system, for a process.

Process Logic   The detailed definition of precisely what a process does, including the way it manipulates information and algorithms, is defined as part of the logic of the process.

Process Logic Language   An English-like pseudo-code for defining in detail the actions that make up an elementary process. The actions may be structured within a syntactic or diagrammatic framework that represents sequence, choice or iteration. Sometimes the term action diagram is used.

Process Name   A short, succinct sentence, starting with a verb, describing what a system does or needs to do. See **Process Label**.

Program   A set of computer instructions, which can enter, change or query database items, and provide many useful computer functions.

Property   Any detail that serves to qualify, identify, classify, quantify or express the state of an element in a repository.

Prototyping   A technique for demonstrating a concept rapidly, to gain acceptance and check feasibility.

Within CASE*Method use of a prototype is recommended during:

- Analysis – to check requirements and then be discarded.

- Design – to check feasibility of alternative options and to agree style (optionally discarding it).

- Build – to incrementally construct modules that need close user involvement.

Quick Build   See **Incremental Development**.

RDBMS   Relational database management system.

Realtime Event   See **Event**.

Realtime System   A system in which events control the mechanisms. These are often found controlling machinery (e.g. a control system for an aircraft) and are often time and/or safety critical. See **Event** and **State Transition Diagram**.

Record   In a non-relational database system, a record is an entry in a file, consisting of individual elements of information, which together provide full details about an aspect of the information needed by the system. The individual elements are held in fields, and all records are held in files. An example of a record might be an employee. Every detail of the employee (e.g. date of birth, department code, full name) will be found in a number of fields.

In a relational system record is an alternative word for row. See **Row**.

Record Type   A predetermined set of fields within a file.

Referential Integrity Constraints   A set of validation rules applied to an entity or table such as uniqueness constraints, domain validation of columns, correspondence of foreign keys to the primary key of their related table and so on.

Relation   A relation is a term that embraces the concepts of both table and view. See **Table** and **View**.

Relationship   What one thing has to do with another.
or
Any significant way in which two things of the same or different type may be associated.

Note that it is important to name relationships.

Repository   A mechanism for storing any information to do with the definition of a system at any point in its life-cycle. Repository services would typically be provided for extensibility, recovery, integrity, naming standards, and a wide variety of other management functions. Modern repositories are implemented using a multi-user distributed database.

Reverse Engineering   An automatic and/or manual procedure that takes a component of an existing system and transforms it into a logical definition within a CASE tool.

Reverse engineering may apply to both data and computer programs. Such a logical definition so derived will often be refined, integrated with some new top-down definition of requirement, and forward engineered or generated to some replacement technology.

Row   An entry in a table that typically corresponds to an instance of some real thing, consisting of a set of values for all mandatory columns and relevant optional columns. A row is often an implementation of an instance of an entity. See **Table** and **Column**.

Schema   A collection of table definitions.

Secondary Index   An optimization technique used on a set of columns (optional or mandatory) which improves the performance of access to rows.

Select   The function of making some object or data current for subsequent use.

A query may result in the selection of one or more rows from a repository or database; for example, to select any functions that contain the word ACCOUNT in their description.

Sequence   A database object created like a table which is used to generate unique keys (sequence numbers). Sequence information is stored in the data dictionary.

SQL   Structured Query Language. The internationally accepted standard for relational systems, covering not only query but also data definition, manipulation, security and some aspects of referential integrity.

Stage   One of the seven major parts of the CASE*Method Business System Life Cycle.

State   A recognizable or definable condition that a system or an object can be in at some point in its life-cycle.

State Transition Diagram   A visual means of modelling an object, the states through which it might go during its life-cycle, events that affect it and interrelationships to other objects and states. Such diagrams may be used to model objects such as an entity, a system, a process/function, a program. These diagrams are particularly useful to model realtime situations.

Storyboard   A technique, borrowed from the film industry, for describing screen dialogues. A storyboard consists of an ordered series of pictures, illustrating stages of the dialogue. The pictures are annotated with notes about logic and user input.

Structure Chart   A diagram that represents how a process or program may be designed in terms of actions and their sequence, choice and iteration.

Sub-entity   Synonymous with sub-type. See **Sub-type.**

Sub-function   A business function that has a parent function.

Sub-process   A system process that has a parent process.

Sub-schema   A subset of a schema. In relational terms, a view is often a more applicable concept.

Sub-type   A type of entity. An entity may be split into two or more sub-types, each of which has common attributes and/or relationships. These are defined explicitly once only at the higher level. Sub-types may have attributes and/or relationships in their own right. A sub-type may be further sub-typed to lower levels.

Success Unit   This term is normally used to mean that component of work carried out by a computer program which takes the database from one state of consistency to another.

Super-type   A means of classifying an entity that has sub-types.

Synonym   A word or phrase with the same meaning as another (in a given context); for example, aircraft and aeroplane.

System   A named, defined and interacting collection of real-world facts, procedures and processes, along with the organized deployment of people, machines, various mechanisms and other resources that carry out those procedures and processes.

In a good system the real-world facts, procedures and processes are used to achieve their defined business purposes with acceptable tolerances. Also see **Application System**.

System Event   See **Event**.

Table   A tabular view of data, which may be used on a relational database management system, defined by one or more columns of data and a primary key. A table would be populated by rows of data. It is often an implementation of an entity. Tables are the logical and perceived data structure, not the physical data structure, in a relational system.

Tablespace   A logical portion of a database used in allocating storage for table data and table indexes.

Task   A task is the first subdivision of a stage. See **Stage**.

Time Event   See **Event**.

Transferable Relationship   A relationship between an object of type A and another object of type B is said to be transferable if there is a business rule that enables an instance of A to be disconnected from one instance of B and connected to another instance of B; for example, a divorce and remarriage. Conversely, a non-transferable relationship would occur if the instance of A must always be connected to a particular instance of B; for example, a child and its natural mother.

Transition   A valid change of a system or an object from one state to another, modelled on a state transition diagram. See also **State**.

Trigger   In CASE*Method the word trigger is used in the sense that an event will trigger one or more functions or that a function may be triggered by the completion of another function (an implied event). See **Event.**

The word trigger is also used within software to denote some computer processing that is also carried out under certain conditions. There are, for example, triggers that may be actioned before or after the insertion of a row. These would be called pre-insert and post-insert triggers. The processing for a trigger would typically be written in SQL or PL/SQL.

In database terms, a trigger is a piece of code executed by a database management system when a defined action occurs; for example, when a row is inserted into a table.

Tuple   A set of values for an attribute, synonymous with row. See **Row**.

Type and Instance   The same word is often used by end users to represent a type (or class) of thing and an instance (or occurrence) of a thing.

For example, the word CAR may be used in the sense of a model or type of car; an instance of this would be uniquely identified by the name 'Silver Cloud Rolls-Royce'. The word CAR may also be used in the sense of defining a vehicle; an instance of this would be a Silver Cloud Rolls-Royce uniquely identified by the registration number 'GWS 1'. In a database one might find two tables: one called MODEL, which has, say, a hundred rows each corresponding to the hundred types of models of cars that we know of; the other called CAR, which has, say, twenty thousand rows, each of which corresponds to an actual vehicle.

Unique Identifier   Any combination of attributes and/or relationships that serves, in all cases, to uniquely identify an occurrence of an entity.
or
Any combination of columns that serves, in all cases, to uniquely identify an occurrence of a row in a table.

Primary keys and unique indexes are alternative ways of implementing unique identifiers on a relational database management system.

User   Any person or group of people with some rights to access a computer facility. The same person may be known to a sophisticated system in several ways; for example, as a database user, CASE user, user of an operating system, package user, user of an electronic mail system, and so on.

User Preferences   In many circumstances in computer systems there may be alternative ways a user can influence the behaviour of a utility, user interface or other system process. These may typically be set by adjusting values in a set of user preferences; for example, in a program generator, preferences may be set for style, performance, user interface behaviour, code standards, and so on.

Version Control   A mechanism to help system engineers handle the problem of a system going into a production (live) state and then moving on to a second or subsequent development state. Version control is a facility that includes the capability of changing the state of a version of an application, archiving a version, creating new versions, and so on.

Version Group   A collection of application systems consisting of one application system at a specified version plus all the dummy application systems that own elements shared by this application system. The version group is significant because to drop an application system, its entire version group must be dropped (i.e. it is not possible to drop part of a version group); this is to retain consistency of shared elements.

View   A means of accessing a subset of the database as if it were a table. The view may:

- be restricted to named columns
- be restricted to specific rows
- change column names
- derive new columns
- give access to a combination of related tables and/or views.

Working Style Requirement   A definition of a manner of working which may apply to different roles of user when performing business functions; for example, use of a few simple easy-to-use buttons for shop-floor working; use of sophisticated workstations for designers.

INDEX

Where a given term has several references, primary references are highlighted in bold. An index entry starting with the letters **Ch** references an entire chapter. A single letter entry references an entire appendix.

A

Abbreviation 30, 70
Access control 177, 204
Access right 113
Accuracy 68, 75, 110, 170
Acronym 30, 70
Action diagram 363
Activity 173, 363
Adaptability 261
Advanced technique 12, Ch7, Ch8, Ch9, Ch13, Ch14, Ch15
Aim 7, 27, **28**, 41, 260, 299, 363
Algorithm 139, 141-143, 154-159, 304, 315
Ambiguity 142
Analogy 64, 296
Analysis 73, 139, 162, 165, 170, 177, 315, **320-323**
    paralysis 10
    scoping 171
Analyst 9, 45, 46, 171
Annotation 152
Applicability 7, 10, 207
Application 264, 334 , 363
    system 363
Approach **73**, 162, 164, 196, 260, 358
    function driven 188
Arc 102, 363, 367
Architecture 184, 185
    diagram 184, 185, 186, 187
    network 184
    system **184**, 188, 197, 324
Archive 131, 158, 204
Argument 267
Array 286
    data structure 287
    -driven state machine 287
Aside 51, 69, 101, 124, 284
Assertion 54, 307
Association 363
Assumption 207
Atomic function 42, **138**, 363
Atomic process 363
Attitude 7, **9**, 53

Attribute / Audit / Availability

Attribute 1, 34, **35**, 41, 45, 113, 126, 141, 146, 153, 168, 192, 193, 276, 299, 362, 363, 364
    change 37, 139
    definition 35
    mandatory 35, 145
    modification 139
    optional 35, 145, 147
    value 147
Audit 174, 177, 204
Availability 207

B

Back-up/recovery 174, 177, 204
Back-up system 280
Base entity 147
Basic technique 12, Ch1, Ch2, Ch3, Ch4, Ch5, Ch6, Ch10, Ch11, Ch12
Benefit 8, 10, 11, 205
    function modelling 11
Block structuring 267
Bottom up 53, **55-59**, 164, 196, 239, 299, 301
Budget 11
Business 1, 5, 358, 364
    activity 173
    aim 1, 27, 364
    algorithm 139, 141-143, 154-159, 304
    awareness 308
    constraint 136, 145, 304, 364
    direction model 41, 319
    knowledge 170
    level 5, 6, 13, 27, 45, 55, 81, 93, 113, 135, 191, 298, 299, 333
    level technique 6, Ch2, Ch3, Ch4, Ch5, Ch6, Ch7, Ch8, Ch9, Ch11
    life-cycle 358
    location 364
    model **28**, 41, 319, 364
    need 1, 5
    objective 1, 27, 41, 45, 61-62, 173, 364
    objective definition 27, 364
    policy 136